The Best Book of:
Lotus™ 1-2-3™

by
Alan Simpson

Howard W. Sams & Co., Inc.
4300 WEST 62ND ST. INDIANAPOLIS, INDIANA 46268 USA

International Standard Book Number- 0-672-22307-4
Library of Congress Catalog Card Number: 83-51529

Edited by *Welborn Associates*
Illustrated by *David K. Cripe*

Printed in the United States of America.

PREFACE

Soon after its release in 1983, Lotus 1-2-3 skyrocketed to the top of the software best-seller lists—and for several good reasons. Firstly, it was among the first of the "integrated" software packages to combine electronic spreadsheet, graphics, and information management into a single program. Secondly, it took advantage of the features of the modern 16-bit microcomputers (such as the IBM PC) for maximum speed and performance. Thirdly, even with its advanced capabilities, it was (and still is) one of the easiest programs to use.

The term "easy to use" is a relative one, however, when talking about computers and programs. While the basics of 1-2-3 are easy to grasp, taking full advantage of this large and sophisticated program takes some time and some practice. And a little guidance doesn't hurt either. The purpose of this book is to provide that guidance. We'll have you writing some useful spreadsheets within the first couple of chapters. By the end of the book, you will have truly mastered all that 1-2-3 has to offer.

So without further ado, let's begin to explore, and master, the Lotus 1-2-3 program.

ALAN SIMPSON

LIST OF TRADEMARKS

CONTENTS

Section II: 1-2-3 Graphics

Section III: Database Management

Section IV: Macros

INTRODUCTION

Lotus 1-2-3 is unquestionably one of the most powerful microcomputer programs available on the market today. It combines electronic spreadsheet power, graphics, information management, ease-of-use, and flexibility as no other product before its time. As a business tool, 1-2-3 is incomparable. The powerful worksheet allows for rapid development of financial models, automated "what-if" scenarios, powerful built-in calculations for business, statistics, trigonometry, and more. As a graphics package, 1-2-3 provides graphs of any data in a worksheet, supports "what-if" graphics scenarios, and even graphic "slide shows." As a database management system, 1-2-3 provides sorting and searching capabilities to instantly organize and retrieve information. 1-2-3 even includes a small programming language, so you can automate your custom worksheets.

Who is 1-2-3 for? Anyone who works with numbers, anyone who needs rapid access to information, anyone who needs to plan. We are not talking about people who are already "into" computers here. We are talking about business owners, managers, financial planners, real estate agents, insurance agents, farmers, college professors—in short—anyone who needs information to make decisions or to make sales. The only prerequisite for using 1-2-3 is a little typing skill, and even that isn't too important. 1-2-3 is as well designed for the non-typist as a software product can be.

Who is this book for? Exactly those individuals described above. Granted, 1-2-3 is an easy-to-use product, but the term "easy-to-use" is a relative one when talking about computers. You can be productive almost immediately with 1-2-3. But, there are also many options (over 300 of them!) to choose from in 1-2-3. To really master the wonderful worksheet, it helps to get some guidance. While the manual is a good reference packed with useful examples, it is primarily a reference. Learning is more effective when you can develop some basic, practical skills and then build upon these acquired skills to achieve mastery. Reference manuals provide necessary information, instructional texts teach. This book is for anyone who wants to learn to use 1-2-3 to its fullest potential.

If you are just thinking about buying 1-2-3, and are wondering what it can do for you, this book can help you make your decision.

GETTING READY

If you already have access to 1-2-3, you should know some things prior to reading Chapter 1. These are:

1. 1-2-3 needs to be installed on your computer.

If you are already working with 1-2-3, then it is already installed on your machine. If not, we've included instructions for installing 1-2-3 in the Appendix. Our instructions are general, because various computers, or new updates by Lotus 1-2-3, may require different installation procedures. Version 1A of 1-2-3 comes with a pamphlet called "Getting Started." That is a good reference for the easy installation procedures.

2. 1-2-3 has a tutorial on disk.

The 1-2-3 program comes with five separate diskettes. The one labeled "Tutorial" gives you a "hands-on" overview of 1-2-3. If it is readily available, you should work through all the lessons on that disk prior to reading this book. The entire tutorial only takes about a half hour, and is time well spent. It is enjoyable as well.

You need to go through the installation procedures before you use the tutorial, so refer to the Appendix or the Lotus "Getting Started" pamphlet first if you haven't already done so. Then you can work through the tutorial following these steps:

(1) If your computer is already on, and the A> prompt is showing on your screen, insert the Lotus Tutorial disk in drive A on your computer, and type:

TUTOR

then press the RETURN or ENTER key (the one with this symbol on it: ↵). If your computer is not already turned on, insert the Tutorial disk in drive A, and turn on the power. This brings up a menu of lessons:

A   **Getting Started**
B   **The Loan-Analysis Worksheet -- I**
C   **The Loan-Analysis Worksheet -- II**
D   **The Loan-Analysis Worksheet -- III**
E   **Handling a Database**
F   **Graphing**

(2) Select a lesson by typing in the appropriate letter (A—F). Obviously, you should probably go through the lessons in order, A through F.

(3) To end your tutorial session, press the Escape key on your keyboard (the one labeled "Esc").

The tutorial provides ample instruction as you work through, so there is nothing else to discuss here. Just follow along and let the tutorial introduce you to 1-2-3. We'll take it from there.

3.   1-2-3 has a built-in "Help" facility.

On the left side of your keyboard are several keys labeled F1, F2, F3, F4, F5, etc. These are *special function* keys, and the one labeled F1 has the special function of providing help when you're working with 1-2-3. Anytime you are working with 1-2-3 and need some help, press the F1 key. The screen will provide help. When you have finished reading the help screen, just press the Esc key. The 1-2-3 worksheet will reappear on the screen.

This book allows you to work interactively with 1-2-3 as you read. You can use the 1-2-3 Help facility in conjunction with this text whenever you feel like exploring a topic in more detail. The Help facility is always there to help, so you might as well use it.

STRUCTURE OF THIS BOOK

This book contains four major sections. Section one contains chapters that deal specifically with the 1-2-3 worksheet. These chapters are designed to make your developing skills productive right off the bat, and then help you expand and refine those skills for faster and more fluent use of the worksheet's potential. We use fairly simple examples to explain and demonstrate new concepts and then provide additional examples that are more complex to help put your new knowledge and skills to work.

Section 2 deals with 1-2-3 graphics. It utilizes many of the skills you learned in the first section, and provides an in-depth tutorial in mastering 1-2-3's graphics capabilities.

Section 3 discusses 1-2-3's database management capabilities as well as basic database management techniques and concepts. You will also find some very powerful techniques for using computerized "what if" capabilities in Section 3.

Section 4 deals with the somewhat esoteric "macro" capabilities of 1-2-3. A macro is a collection of keystrokes stored in a worksheet that can be executed by typing a single command. Macros are not essential to using 1-2-3, but they provide one more added attraction that those of you interested in computer programming may want to explore. Information about macros is more in the "nice-to-know" arena than the "need-to-know." But just in case you happen to be curious enough, we dealt with the topic in considerable detail. The section on macros brings new meaning to the term "graphics slide show," among other things.

One last tidbit of advice I might offer before starting in Chapter 1. Learning about a new computer program is an enjoyable experience if you allow yourself to work at a comfortable pace. One of the best techniques for learning any computer skill is to *play.* Many people are afraid to do so because they fear that they will break or ruin something. If you are such a person, let me tell you something, and this is for certain. No matter what you type on the keyboard, even if you close your eyes and pound on the keys for half an hour, there is absolutely no possibility of your damaging the computer. There are no secret words or commands you can accidentally type to hurt the computer. So enjoy your learning. Play and experiment. The worst that can happen is that the computer will tell you that it doesn't understand what you mean. And that is only because the computer is not as smart as you are, not vice versa.

THE 1-2-3 WORKSHEET

CREATING THE WORKSHEET

The LOTUS system includes five separate disks: System, Utility, PrintGraph, Tutorial, and System Backup disk. 1-2-3 is stored on the one labeled System Disk. It is the main program of the system. The 1-2-3 program turns your computer into a giant worksheet which can perform calculations at amazing speeds. The worksheet has rows and columns of cells, and each row and column title provides an address for each cell. You can fill in the cells with whatever information you need: numbers, formulas for calculations, and even labels to make the display look nice.

The actual worksheet is 256 columns across, and 2048 rows long. Your computer's screen can't actually display this many rows and columns, so 1-2-3 displays only a portion of the worksheet. Of course, you can move to any part of the worksheet you like by giving 1-2-3 the appropriate commands. In this chapter, we will demonstrate some techniques you can use to put 1-2-3 to work right away, by moving around the worksheet and filling in some cells.

GETTING STARTED

Before we can work with 1-2-3, you need to have it up and running in the computer. That is, you need to get a copy of 1-2-3 from the disk into the computer's main memory. For now, we'll assume that 1-2-3 is already configured to your computer. If it isn't you can find general guidelines for configuring 1-2-3 in the Appendix.

To use 1-2-3 is to follow these steps:

1. Insert your Lotus System Disk in drive A of your computer, and turn on the computer (this is called "booting up"). If computer is already on, and the A> prompt is showing, put the Lotus System disk in drive A and type LOTUS, followed by pressing the RETURN (↵) key.
2. If you have a printer and continuous-form paper, roll the paper in the printer to a point where there is a page perforation just above the printer's print head, and *then* turn on the printer. This assures that any pagination that may occur will always be on one page, rather than split across two separate pages.
3. Insert a formatted data disk in drive B. (If you are using a hard disk system, you need not bother with this step.) At this point, you should see the Lotus Access System Main Menu, which looks like this at the top of the screen:

Lotus Access System V.1A   (C) 1983 Lotus Development   MENU

1-2-3 File-Manager   Disk-Manager   PrintGraph   Translate   Exit

==

Besides the 1-2-3 worksheet, Lotus provides the other capabilities shown in the menu. For the time being, however, we'll only be concerned with the 1-2-3 worksheet. Notice that the 1-2-3 option is highlighted. This means that if you press the RETURN (labeled ↵ on your keyboard), then 1-2-3 will be put into use. To select other options, press the right arrow (→) key on the numeric keypad on your keyboard, moving the highlight to various other choices. When you highlight the choice you want, press the RETURN key to call up that option.

Now, with 1-2-3 as the highlighted option, press the RETURN key, and 1-2-3 will load. A brief copyright notice will appear. Just press any key, and the 1-2-3 worksheet will appear on the screen and ready to use.

Now let's discuss what we see on the screen when 1-2-3 is in control.

THE SCREEN

When you first call up 1-2-3, your screen will display the upper-lefthand portion of the worksheet as shown in Fig. 1-1. All of the cells

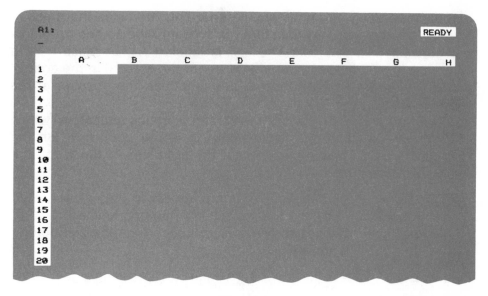

Fig.   1-1

are empty, of course, because we haven't filled any of them yet. But other parts of the screen have important information in them, which we'll discuss now.

At the upper left corner of the screen is an area called the "control panel." The upper left corner of this area contains the symbol A1:, which indicates that the cell pointer is presently in column A, row 1. This line will also display the contents of a cell when we start filling in the worksheet. Just below the A1 is the cursor. Anytime you type commands into 1-2-3, they will be displayed in this section of the screen as you type. When you start working with 1-2-3 commands, menus of options and a brief explanation of each menu item will appear in the two blank lines below the cursor. In the upper right corner of the screen is a box which contains the *mode* that 1-2-3 is in at the moment. Right now, the worksheet is in the "READY" mode (Fig. 1-1), indicating that it is ready to take commands from you.

Below the control panel are the worksheet *borders.* Across the top are columns A through H. Columns are labeled with letters and extend to column IV. After column Z, columns are labeled with two letters. That is, the 27th column is AA, followed by AB, AC, etc. The columns beyond these are labeled BA through BZ, CA through CZ, etc., until the right-most column, which is IV. There is also a border which labels the rows, numbered 1 through 20. The row numbers extend to 2048, but only 20 can fit on the screen. Just inside the border, the upper left cell is highlighted. This indicates that the *cell pointer* is in this cell. Any data that you type into the screen right now will be placed in this cell. The cell is labeled A1, because it is in column A, row 1. In the upper left corner of the screen, in the control panel, the letters A1 indicate that this is indeed the position of the cell pointer.

The bottom right corner of the screen contains indicators, which will light if the Cap Lock, Num Lock, or Scroll Lock keys on the keyboard are on. These keys are near the right side of the keyboard, and have these effects when on:

Cap Lock: Alphabetic characters appear in upper case.
Num Lock: Activates the keyboard's numeric keypad.
Scroll Lock: Causes screen to scroll each time the cell pointer is moved.

Pressing any of these keys will turn them on, pressing again turns them back off.

The lower left corner of the screen will display messages should you provide 1-2-3 with some information that it cannot compute.

As we've mentioned, the screen can only display a portion of the actual worksheet, as much as will fit comfortably on the screen. The screen, then, is a "window" into a section of the screen, as shown in Fig. 1-2.

You can use a number of keys to move the screen around the worksheet to display any portion we wish.

MOVING AROUND THE WORKSHEET

Use the arrow keys on the numeric keypad to move the cell pointer from one cell to another. The keypad is on the right side of the keyboard, as shown in Fig. 1-3. Notice that the keys labeled 8, 6, 2, and 4 also have arrows. Pressing these keys will move the cell pointer in the direction of the arrow. These *only* work if the Num Lock key is in the "off" position. If you try to move the cell pointer using these keys, and end up with numbers displayed on your screen instead, then you need to press the Num Lock key to activate the arrows again.

If you attempt to move the cell pointer off the right edge of the screen or past the bottom, the window will simply adjust itself accordingly. For example, if you move the cell pointer to row 20, col-

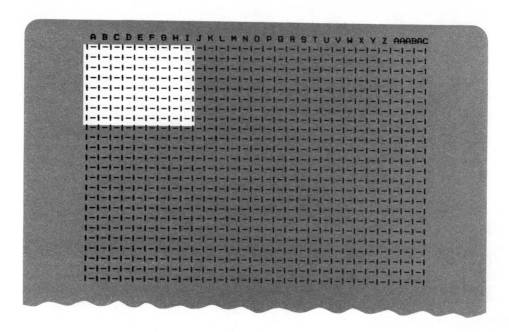

Fig.   1-2

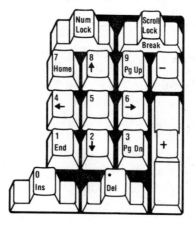

Fig.   1-3

umn A (by pressing the down-arrow key 19 times), the cell pointer
will be positioned as shown in Fig. 1-4.

Now, if you again press the down-arrow key, the cell pointer will
move to row 21, and the windows will adjust accordingly, as in Fig.
1-5. If you attempt to move past a border, as if attempting to move to

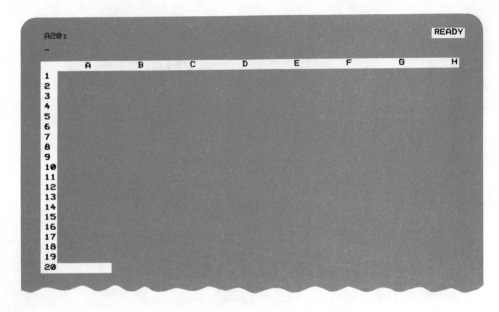

Fig.   1-4

a column left of column A, the computer will beep at you to remind you that there is no cell there.

Often you need to travel much further than one cell at a time, and it isn't very efficient to type lots of arrow keys to get to your destination. Instead, you can just jump to a cell by giving 1-2-3 the cell's column and row number. Use the "GoTo" key for this type of movement. This key is special function key number five (F5) on the keyboard, as shown in Fig. 1-6. The figure shows the function keys with the 1-2-3 template installed on the keyboard. The template comes with 1-2-3, and should be used so that you don't have to memorize what all these keys do.

When you first press the GoTo key, the control panel at the top of the screen asks which cell you wish to move the pointer to, like so:

A1:   **Ready**
Enter cell to go to:

        A   **B**   **C**   **D**   **E**   **F**   **G**   **H**

2
3

All you need to do now is type in the position of the cell you wish to jump to. For example, if you wish to position the pointer in column D,

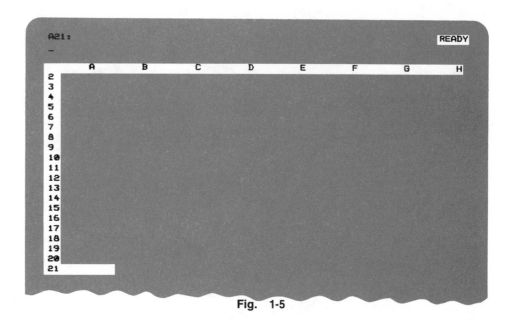

Fig.   1-5

row 3, you just type in D3 and press the RETURN key. (The RETURN key is the one with the symbol ⏎ on the keyboard. To simplify, we'll use the symbol <RET> to stand for "Press the RETURN key." Don't type the <RET> symbol on the screen.) After <RET>, the screen looks like Fig. 1-7, with the cell pointer in column D row 3, and the control panel indicating that the pointer is in cell D3.

Notice that a key on the numeric keypad (shown in Fig. 1-3) is labeled "Home." Pressing this key will cause the cell pointer to return to its "home" position, which is usually cell A1. There is also a key labeled "End." That key, when pressed and followed by another press on one of the arrow keys, will move the cell pointer to the end of the worksheet. For example, typing End down-arrow will put the cell pointer to the bottom of the worksheet. Typing End → will move the pointer to the right corner of the worksheet.

Sometimes you will want to move the window (screen) to another section of the worksheet. If you consider the portion of the worksheet presently displayed on the screen as one *page* of the worksheet, you may want to move down one page, or to the right one page. Several keys allow you to move the screen through the worksheet in a page-like fashion. To move up one page, use the "PgUp" key (key number 9 on the numeric keypad). To move down one page, use the "PgDn" key (number 3 on the numeric keypad). To move the

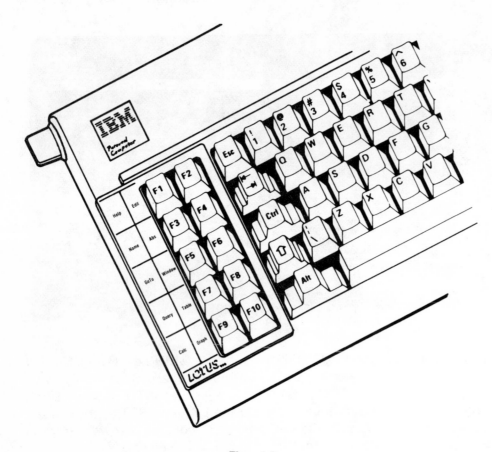

Fig.   1-6

screen to the left or right, use the control key (labeled Ctrl on the keyboard) combined with an arrow key. To move the screen one page to the right, hold down the Ctrl key and press the right-arrow key. To move the screen one page to the left, hold down the Ctrl key and press the left-arrow key. Let's try an example. Right now, press the ''Home'' key to put the cell pointer in cell A1. If you press the PgDn key, you would see that the screen has indeed moved down a page, as shown in Fig. 1-8. Notice that the column titles are still A to H, but the row numbers are 21 to 40.

Now you can move one page to the right by holding down the Ctrl key and pressing the right-arrow key. Now the screen looks like Fig. 1-9. The row numbers are the same, but the column headings range from the letter I to P.

To move up a page, press the PgUp key, and the row numbers

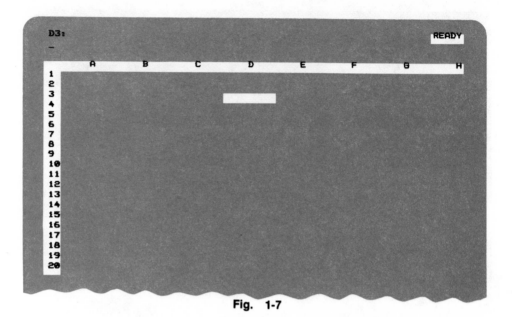

Fig. 1-7

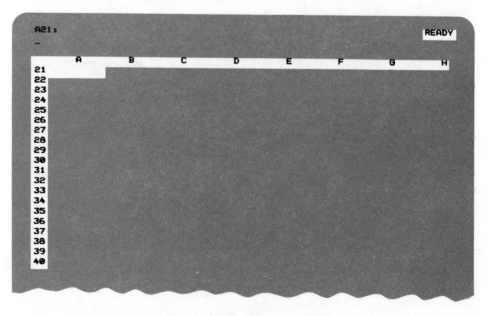

Fig. 1-8

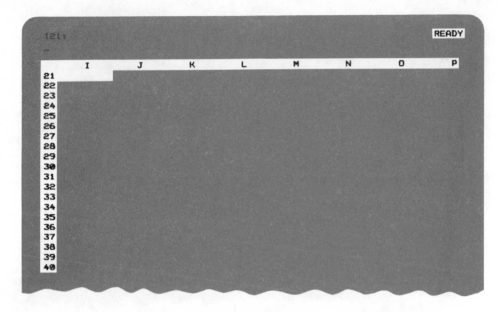

Fig.   1-9

change back to 1 through 20, while the column headings do not change, as shown in Fig. 1-10.

Now you can move the screen to the left a page, by holding down the Ctrl key and pressing the left-arrow key, which will return you to your original page (Fig. 1-11).

You have actually completed a circle around a section of the worksheet. Fig. 1-12 shows the entire series of events that has occurred with these four page movements.

In addition, 1-2-3 also allows you to move the screen to the left and right using other key strokes. For example, pressing the tab key (labeled with both a left and right arrow) will move the screen a page to the right (equivalent to Ctrl →). Holding down the shift key while pressing the tab key will move the screen a page to the left (identical to Ctrl ←).

Once you get the hang of moving the cell pointer and window around the worksheet, you can start filling in some cells. However there are a few things you need to know about how 1-2-3 views data first.

TYPES OF DATA

Data on the worksheet comes in three types: "labels," "numbers" and "formulas." Labels are simply "nonnumeric" pieces of in-

Fig. 1-10

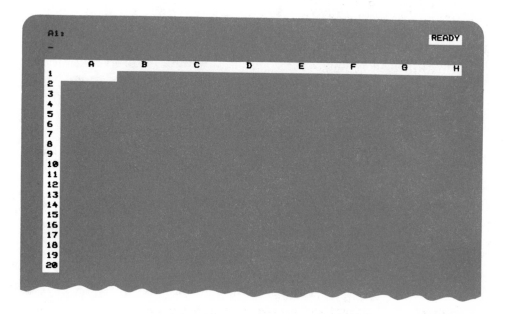

Fig. 1-11

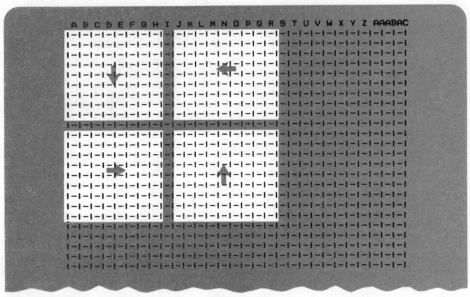

Fig.   1-12

formation that are used to describe information on the worksheet. For example, if a worksheet had a column of numbers for each month of the year, you would want to label each column with the appropriate month so that the display would be easier to read. Numbers are actual numeric values, and are generally used in calculations. Formulas are used to perform math on numbers, and to display the results of the math in a cell. There are few rules that go along with each type of data. 1-2-3 considers any data entered that "looks like" a number to be a number. Therefore, the number must begin with a numeric character (0 to 9), or a plus sign, a minus sign, a decimal point, or a dollar sign. A number may contain only one decimal point and may not contain a comma or a space. Numbers cannot include alphabetic characters, except the letter E, which is used for scientific notation. Below are examples of valid and invalid numbers:

Valid Numbers	Invalid Numbers	
.99	.99.1	(too many decimal points)
1234	1,234	(can't have comma)
123.45	A123.45	(has an alphabetic letter)
−9999.99	321 34	(contains a space)
1.2E+05	64K	(contains a letter)

$123.45   (O.K., indicated dollar amount)
22%   (O.K., indicates percent)

Specify labels by making sure that the first character in the data is NOT one of the characters used to specify a number. Quite simply, a label should always begin with an alphabetic character. However, if you must start a label with a number (i.e., 123 A St.), you can use a "label prefix" so that 1-2-3 doesn't get confused. Label prefixes specify that a data item is a label and affects the way in which the label is displayed. The label prefixes are:

'   apostrophe: left—justifies a label in a cell.
"   quotation mark: right—justifies a label in a cell.
^   caret: centers a label in a cell.
\   backslash: repeats the label within the cell.

Some valid and invalid labels are shown below:

Valid Label	Invalid Label	
January 1, 1983	1/1/83	(starts with a number)
'123 A St.	123 A St.	(starts with a number)
Interest	—Interest	(starts with minus sign)

Preceding a label with a backslash fills the entire cell character. For example, entering \- into a cell will produce ---------.

Formulas generally contain cell reference numbers and arithmetic operators to perform math. Like numbers, formulas may not contain any spaces. The arithmetic operators that 1-2-3 uses in performing math are summarized below. These operators follow the normal order of precedence that the rules of math dictate. That is, if a formula contains both multiplication and addition, then the multiplication takes place first. Operations of equal precedence take place from left to right. The operands below are displayed in order of precedence:

( )   :parentheses used for grouping
^   :caret used for exponentiation
—   :negative number
*   :multiplication
/   :division
+   :addition
—   :subtraction

We can see how operators are used in formulas by looking at some examples, as follows:

1+1	:produces 2, the sum of 1 + 1.
A1+B1	:the sum of the contents of cell A1 plus the contents of cell B1.
A1+A2*A3	:the contents of cell A1 added to the product of the contents of cells A2 and A3.
(A1+A2)/A3	:the sum of the contents of cells A1 and A2 divided by the contents of cell A3.
C3^ (1/3)	:the cube root of the contents of cell C3.

Formulas follow the same rules as numbers. The examples above are "logically" correct, but some of them break the rules for defining formulas. Like a number, a formula must not begin with an alphabetic letter. A formula may begin with any of these characters:

$$0\ 1\ 2\ 3\ 4\ 5\ 6\ 7\ 8\ 9\ .\ (\ @\ \#\ \$\ +\ -$$

Below are examples of valid and invalid formulas:

Valid Formula	Invalid Formula	
+A1+A2	A1+A2	(starts with a letter)
(C3+C4)*2	(C3+C4) *2	(contains a space)
10+10	'10+10	(starts with an apostrophe)

In general, if you get in the habit of beginning all formulas with a + sign or open parenthesis, you will have no trouble.

Now, before we provide you with more basic information, we will put all of this together with some practical applications in mind.

ENTERING DATA INTO THE WORKSHEET

Entering data into the worksheet is a three-step process:

1. Position the cell pointer into the cell where the data will appear.
2. Type the data to be entered onto the screen.
3. Press the RETURN (↵) key, or an arrow key when finished typing the cell's contents.

We will begin with a simple example using a teacher's grade book. First, we'll need a blank screen to work with, as in Fig. 1-13. Notice that the cell pointer is in cell A1.

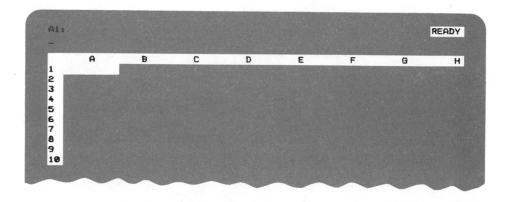

Fig.   1-13

First, type in the students' names down the left column. These will be labels, because they will not be used in any calculations, nor will they perform calculations. So here is a list of our students:

> Adams
> Brown
> Cass
> Davids
> Edwards

First, type in Adams. As you are typing, the name appears in the control panel, as shown in Fig. 1-14.

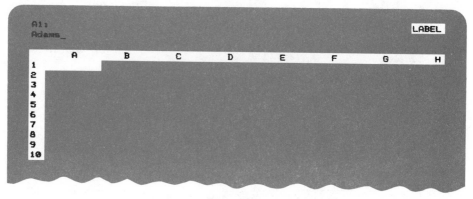

Fig.   1-14

If you make a mistake while typing in a name (or any data into any cell, for that matter), you can use the backspace key to back up and re-type your entry. The backspace key has a large, dark back-arrow

(♦) on it. Once Adams is typed on the screen, press the down-arrow key, which will cause his name to appear in cell A1, and the cell pointer to move down to cell A2. (Fig. 1-15).

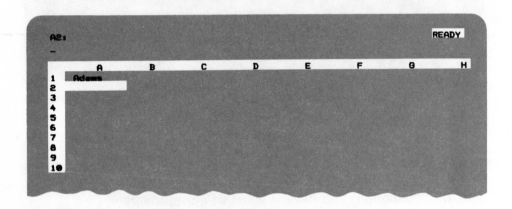

Fig.   1-15

Now type in the name Brown, followed by a press on the down-arrow key, and the same thing occurs, but his names goes into cell A2, and the pointer moves to cell A3, as shown in Fig. 1-16.

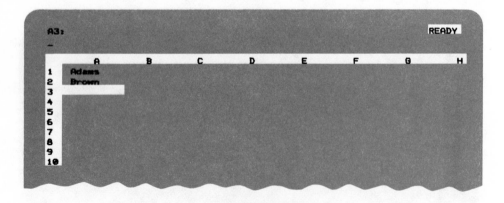

Fig.   1-16

Now simply type in each name, one at a time, following each name with a press on the down-arrow key. When you're done, the screen looks like Fig. 1-17.

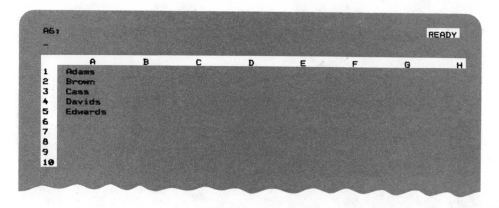

Fig. 1-17

Now you can type in some test scores, like these:

Adams	100	90
Brown	90	80
Cass	100	95
Davids	98	80
Edwards	90	75

You need to put these in the second and third columns of the worksheet. Use the arrow keys (or the GoTo key) to position the cell pointer to cell B1, as shown in Fig. 1-18.

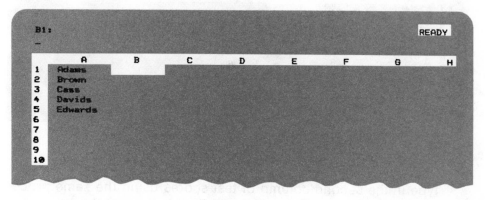

Fig. 1-18

Type in the numbers just as you did the labels. You can type in the first set of scores by typing in each number one at a time, following each number with a press on the down-arrow key, which will make the worksheet look like Fig. 1-19.

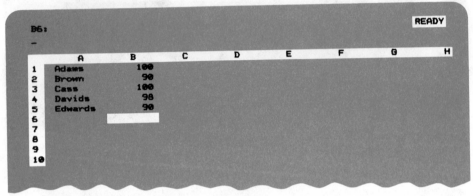

Fig.   1-19

Notice that the cell pointer is down in row 6. To type in the next set of scores, you need to get the pointer up to cell C1, either by using some arrow keys or the GoTo key. Once that's done, the worksheet will look like Fig. 1-20.

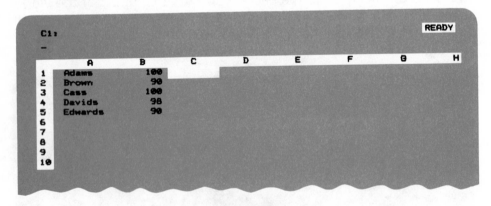

Fig.   1-20

Type in the second column of test scores using the same procedure as for the first column of scores. That is, type in the first score in the column, followed by a press on the down-arrow key; the second score, followed by a press on the down-arrow key; and so forth, until the screen looks like Fig. 1-21.

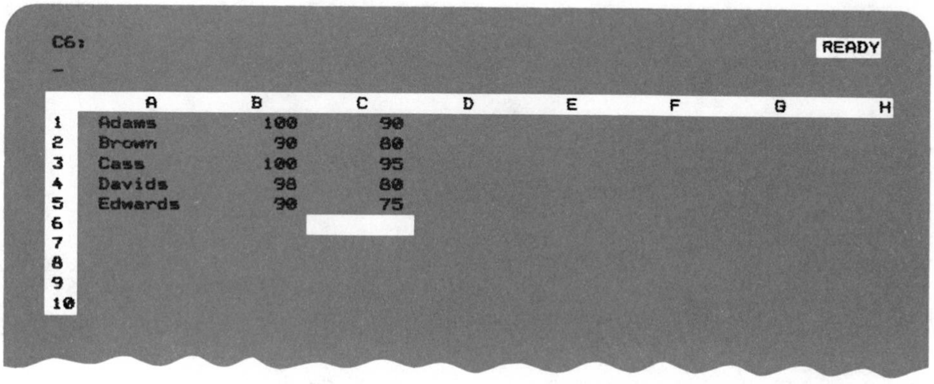

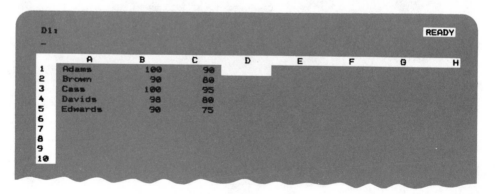

Fig. 1-21

And now we have the basic data of a grade book. But we don't have the students' average test scores. We're certainly not about to figure them out by hand when we have a computer at our finger tips. We'll have to add some formulas to have 1-2-3 do this work for us.

First we need to figure out a formula. Adams' average test score is the sum of the contents of B1 and C1 divided by two. In a 1-2-3 formula, that looks like this:

$$(B1+C1)/2$$

To type it in, position the cell pointer to column D, row 1, as in Fig. 1-22.

Fig. 1-22

Next, type in the formula (B1+C1)/2, followed by a press on the down-arrow key. This gives the result shown in Fig. 1-23. The result of the formula—not the formula itself—is displayed in that cell.

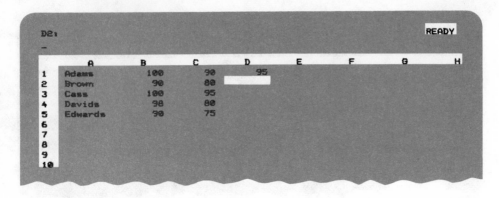

Fig.   1-23

Adams' test average (95) is displayed in cell D1. The pointer is now in cell D2. The formula for Brown's average test score is:

(B2+C2)/2

So if you type in this formula, and press the down-arrow key, Brown's average is displayed in cell D2 (as in Fig. 1-24), and the pointer has advanced to cell D3.

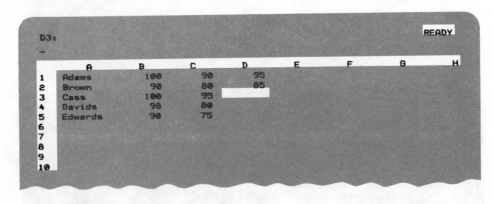

Fig.   1-24

Now we can type in the rest of the formulas in the usual fashion. The remaining formulas are:

(B3+C3)/2
(B4+C4)/2
(B5+C5)/2

As you type in each one, the result appears on the screen.

Now here is the real beauty of an electronic worksheet. Suppose you discover an error in Davids' first exam score. All you need to do is position the pointer to the appropriate cell as shown in Fig. 1-25.

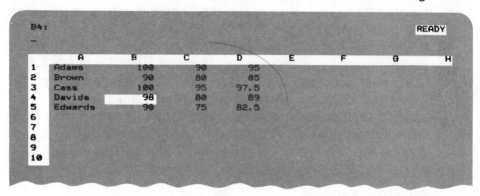

Fig.   1-25

Let's change that to 100. Since the pointer is already in this cell, we just type in 100, and press the RETURN key. The 100 replaces the 98 in the cell, and 1-2-3 instantly updates his average! Fig 1-26 shows this result.

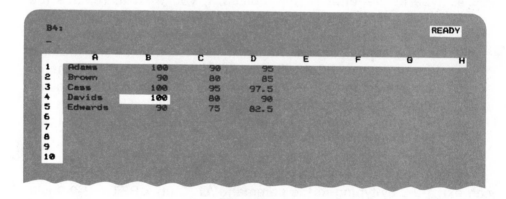

Fig.   1-26

Any time you change an item of data on the worksheet, all formula cells recalculate and present the proper results.

SAVING THE WORKSHEET

Keep one very important point in mind when you use the worksheet. If you exit 1-2-3, or turn off the computer prior to saving the worksheet, it will be gone for good. Saving the worksheet requires a few simple steps:

1. You need to think of a file name to store the worksheet under. The file name should be no more than eight characters in length. For example, a good file name for this worksheet might be GRADES.
2. Decide which disk to store the worksheet on. If you have a computer with two disk drives, (A and B), 1-2-3 will store the worksheet on the disk in drive B. If you want to store the worksheet on some other drive, such as a hard disk, you can specify that drive in the file name. For example, to store GRADES on drive C, make the file name C:GRADES.
3. Type in the command /FS (File Save). The 1-2-3 control panel will ask you to:

Enter save file name:

Type in the name of the file (RET). If you select a file name that already exists, 1-2-3 will ask:

Cancel   Replace
Cancel Command—Leave existing file in place

4. Type in the letter R (for replace) if you wish to replace the existing file's contents with the current worksheet's contents. You can either select R to replace, thereby erasing the old file, or C to cancel, which will allow you to save the file under a different name. 1-2-3 will store the file on disk with the name you provide and the extension .WKS. So the GRADES file will actually be saved as GRADES.WKS. The WKS is short for "worksheet," and is used to tell 1-2-3 that this file contains a worksheet.

When you have finished creating and saving a worksheet, you can exit 1-2-3 by typing in the command /Q (Quit) <RET>. 1-2-3 will double-check to make sure this is what you meant. Just answer Yes, and the Lotus Access System menu will reappear on the screen. From the Lotus Access menu, you can choose Exit to get back to the A> prompt.

If you now perform a directory of the disk on which you saved the file, you will see that the file does indeed exist on the disk. That is, if you originally saved the current worksheet with the file name GRADES, and you now type in the command DIR B: <RET>, you will see the GRADES.WKS on the directory which appears on your screen.

In the future, when you want to use 1-2-3 again, just put the Lotus System Disk in drive A, and type in LOTUS (RET) next to the A> prompt. At that point, you will see the Lotus Access System menu again, and you can select the 1-2-3 option to get a blank worksheet to work with. If you wish to resume working on a previous worksheet (such as GRADES), you can use the /FR (File Retrieve) command to call it back onto the screen. Just type in /FR and the file name to retrieve (e.g., GRADES) and press the RETURN key. We'll discuss commands such as /FS and /FR in more detail later.

There is a great deal more to 1-2-3 than what we've covered here of course. In the next chapter, we'll discuss 1-2-3 *functions,* which will expand our calculating powers beyond simple formulas.

Chapter 2

FUNCTIONS AND FORMULAS

If your pocket calculator cost more than $1.98, or came as a prize in a breakfast cereal box from a reputable company, chances are it has some built-in function keys on it, such as a square-root key, or perhaps even some trigonometric functions. These are provided because it is pretty difficult to do these calculations using add, subtract, multiply, and divide. The 1-2-3 worksheet has many built-in functions too. However, you don't press a key to use a 1-2-3 function. You type the name of the function (preceded by the @ symbol) into a cell, and 1-2-3 handles it from there.

Most functions require an *argument*. An argument in computer jargon is simply some value for the function to work upon. (Personally, I have had other types of arguments with my computer—none of which I've ever won.) The argument to a function is always placed in parentheses after the function. For example, the function to determine the square root of a number in 1-2-3 is @SQRT. The function can't do much by itself, it needs to know what to find the square root of. That is, it needs an argument. To ask 1-2-3 for the square root of nine, simply put this formula (the function with its argument) into any cell of the worksheet:

@SQRT(9)

Whichever cell you place this formula into will display the number 3, the square root of nine. The (9) is the argument. The argument need not be a specific number. It can be another cell's value. For example, if cell A1 contained the number 64, then the formula:

@SQRT(A1)

would display 8, the square root of 64.

The argument need not be a single cell either. For example, if cell A1 contained the number 90, and cell A2 contained the number 10, then the formula:

@SQRT(A1+A2)

would display 10, the square root of cell A1 (90) plus A2 (10).

In some cases, the argument may actually be a whole row or column of numbers. For example, the SUM and AVG (average) functions are usually used with numerous arguments. Fig. 2-1 shows a worksheet with a column of numbers typed in.

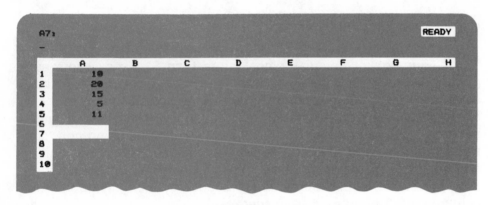

Fig.   2-1

We can use the symbol .. to stand for "all the values between one cell and another." Therefore, to sum all of the values between A1 and A5 (inclusive), type in the formula:

@SUM(A1..A5)

More specifically, position the cell pointer A7 (as shown in Fig. 2-1), type in the formula, press RETURN, and get the result displayed in Fig. 2-2. The sum is displayed in cell A7.

Similarly, you can place the cell pointer to cell A8, type in the formula:

@AVG(A1..A5)

press RETURN, and the average of the column of numbers would appear in cell A8 as shown in Fig. 2-3.

We selected cells A7 and A8 at random. No rule states that these formulas must appear at the bottom of the column or even in the

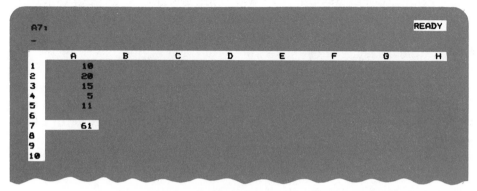

Fig. 2-2

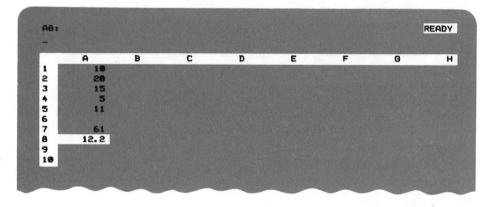

Fig. 2-3

same column. We could have placed these formulas in any cell on the entire worksheet and still come up with the same answer.

Functions can also use other functions as their argument. For example, the @ABS function converts a number to its absolute value (i.e., if it is a negative number, ABS will change it to a positive number). So, if cell A1 contained the number −90, and cell A2 contained the number −10, then the function:

@SQRT(@ABS(A1+A2))

would display 10, the square root of the absolute value of −100 (−90 + −10). We call these *nested* functions, because one is inside the other. Any formula that contains parentheses must have exactly the same number of open and closed parentheses. Hence the formula:

@SQRT(@ABS(A1+A2)

won't work, because there are two open parentheses, and only one closed parenthesis. 1-2-3 would beep at you if you typed in this formula, and wouldn't accept it until it was fixed.

A quick easy way to make sure you have equal parentheses in a formula is to start counting from zero at the left, add one for each open parenthesis, and subtract one for each closed parentheses. If you end up wth zero at the end, you have entered the formula correctly. For example, when we try it with the formula below, the end result is zero:

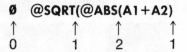

However, with this formula, the end result is one because a closed parenthesis is missing:

$$\emptyset \quad \text{@SQRT(@ABS(A1+A2)}$$
$$\uparrow \qquad\qquad \uparrow \qquad \uparrow \qquad\qquad \uparrow$$
$$0 \qquad\qquad 1 \qquad 2 \qquad\qquad 1$$

This concentration on precision may seem trivial now, but when you nest functions five or six deep, parentheses can become a real chore. Programmers use this technique all the time when writing software because it is easy, and it works.

Arguments may also be quite complex. For example, the following formula:

@ABS(@SUM(A1..A5)+G7/4)

states that the absolute value of the sum of columns A1 through A5, plus the quotient of cell G7 divided by four, is to be displayed. Again, notice that an equal number of open and closed parentheses occur within the argument list.

Functions do not always display results in a cell immediately. For example, the function:

@SQRT(@ABS(A1))

only displays the square root of the absolute value of the contents of cell A1. The absolute value, per se, is never displayed. Therefore, we often use the term *returns* when discussing the effect of a function on a value. That is, we "send" the function some numeric value, and it "returns" another value. In the expression below:

@SQRT(81)

we send the value (81) to the SQRT function, and it returns the value, 9 (the square root of 81). We'll use the term "returns" often throughout this chapter.

Functions are a tool you can use with your worksheet. Before you start to build a worksheet, it's good to know what tools you have available to work with. In this chapter, we'll summarize some of the more commonly used 1-2-3 functions. Don't worry about memorizing them. Just scan through and make a mental note of those which you may want to use in your profession.

As in the foregoing examples, some functions require only a single argument. Others require a range of values (e.g., A1–A5), while others require combinations of single arguments and ranges.

We will separate the various functions into types to help you more easily spot functions relevant to your particular needs. The 1-2-3 manual discusses all the functions in more technical detail.

SUMMARY OF FUNCTIONS

This summary shows the name and proper argument for many of the 1-2-3's more commonly used functions. Some functions operate on entire ranges of numbers (either a row, column, or even a block). When this is the case, we use the word "range" in the argument list [e.q., @SUM(range)]. Otherwise, we use a single variable name [e.g., @SQRT(x)]. Some functions require two or three arguments in which case we separate the arguments with commas [e.g., @IRR(guess, range)]. Some functions require no arguments, and appear without an argument list (e.g., @RAND).

Wherever a single argument is required, the argument can be either an actual number or a reference to a cell. Whenever a range is required, you should use the beginning and end points in the range (e.g., A1..A10).

We provide a brief description of each function along with examples of proper *syntax* (grammatical rules). We use the words "calculates," "displays," and "returns" interchangeably.

General Mathematical Functions

1-2-3 provides these general mathematical functions:

@SUM(range)   **Sum of a Group of Numbers**

Returns the sum of a group of numbers specified in the range. Example:

@SUM(A1..A25) gives the sum of all numbers in the column A1 to A25.

@AVG(range)

Average of a Group of Numbers

Returns the average of a group of numbers (including zeros, but not blanks). Example: @AVG(A1..Z1) returns the average of all numbers in row A1 to Z1.

@ABS(x)

The Absolute Value of a Number

Returns the absolute value of a number or a single cell. Example: @ABS(B2) returns the absolute value of the contents of cell B2.

@ROUND(x,places)

Round a Number

Rounds the value to the number of places specified. Example: @ROUND(9.129,2) returns the value, 9.13. Either x or places may be cell locations [[@ROUND(A1,A2)   ].

@INT(x)

Integer Portion of a Number

Removes the decimal portion of a number. Example: If cell B1 contains 1.23456, @INT(B1) returns 1.

@RAND

Random Numbers

Returns a random number between 0 and 1. Does not use an argument. Example: @RAND returns the value 0.147506 or any other number between 0 and 1.

@SQRT(x)

Square Root

Displays the square root of a number. Example: @SQRT(x).

Business Functions

The business functions provide built-in financial calculations commonly used in business.

@IRR(guess,range)

Internal Rate of Return

Returns the approximate internal rate of return for a series of evenly distributed payments, starting at the value of guess. If convergence to within .0000001 does not occur within 20 iterations, 1-2-3 gives up and returns the message ERR. Example @IRR (.19,A1..A12) attempts to find the internal rate of return for values in cells A1 to A12, starting at an estimated IRR of .19.

@FV(payment,interest,n)

Future Value

Calculates the future value of fixed payments over a number of periods. Example: @FV(A1,B1,C1) where A1 is the amount of each payment, B1 the interest rate, and C1 the number of periods.

@NPV(x,range)

Net Present Value

Calculates the net present value of a series of future cash flows. x is the per-period interest rate, range is any single column or row of numbers. Example: @NPV(16.5,A1..A12).

@PMT(principal,interest,n)

Payment on a Loan

Calculates the individual payments on a loan with known principal, interest rate and term. Example: @PMT(A1,B1,C1), where A1 contains the principal, B1 the interest rate, and C1 the number of payments to be made.

@PV(payment,interest,term)

Present Value

Returns the present value of loan. Example: @PV(C1,C2,C3), where C1 is the amount of each payment, C2 is the interest rate, and C3 the number of payments to be made.

Statistical Functions

1-2-3 includes a number of functions for performing basic statistical analyses of data. Section III of this book discusses addition statistical functions that are used with 1-2-3's database management capability.

@COUNT(range)

Count the Items in a List

Counts how many nonblank cells there are in a range of cells, and returns that number. Example: @COUNT(A1..A10) would return 10 if all cells were filled. It would return 6 if four cells were blank.

@STD(range)

Standard Deviation

Returns the standard deviation of a range of numbers (it ignores blank cells in the list). Example: @STD(Z1..Z28) provides the standard deviation of all values between cells Z1 and Z28 (inclusive).

@VAR(range)

Variance

Calculates the variance in a series of numbers. Example: @VAR(A1..A5) determines the variance of the numbers in cells A1 to A5. Ignores blank cells.

@MIN(range)

Smallest in a Range

Displays the smallest number in a series of numbers. Example: @MIN(A1..A20) displays the smallest value in the series from cell A1 to cell A20.

@MAX(range)

Largest in a Range

Displays the largest number in a series of numbers. Example: @MAX(A1..A20) displays the largest value in the series from cell A1 to cell A20.

Trigonometric Functions

The trigonometric functions are used in scientific and engineering settings. Besides the three summarized here, 1-2-3 includes natural log, log base 10, arc cosine, arc sine, 2-quadrant arc tangent, 4-quadrant arc tangent, exponent, modulus, and pi.

@COS(x)   **Cosine**

Returns the cosine of the argument in radians. Example: @COS(E2) returns the cosine of the value in cell E2.

@SIN(X)   **Sine**

Calculates the sine of x. The answer is expressed as an angle in radians. Example: @SIN(B3) returns the sine of the contents of cell B3.

@TAN   **Tangent**

Returns the tangent interpreted as an angle in radians. Example @TAN(C3) returns the tangent of cell C3.

Logical Functions

The logical functions are used to make decisions within the worksheet. The IF function allows you to use a number of *logical operators* for making decisions. These are:

=	Equal
<	Less than
<=	Less than or equal to
>	Greater than
>=	Greater than or equal to
<>	Not equal to
#NOT#	Not
#AND#	And
#OR#	Or

We'll see some examples of their use after the summaries below.

@IF(condition, true, false)

Make a Decision

Tests to see if a value in condition is true. If so, the first argument in the list is selected. If the condition is false the second argument in the list is selected. Example: @IF (B1>0,C3/B1,0). This argument says "If the value of cell B1 is greater than 0, then display the quotient of the contents of cell B3 divided by the contents of cell B1, otherwise, just display a zero."

@CHOOSE(x,option1, option2. . . .optionn)

Choose an option

Chooses an argument based on the value of x. If x is 1, the first argument is performed. If x is 2, the second argument is performed, and so forth. Example: @CHOOSE(A1,01,02,03,04, 05). In this example, if cell A1 contains a 3, the content of cell 03 is displayed.

With the addition of logical operators in the logical functions, we can be very specific about making decisions in the spreadsheet. Some examples of decision-making formulas and their English equivalents are listed below:

Formula	English Equivalent
@IF(B4<>C4,A1,A2)	If cell B4's contents do not equal cell C4's contents, display the contents of cell A1; otherwise, display the contents of cell A2.
@IF(BA>1#AND#C4>1, A1,A2)	If both cell B4 and C4's contents are greater than 1, display cell A1; otherwise, display cell A2.
@IF(B4>1#OR#C4>1,A1,A2)	If either cell B4 or C4's contents are greater than 1, display cell A1; otherwise, display cell A2.

We'll see some practical applications for these functions in due time.

Table Functions

Sometimes an exact mathematical relationship does not exist between two related sets of numbers. For example, the tax tables have an income range and a base tax fee and percentage rate for each income. To determine our taxes, we need to look them up in the table; there is no direct mathematical correlation. 1-2-3 can also look up information in tables, using the table functions.

@HLOOKUP(x,range,offset)

Horizontal Table Lookup

Looks up the value of x in the specified range, and returns the value in the range "offset" number of rows below. If x is a value between two numbers in the range, the function selects the lesser of the two possible values. For example, there are three rows of figures below, composing a range whose upper left corner is cell A1, and whose lower right corner is cell E3:

	A	B	C	D	E
1	10	20	30	40	50
2	123	234	345	456	567
3	0	0.05	0.1	0.15	0.2

The @HLOOKUP function can look up data in either rows two or three. Example: @HLOOKUP(30,A1..E3,2) will return 0.1, since this value is 2 rows directly below 30.

@VLOOKUP
(x,range,offset)

Vertical Table Lookup

Is the same as the HLOOKUP function, but works with vertical ranges of numbers (columns).

Error-Trapping Functions

The error-trapping functions respond to errors that occur when we make the worksheet attempt to do something impossible, such as take the square root of a negative or nonexistent number.

@ERR

Error

Makes the value of the cell ERR (error). Example: @IF(B1>0,@SQRT(B1), @ERR). This functions says, "If the contents of B1 are greater than zero, display the square root, otherwise, display ERR."

@NA

Not Available

Makes the value of the cell NA (not available). Example: @IF(B1>0,@SQRT(B1),@NA). This function says, "If the contents of B1 are greater than zero, display the square root of cell B1, otherwise, display NA."

@ISERR(x)

Detect an Error

Returns a "true" (1.0) if an error occurred in the named cell, otherwise it returns "false" (0). Example: @IF(@ISERR(B1),0,B2/B1). This function says, "If cell B1 contains an error, display 0; otherwise display the quotient of cell B2 divided by cell B1."

@ISNA(x)

Detect Unavailable Data

This function returns a "true" (1.0) if data in the named cell is Not Available; otherwise it returns "false" (0). Example: @IF(@ISNA(B1),@NA,B2/B1). This function says, "If cell B1 is NA (not available) display NA, otherwise display the quotient of cell B2 divided by cell B1."

Date Functions

Computers generally have a hard time dealing with our calendar system. Computers like nice even series of numbers, and have a very difficult time with concepts such as "Thirty days hath September, April, June, and November. . . ." To help the computer along, 1-2-3 has a built-in "serial date" system. In the serial system each day from January 1st, 1900 to December 31st, 2099 has a number associated with it. 01/01/1900 is number 1, 12/31/2099 is number 73049. All the dates in between are numbered appropriately. The 1-2-3 date functions allow you to translate dates back and forth from the calendar system to the serial system.

@DATE(year,month,day)

Determine the Serial Date

Translates a calendar date to a serial date. Example: @DATE(84,03,31) returns the serial date for March 31st, 1984, which is 30772.

@TODAY

Today's Serial Date

Most computers usually ask for today's date when you first turn them on. This function turns that date into a serial date. Example: @TODAY returns the serial date for today.

SAMPLE WORKSHEETS USING FUNCTIONS

Take some time now to look at some useful worksheets that combine numbers, labels, formulas, and functions. For purposes of illustration, we'll display the actual formulas on the screen in some cases rather than their output, so you can analyze the worksheet's actual contents. 1-2-3, of course, will just display the calculated value.

The first is a simple loan-analysis worksheet that calculates the payment on a loan for various terms, 1 to 5 years. This worksheet appears in Fig. 2-4.

Notice that there is a separate formula for each term:

@PMT(B1,B2/12,A?*12)

This formula calculates the payment for the principal, stored in cell B1; interest rate divided by 12 (months), which is stored in cell B2; and the term (times 12 months); which is stored in column A for this particular row.

Of course, what you type in will not appear as you typed it, because 1-2-3 always shows the results of a formula rather than the

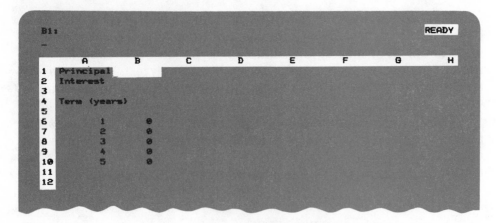

```
B1:                                                              READY
─

         A        B         C          D        E        F       G        H
1  Principal
2  Interest
3
4  Term (years)
5
6            1            @PMT(B1,B2/12,A6*12)
7            2            @PMT(B1,B2/12,A7*12)
8            3            @PMT(B1,B2/12,A8*12)
9            4            @PMT(B1,B2/12,A9*12)
10           5            @PMT(B1,B2/12,A10*12)
11
12
```

Fig.   2-4

formula itself. [Actually, you can make 1-2-3 display formulas rather than their outcomes by typing in the command /WGFT (Worksheet Global Format Text)]. If you position the cell pointer to each location where something appears in Fig. 2-4, and type in the displayed labels and formulas, you will end up with a worksheet that looks like the one in Fig. 2-5. Notice that all values are presently 0, because we've only typed in the labels and formulas.

```
B1:                                                              READY
─

         A        B         C          D        E        F       G        H
1  Principal
2  Interest
3
4  Term (years)
5
6            1         0
7            2         0
8            3         0
9            4         0
10           5         0
11
12
```

Fig.   2-5

To use the worksheet position the cell pointer to cell B1 and type in a principal amount, say 5000 <RET>. Then move the cell pointer in cell B2 and type in an interest rate, say 16.5% (don't forget the percent sign, since this is a percentage figure). The result, shown in

Fig.2-6, is the monthly payment for the loan for each of the five possible terms.

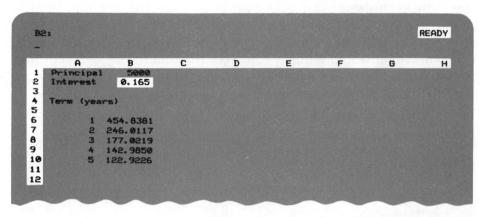

Fig.   2-6

Of course, if you were to change any of the assumptions (principal, interest, or term), the calculated cells would recalculate immediately, and display the new results.

Let's look at another worksheet that uses some of the statistical functions, and deals with rows and columns of data. Fig. 2-7 displays another grade book example, but with many calculations.

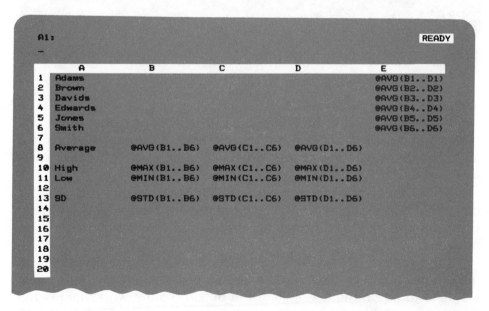

Fig.   2-7

Notice that the cells in column E1 to E6 calculate the averages for each student. The cells in row B8 to D8 calculate the average score on each exam. The cells in row B10 to D10 and C10 to D10 calculate the highest (MAX) and lowest (MIN) scores on each exam. Row B13 to D13 calculates the standard deviation for each exam. This worksheet would actually look like the one in Fig. 2-8 with just the labels and formulas typed in. Note that the results of all formulas are ERR because there are no data in the grade book.

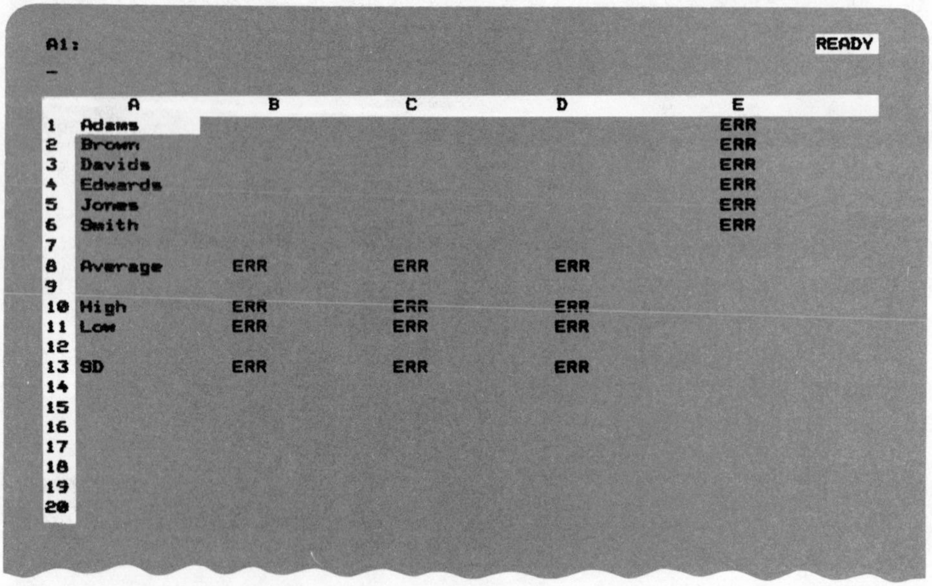

Fig. 2-8

When you fill in some test scores, the proper results of the formulas will appear as shown in Fig. 2-9. And of course, if you make any changes to existing scores, 1-2-3 will update all calculations immediately.

There are quite a few more decimal places than we need on most calculations. Perhaps two would be sufficient, and would certainly clean up the display. Formatting displays is the topic of the next chapter.

Let's look at an example of 1-2-3's ability to look up data in a table now. We'll use the classic example of a tax table. In this case, we need to put in the tax table at the outset, so the worksheet looks like the one in Fig. 2-10. Notice that most formulas refer to cell B16

A1:   READY
—

	A	B	C	D	E
1	Adams	100	90	80	90
2	Brown	90	80	90	86.6666
3	Davids	100	85	90	91.6666
4	Edwards	90	90	80	86.6666
5	Jones	90	100	100	96.6666
6	Smith	90	100	100	96.6666
7					
8	Average	93.3333	91.6666	90	
9					
10	High	100	100	100	
11	Low	90	85	80	
12					
13	SD	4.71495	6.236095	8.164965	
14					
15					
16					
17					
18					
19					
20					

Fig.   2-9

B16:   READY
—

	A	B	C	D	E	F	G	H
1	Taxable	Tax	Plus %					
2	Income	Owed	Over					
3	————————————————————————							
4	0	0	0.01					
5	3120	31.2	0.02					
6	5450	77.8	0.03					
7	7790	148	0.04					
8	10160	242.8	0.05					
9	12500	359.8	0.06					
10	14850	500.8	0.07					
11	17170	663.2	0.08					
12	19520	851.2	0.09					
13	21860	1061.8	0.1					
14	24200	1295.9	0.11					
15								
16	Income:		(————— Enter income here					
17	Base owed:	@VLOOKUP(B16,A4..C14,1)						
18	Plus:	+B16-@VLOOKUP(B16,A4..C14,0)						
19	Percent:	@VLOOKUP(B16,A4..C14,2)						
20	Total tax:	+B17+(B18*B19)						

Fig.   2-10

as a piece of data. This is the cell into which you type an individual's income to figure his taxes. Let's study this worksheet in more detail before trying it out.

Notice that cells in the table from A4 to C14 contain the actual tax table. Column A of the table holds a range of incomes, column B holds the base tax rate, and column C holds the percentage figure for calculating taxes on the amount of income over the base rate. Cells B17 to B20 do all the calculating.

Cell B16 will contain an income. Cell B17 contains this formula:

@VLOOKUP(B16,A4..C14,1)

The formula looks up the income stored in B16 in the tax table. It returns the base tax rate, because the third argument (1) instructs the formula to return the value in column B (1 column to the right of column A). If the formula can't find the exact income in the tax table, it picks the next-lowest income in the range of incomes (e.g., if income is 15000, the table lookup will select 14850). The formula will then return the base tax rate for 14850, (which is 500.8), and place that amount into cell B17.

In cell B18, the formula determines how much over the income cutoff the individual made. It looks like this:

+B16−@VLOOKUP(B16,A4..C14,Ø)

This formula subtracts the cutoff value in the table from the actual income. For example, if actual income were 15000, then this formula would become 15000−14850, because the @VLOOKUP value of 15000 with a zero offset is 14850 (closest to, and below 15000).

Cell B19 looks up the appropriate percentage rate for the actual income. The formula looks like this:

@VLOOKUP(B16,A4..C14,2)

This is basically the same as looking up the base tax rate, however the offset argument is two, so the value returned is the percentage figure from column C. Therefore, if the actual income were 15000, then the percentage rate returned by this formula will be 0.07.

Finally, cell B20 determines the total tax owed. Its formula looks like this:

+B17+(B18*B19)

which simply adds the base tax owed to the percentage figure times the amount over.

The worksheet, without an income figure in it, will look like Fig. 2-11. The Income cell is empty, and calculations are zero (except for the percentage figure, which is 0.01, and correctly so).

```
B16:                                                              READY
-

        A           B           C        D       E       F       G       H
1   Taxable      Tax         Plus %
2   Income       Owed        Over
3   ------------------------------------
4         0          0           0.01
5      3120       31.2          0.02
6      5450       77.8          0.03
7      7790        148          0.04
8     10160      242.8          0.05
9     12500      359.8          0.06
10    14850      500.8          0.07
11    17170      663.2          0.08
12    19520      851.2          0.09
13    21860     1061.8           0.1
14    24200     1295.9          0.11
15
16  Income:              (------- Enter income here
17  Base owed:       0
18  Plus:            0
19  Percent:         0
20  Total tax:       0
```

Fig.   2-11

```
B16:                                                              READY
-

        A           B           C        D       E       F       G
1   Taxable      Tax         Plus %
2   Income       Owed        Over
3   ------------------------------------
4         0          0           0.01
5      3120       31.2          0.02
6      5450       77.8          0.03
7      7790        148          0.04
8     10160      242.8          0.05
9     12500      359.8          0.06
10    14850      500.8          0.07
11    17170      663.2          0.08
12    19520      851.2          0.09
13    21860     1061.8           0.1
14    24200     1295.9          0.11
15
16  Income:      15000   (------- Enter income here
17  Base owed: 500.8
18  Plus:          150
19  Percent:      0.07
20  Total tax: 511.3
```

Fig.   2-12

If you position the cell pointer to cell B16, and type in a hypothetical income, such as 15000, 1-2-3 will immediately calculate the entire tax due, as shown in Fig. 2-12.

Of course, if you position the cell pointer to cell B16 and type in someone else's income, then this worksheet will immediately calculate his or her own taxes, too.

If this last example seems a bit too abstract to grasp in a single reading, don't worry about it. Table lookups are by nature a bit abstract and are rarely used in practical situations. However, you might make a mental note of this example should you ever need to refer to it for a future worksheet you create.

The worksheets displayed here are relatively small and simple. 1-2-3 allows us to create worksheets of enormous size and complexity. With the knowledge gained so far, you can probably create just about any worksheet you heart desires. It is simply a matter of positioning the cell pointer to where you want to add data, and typing in whatever label, number, or formula you wish. It helps to know what functions you have available to you to make the work easier.

In the next chapter, we'll discuss techniques for formatting the worksheet.

Chapter 3

FORMATTING THE WORKSHEET

In this chapter we'll be working with 1-2-3 *commands.* A command always begins with a slash (/). Commands never appear in cells. Rather, they are used to work with the worksheet as a whole. The commands are hierarchically arranged in menus. The 1-2-3 main menu of commands appears on the screen, as soon as you type in a slash, as shown in Fig. 3-1.

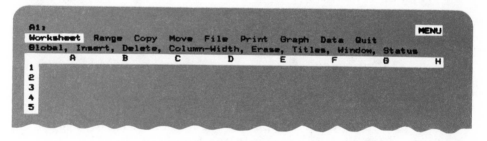

Fig. 3-1

Notice that the prompt in the upper right corner of the screen now reads "Menu," indicating that you are in the menu mode. There is a cell pointer in the menu itself, and right now it is highlighting the menu option Worksheet. Worksheet is a command that has a whole series of subcommands associated with it. These are displayed just below the main menu. You can use the left- and right-arrow keys to move the menu pointer to other options. If you move the menu pointer to Range, a submenu of commands that go along with the Range command appears in the control panel. To select a command, position the pointer to the appropriate option and press the RETURN key.

For example, in the first chapter we used the /FS (File Save) command to save a worksheet. We could have optionally done the following:

1. Type in a slash (/), which would make the Main Menu appear as such:
   WORKSHEET   Range Copy Move File Print Graph Data Quit Global, Insert, Delete, Column-Width, Erase, Titles, Window, Status

2. Press the right arrow key four times until the menu pointer is highlighting the File command, as below:
   Worksheet Range Copy Move FILE Print Graph Data Quit Retrieve, Save, Combine, Xtract, Erase, List, Import, Directory

3. Press RETURN, which makes the File subcommand menu replace the main menu, like so:
   RETRIEVE   Save Combine Xtract Erase List Import Directory Erase the worksheet and read a worksheet file
   Now the Retrieve subcommand is highlighted, and a brief description of its purpose is displayed beneath the menu.

4. Press the right arrow key once, so the pointer moves to the Save option. Now its purpose is briefly described beneath the menu, as such:
   Retrieve SAVE Combine Xtract Erase List Import Directory Store the entire worksheet in a worksheet file

5. Press RETURN. This selects Save as the command to perform. 1-2-3 then asks:
   Enter save file name:
   Also, any existing file names are displayed below this prompt. At any point, you can type in a file name, press RETURN. 1-2-3 saves the file and returns to the Ready mode.

So you actually have two methods of giving commands to 1-2-3. One is by typing in a slash and the first letter of each command. For example, to save a file, you could quickly type in /FS, and the control panel would ask for the name of the file to save. The second method, as described above, is to type in commands by pointing to menu options. That is, type in a slash to display the Main Menu, then move the menu pointer to appropriate command and press RETURN. You may prefer the latter until you have memorized the commands, or if you are not a good typist.

For the sake of simplicity, we'll use the following method of expressing commands in this book: Whenever a new command is introduced, we'll display both its abbreviated form and longer pointing form in parentheses. For example, when you see a command like this:

/FS (File Save)

you can use either method. You can either type in the /FS, or you can type in the slash: move the menu pointer to the File command in the main menu, and press RETURN. Then move the menu pointer to the Save command in the next menu, and press return again. Whichever method you prefer is up to you.

Remember, we'll always present commands in this format:

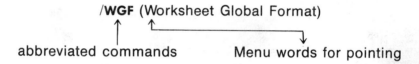

In this second example, you can either type in /WGF, or type in a slash, press RETURN when the menu pointer is highlighting the word Worksheet; move the menu pointer to the word Global in the next menu that appears, the press RETURN; then move the pointer to the word "Format" in the next menu to appear on the screen, and press RETURN again.

If you ever get a bit lost using the pointing method of selecting menu options, press the escape (Esc) key. The escape key unselects commands. So if you get lost, the escape key can back you up into more familiar territory. So now, just remember this important saying:

If in doubt, ESCape key out.

If you're ever lost, just keep pressing the escape key until you are back in familiar territory.

OK, now let's get on with the business of custom formatting the worksheet to our liking.

When you first call up 1-2-3, it displays a blank worksheet with an initial format: each column is nine spaces wide. Labels are automatically left-justified in a cell, and numbers appear with as many decimal places as will fit in the cell. Formulas display results rather than themselves. You can change one or all of these format settings for a single cell, a column or *globally* (on the entire worksheet).

FORMATTING COLUMNS

There are several ways to format a column in the worksheet. The simplest is to define a new width for the entire column. 1-2-3 usually assigns a standard width of nine characters to each column on the worksheet, but you can change that. For example, in the grade book worksheet, nine characters is a little slim for displaying the students' names. A column width of 20 would be better for the names. The /WC (Worksheet Column-width) command allows you to assign a column a width of one (minimum) to 72 (maximum) characters.

Fig. 3-2 shows part of a blank worksheet that has not been formatted in any fashion.

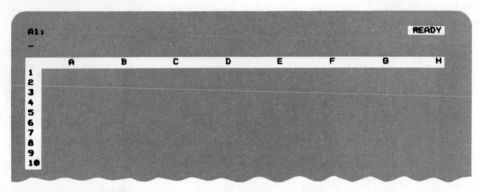

Fig. 3-2

To widen column 1 to 20 characters, perform the following steps:

1. Position the cell pointer to the column you wish to format. (The cell pointer is already in cell A1, so you need not do anything in this case.)
2. Type in the command /WC. The screen will display two options: Set and Reset. Select Set. 1-2-3 asks you to:

Enter column width (1 . .72): 9

and displays the current column width.
3. Type in the new column width, 20 <RET>.

The column width adjusts accordingly, as in Fig. 3-3.
Note that columns G and H have been bumped off the screen, because the additional width in column A takes up more room in the window.

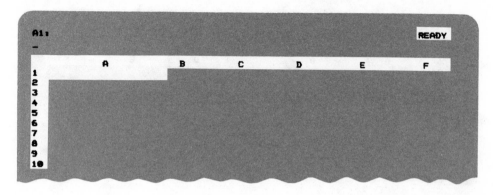

Fig. 3-3

Another way to set the column width is to position the pointer to the column and type in the /WC command. When 1-2-3 asks for a new column width you can use the right-arrow key to widen the column, and the left-arrow key to slim it. Each time you press an arrow key, the column will widen or shrink by one space. Press RETURN when the column is at the desired width.

The other option on the /WC menu is Reset. If you select this option, the column will be reset to the initial width of nine.

You can also format the way in which numbers and labels are displayed in columns. For example, you can specify that all labels in a given cell be either left-justified, centered in the column, or right-justified. You can specify that labels be right-justified, like so:

Adams
Brubaker
Carlson
Decker
Smithsonian

For this type of formatting use the /RLP (Range Label Prefix) command. This command only works with labels that are already in the column as shown in Fig. 3-4.

Here are the steps for re-aligning the labels:

1. Type in the command /RL.
2. Select an option from the menu; Left, Right, or Centered.
3. Specify the Range (in this case, A1..A5) <RET>.

All labels shift to right-justification as shown in Fig. 3-5.

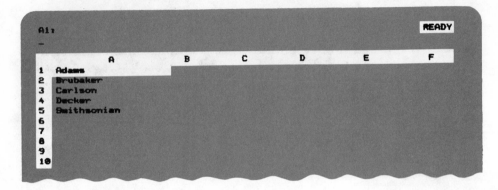

Fig.   3-4

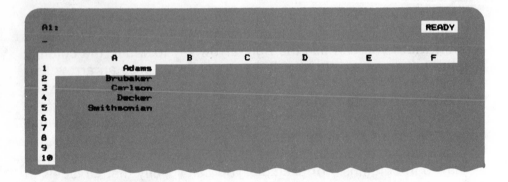

Fig.   3-5

The Center option from the /RL menu of choices centers all the labels in the column, as shown in Fig. 3-6.

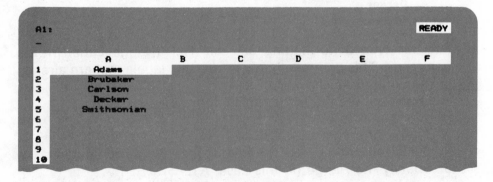

Fig.   3-6

Keep in mind that only the existing labels will be right-justified or centered. Any new labels added to the column will be left-justified, because 1-2-3 "naturally" aligns labels this way.

You can format columns of numbers in a similar fashion. While labels may be centered or left- or right-justified, numbers can be formatted in 9 different ways. 1-2-3 naturally displays numbers in the General format, given in Table 3-1, but you can change that to any of the other eight options. On the following page are the options for formatting numbers.

Fig. 3-7 displays a worksheet with individuals' names and some sales figures.

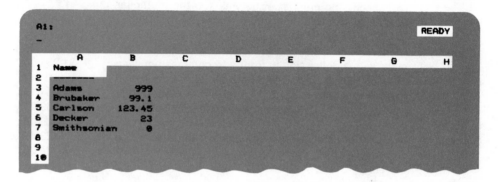

Fig. 3-7

The numbers in this example would look better if displayed in the Currency format. The command to format an existing column of numbers is /RF (Range Format). Here are the steps involved:

1. Select the /RF command.
2. From the menu of choices, move the pointer to the Currency option. Press RETURN. 1-2-3 will ask:

    Enter number of decimal places (0..15): 2

3. The number of decimals for the numbers is displayed as 2. You could change this by typing in another number, but since 2 is adequate just <RET>. 1-2-3 asks:

    Enter range to format: XX..XX

4. Specify the range of numbers to be formatted, in this case B1..B7 <RET>

The numbers in column B are redisplayed in currency format, as in Fig. 3-8.

Table 3-1. Number Formats

Format	Description	Examples
General	Zeros after the decimal point are not displayed. Very large and small numbers are displayed in scientific (exponent) format.	123.456 123.45 1.2E+12 9999.99
Fixed	Numbers are displayed with a fixed number of decimal places (between 0 and 5, inclusive). Zeros behind the decimal point are displayed.	123456 1234.5 123.45 12.345
Scientific	Numbers are expressed in scientific notation. You can specify the number of decimals in the multiplier (from 0 to 15). Exponent of 10 from −99 to +99.	1.23E+04 −1.2E−00 1.234E+15 −3.45E−24
Currency	Numbers are displayed in "dollars and cents" formats, with a dollar sign in front and commas between units of 1000. Negative numbers are displayed inside parentheses. Fixed number of decimal places (0-5) with zeros after the decimal point are displayed.	$123.45 $1,234.00 ($123.45) $1,234.10 $99.01 ($1.00)
, (comma)	Numbers are displayed in the same fashion as in the currency format, except the dollar sign is not displayed.	123.45 1,234.00 (123.45) 99,999,999.99
Percent	Displays the value of the cell, multiplied by 100, followed by a percent sign. Decimal places displayed can range from 0 to 15.	12.00% 10% 123.45% .00001%
Text	Formulas are shown as entered (as in the worksheet examples in the previous chapter). Numbers are displayed in the General format.	@AVG(A1..A5) 95 @SQRT(A1) 123.456
+/−	Each digit in the integer portion of the number is displayed as a + (if positive), − (if negative), or decimal point (if zero). Creates a small horizontal bar graph.	+++++ ++ − − − − − − . . . +
Date	Displays serial dates (discussed in the last chapter) in various formats, as described below: D1 Day-Month-Year format D2 Day-Month format D3 Month-Year format	 31-Mar-55 31-Mar Mar-55

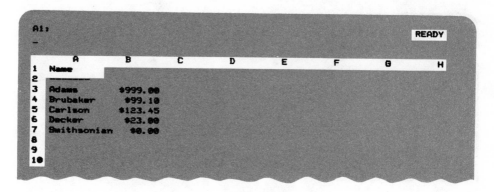

A1:   READY

	A	B	C	D	E	F	G	H
1	Name							
2								
3	Adams	$999.00						
4	Brubaker	$99.10						
5	Carlson	$123.45						
6	Decker	$23.00						
7	Smithsonian	$0.00						
8								
9								
10								

Fig. 3-8

If you end up with a symbol like ********* in a cell instead of the number, that means that the column is not wide enough to display the number. Use the /WC (Worksheet Column-Width) command described before to widen the column.

These commands only affect the format in which the numbers appear. 1-2-3 still performs calculations in full precision, about 15 decimal places of accuracy.

FORMATTING THE ENTIRE WORKSHEET

In this section, we'll discuss commands for formatting the entire worksheet. As with single columns, you can format column widths, label justification, and number displays. We'll begin by formatting all the columns on the worksheet.

1-2-3 always presents a new worksheet with 9 characters per column, and a worksheet typically displays columns A through H on the screen. We can change this to any column width between one and 72 characters. The command we use to do so is /WGC (Worksheet Global Column-width). Here are the steps:

1. Type in the command /WGC. 1-2-3 will display the current width setting and ask for the new column width.
2. Type 20 <RET>. The worksheet is redisplayed with the appropriate column widths, as in Fig. 3-9.

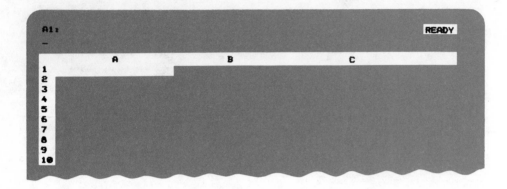

Fig. 3-9

As you can see, only columns A to C are now displayed on the screen, because these are all that will fit in the 1-2-3 window.

If you prefer, you can use the left- and right-arrow keys to draw the column width on the screen, rather than typing in the number for column width. To do so, select the /WGC command, then press the arrow keys to either expand or shrink the column. 1-2-3 will display the effect of the arrow keys on the screen. When the columns appear to be the width you desire, press the RETURN key.

The /WGC command will format all the column widths on the screen, except those which have already been set by a /WC (Worksheet Column-width) command.

You can format all labels in the worksheet also, using the command /WGL (Worksheet Global Label-prefix). Here is how to do that:

1. Type in the command /WGL. This will display three options: Left, Right, Center.
2. Choose the format you desire by moving the pointer or typing in the first letter of the desired format.

Any labels that are presently on the worksheet will not be affected. However, any new labels that you type in will be displayed in the format requested in step 2 above.

You can also specify a format for displaying numbers on the entire worksheet. To do so, use the /WGF (Worksheet Global Format) command. Here are the steps involved:

1. Type in /WGF. This will display your options for displaying numbers: Fixed, Scientific, Currency, ,(comma), General, +/−,

Percent, Date, or Text. (We described these earlier in this chapter.)

2. Select a Format from the options. For some formats, 1-2-3 will ask you for the number of decimal places to display. Type in a number between 0 and 15. If you select Date format, you'll have to specify the 1 (Day-Month-Year), 2 (Day-Month), or D3 (Month-Year) format.

All numbers on the screen, as well as any new numbers added, will appear in the format requested. However, any cells you have formatted with the /RF (Range Format) command will not be affected by the Global Format.

PROTECTING CELLS

You can format cells in the worksheet so that they are protected from accidental change. You will find this feature especially useful for cells with formulas in them, where you don't want to accidentally erase the formula by mistakenly typing a number directly into the cell. If you're going to let other people use your worksheets, then you'll probably end up liking this feature (and the people who use your worksheet) even more.

It helps to think of cells as being for either *input* or *output*. Cells with labels and numbers in them are usually input cells. That is, we enter data into them, such as entering names and test scores into our electronic grade book. Cells with formulas are typically output cells. That is, they display the results of calculations based upon numbers in the cells, such as our average scores in the grade book example. Generally, you should protect output cells, and leave the input cells unprotected for easy data entry and modification.

The analogy to electric fences used in the 1-2-3 manual is good for envisioning what happens when you protect cells. Initially, all cells have the equivalent of an electronic fence around them, but the electricity is off (Fig. 3-10). Since the power is off in the electric fence, it is easy to "jump in" and change the cell's contents.

You can "turn on the juice" in any cell, range of cells, or even all the cells on the screen, which makes it difficult to "jump in" and modify the contents of the cell. In Fig. 3-11, Cell B1 has the power in the fence turned on, and therefore is protected from accidental modification or deletion.

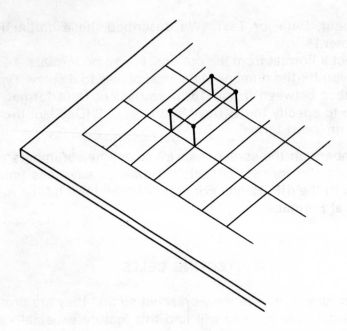

Fig.   3-10

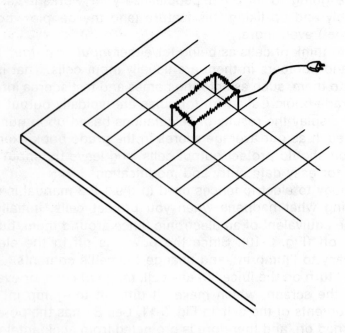

Fig.   3-11

In its normal state each cell in the worksheet has an electronic fence built around it, but the electricity is turned off. 1-2-3 has four commands for protecting cells. Some turn the electricity on and off in the fences, others tear down and rebuild fences around cells. The commands are summarized below:

/RP   Range Protect: Builds electronic fences around a range of cells, but does not "turn on the juice."

/RU   Range Unprotect: Tears down the electronic fences around a range of cells.

/RI   Range Input: Makes it impossible to move the cell pointer into protected cells.

/WGP   Worksheet Global Protection: Turns the electricity on and off in all cells in the worksheet that have electronic fences around them.

Fig. 3-12 shows the loan payment worksheet with the formulas displayed in their cells. Since we have not tampered with the protection facilities at all yet, all cells are in their natural state. That is, each has an invisible electronic fence around it, but the power is off. We'll only need fences around the Output fields (the cells with formulas in them), so let's begin by first tearing down all the electronic fences, and then we'll build fences around only the output cells.

The /RU (Range Unprotect) command will tear down the electronic fences. Here is the procedure:

1. Type in the Command /RU. 1-2-3 asks that you:

   Enter range to unprotect: XX..XX

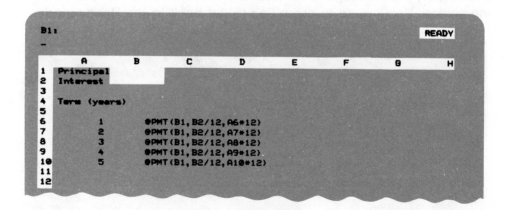

Fig. 3-12

2. Enter the Range to tear down the fences on. (For the sake of example, tear down all the fences.) The range, in this case, is A1..B10 <RET>.

At this point, none of the cells have electronic fences around them. You may notice that the display got a little brighter, or perhaps changed color. Unprotected cells are always displayed at a brighter intensity or in a contrasting color.

To put some fences around the formula cells, use the /RP (Range Protect) command. Here are the steps:

1. Type /RP (Range Protect). 1-2-3 asks that you:

   Enter range to protect: XX..XX

2. Specify the Range to protect. In this example, we'll want to protect the formulas in cells (B6..B10). Type in B6..B10 <RET>.

The cells in the protected range will return to their normal intensity or color. At this point, the formula cells all have electronic fences around them, but the power is off so we can still jump in.

You can turn on the juice in the electric fences with the /WGP (Worksheet Global Protection) command, following these steps:

1. Type /WGP. Two options appear, Enable and Disable.
2. Select the Enable option.

Now all the cells with fences around them have the power on, as shown in Fig. 3-13. You can still move the pointer into those cells, but you can't modify their contents. If you try, 1-2-3 will beep at you and display the message "Protected cell" in the lower left portion of the screen. You'll need to press Esc to get back to the Ready mode.

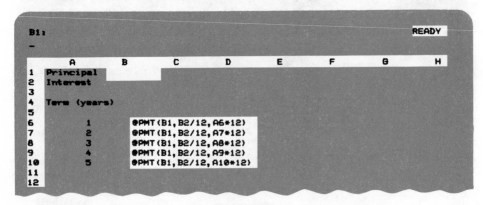

Fig.   3-13

Of course, at some time in the future you may need to change the contents of a protected cell. To do so, you merely have to turn off the power in the "electric fences." This is accomplished by typing in the /WGP command, and selecting the Disable option from the menu choices. When done changing the formula in the protected cell, type in the /WGP command again, select Enable, and once again all output cells are protected.

We can carry it a step farther and make it impossible to even put the cell pointer in the protected cells. We use the /RI (Range Input) command for this. Here are the steps:

1. Type in the /RI command. 1-2-3 asks that you:

   Enter data input range: XX . . XX

2. Type in the range of the entire worksheet (A1..B10)   <RET>.

When you move the cell pointer around the worksheet, it will skip over cells in the range not specified in the /RI command.

To terminate the Range Input command, press the Esc key prior to filling data into a cell.

CREATING FIXED TITLES

When worksheets become large, you need to scroll around with the "window" to see all the data on the worksheet. For example, the worksheet in Fig. 3-14 shows a ten year projection for a piece of commercial property. However, you can only see seven columns: the titles at the left and six years of data.

Of course, you can scroll the window to the right, using the CTRL-right arrow (→) key, but as you move across the worksheet, the labels disappear from the screen, as shown in Fig. 3-15.

This makes it difficult to read the screen, unless you happened to have memorized exactly what is in each row. A simple solution to the problem is to lock the titles into position on the screen, so that as you scroll to the right, the titles remain on the screen. You can "freeze" the left-most column or top-most row of labels onto the screen using the 1-2-3 /WT (Worksheet Titles) command.

First, you need to position the pointer to the upper-left cell of the column that will be allowed to scroll (not the parts that will be locked). In this example, you want to lock the titles in the left column.

```
A1:                                                              READY
─
         A           B         C         D         E         F         G
1   Ten Year Projection for Commercial Real Estate
2
3   Square Feet:      1200
4   $/Sq. Ft.          .99
5
6                     1984      1985      1986      1987      1988      1989
7   ───────────────────────────────────────────────────────────────────────
8   Rent:           $1,188    $1,331    $1,490    $1,669    $1,869    $2,094
9
10  Insurance:        $200      $224      $251      $281      $315      $352
11  Mgmt. Fee:         $90      $101      $113      $126      $142      $159
12  Debt Serv.:       $100      $112      $125      $140      $157      $176
13  ───────────────────────────────────────────────────────────────────────
14  Cash Flow:        $789      $894    $1,001    $1,221    $1,256    $1,406
15
16
17
18
19
20
```

Fig. 3-14

```
         E         F         G         H         I         J         K         L
1
2
3
4
5
6      1987      1988      1989      1990      1991      1992      1993      1994
7   ─────────────────────────────────────────────────────────────────────────────
8    $1,669    $1,896    $2,049    $2,345    $2,626    $2,941    $3,294    $3,690
9
10     $281      $315      $352      $395      $442      $495      $555      $621
11     $126      $142      $159      $178      $199      $223      $250      $280
12     $140      $157      $176      $197      $221      $248      $277      $311
13  ─────────────────────────────────────────────────────────────────────────────
14   $1,121    $1,256    $1,406    $1,575    $1,764    $1,976    $2,213    $2,478
15
16
17
18
19
20
```

Fig. 3-15

So you need to position the pointer to cell B1. Next, use the /WT
(Worksheet Titles) command to lock the titles. Here are the steps to
do so:

1. Type in the command /WT.
2. This displays four options:

Horizontal   Vertical   Both   Clear

For this example, select Vertical.

That's all there is to it. All titles to the left of the pointer will be fro-zen. So if you scroll clear over to the tenth year of the projection, the screen will look like Fig. 3-16, with the titles still displayed on the screen.

The Horizontal option on the /WT menu allows you to fix a single row. The Both option allows freezes to both a top column and a row. The Clear option "unfreezes" fixed rows and columns.

Note one quirk of these frozen titles. You can't easily move the cell pointer into the title area. 1-2-3 will just beep, and keep the cell pointer out. The GoTo (F5) key will move the pointer into the titles area, but sometimes with unpredictable results. The best bet is to use the /WTC (Worksheet Titles Clear) Clear option to unfreeze the titles, make the change, then refreeze the titles with the /WT command.

SPLIT SCREENS

Another way to format the screen is to split it into two separate screens. This comes in handy with large worksheets. For example, Fig. 3-17 shows the ten-year projection worksheet in its normal state.

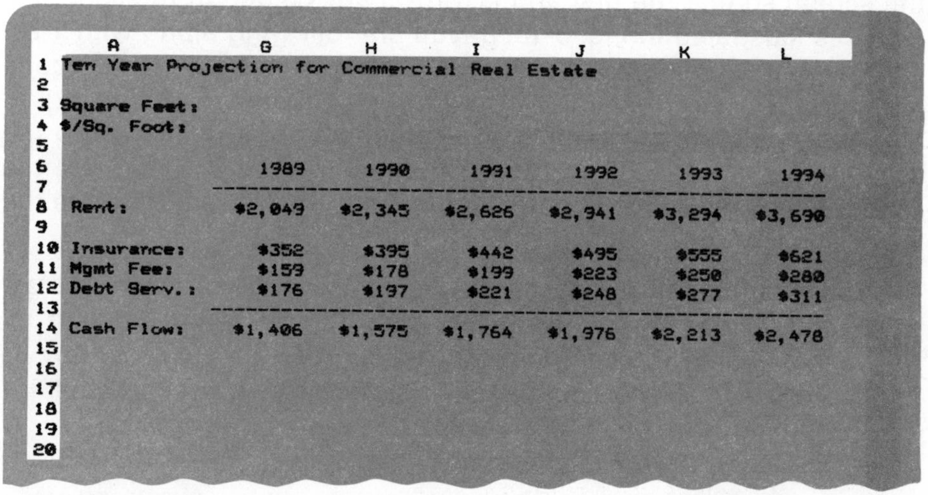

Fig. 3-16

```
A1:                                                              READY
 ─
            A          B          C        D        E        F        G
 1  Ten Year Projection for Commercial Real Estate
 2
 3  Square Feet:      1200
 4  $/Sq. Ft.          .99
 5
 6                     1984       1985     1986     1987     1988     1989
 7  ────────────────────────────────────────────────────────────────────
 8  Rent:           $1,188     $1,331   $1,490   $1,669   $1,869   $2,094
 9
10  Insurance:        $200       $224     $251     $281     $315     $352
11  Mgmt. Fee:         $90       $101     $113     $126     $142     $159
12  Debt Serv.:       $100       $112     $125     $140     $157     $176
13  ────────────────────────────────────────────────────────────────────
14  Cash Flow:        $789       $894   $1,001   $1,221   $1,256   $1,406
15
16
17
18
19
20
```

Fig.   3-17

If you were to change a value in square feet or price, this would affect all the years down the line. However, if you especially wanted to see the effect in year 10, you'd need to scroll over to the right to observe the change. To try another value, you'd need to scroll to the left, make another change, then scroll to the right again. All this scrolling can become tiresome. A better approach is simply to split the screen so that the first and last rows are visible on the screen at once, as illustrated in Fig. 3-18. (If you are following along with 1-2-3 on-line, you will have to use the /WTC (Worksheet Title Clear) command to clear the frozen titles before the split-screen will work.)

This way, you can immediately see the effects of any change to the assumptions in cells B3 and B4 in the tenth year's column. Use the /WW (Worksheet Window) command to split the screen. Here are the steps.

1. Move the cell pointer to the column where you want to start the split. In Fig. 3-18, we selected column C for the split by positioning the cell pointer to column C1.
2. Type in the /WW command. This presents several options, including Horizontal and Vertical.
3. Select an option (Vertical in this example). Press RETURN.

The screen will split, and the cell pointer will be in cell B1. You can scroll either window independently using the usual arrow keys.

	A	B		H	I	J	K	L
1	Ten Year Projection for		1					
2			2					
3	Square Feet:	1200	3					
4	$/Sq. Foot:	0.99	4					
5			5					
6		1984	6	1990	1991	1992	1993	1994
7		----------	7	----------	----------	----------	----------	----------
8	Rent:	$1,188	8	$2,345	$2,626	$2,941	$3,294	$3,690
9			9					
10	Insurance:	$200	10	$395	$442	$495	$555	$621
11	Mgmt Fee:	$90	11	$178	$199	$223	$250	$280
12	Debt Serv.:	$100	12	$197	$221	$248	$277	$311
13		----------	13	----------	----------	----------	----------	----------
14	Cash Flow:	$1,406	14	$1,575	$1,764	$1,976	$2,213	$2,478
15			15					
16			16					
17			17					
18			18					
19			19					
20			20					

Fig.   3-18

To move the cell from one window to the next, use function key F6 (Window).

If you scroll up or down in one window, the second window will also scroll in the same direction. This is because the windows are initially synchronized. If you would like to be able to scroll around one window without affecting the other, you can unsynchronize the two windows. To do so, type in the /WW command, and select Unsynchronize from the menu of choices. To reinstate synchronization, select the Synchronize option.

If you already have a split screen and want to return to a normal screen, you can type in the /WW command and select the Clear option from the menu of choices.

We've dealt with a number of *ranges* in this chapter, specifying a range of cells with two dots between individual cell addresses (e.g., A1..A20). In the next chapter, we'll discuss other techniques for specifying ranges.

Chapter 4

RANGES

A range is simply a rectangular collection of cells on the worksheet. The smallest possible range is a single cell, the largest possible range is the entire worksheet. Fig. 4-1 shows several possible ranges on a worksheet. Note that each has an even, rectangular shape.

We've used ranges in several formulas already, such as @SUM(A1..A10). This formula displays the sum of all numbers in the

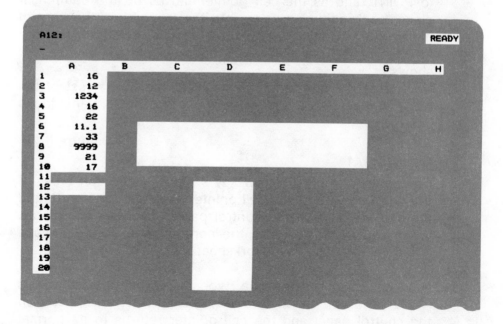

Fig. 4-1

range of cells from A1 to A10. Let's look at some other interesting ways to put ranges into formulas.

RANGES IN FORMULAS

In this exercise, we'll discuss techniques for "drawing" the contents of a range into a formula. For example, Fig. 4-1 has a column of 10 numbers, A1 to A10. If you want to put the formula @SUM(A1..A12) into cell A12, you could just type it in as you have in the past. But let's explore a new technique.

With the cell pointer in cell A12, type the first portion of the formula into the control panel as such:

A12   **VALUE**
@SUM(___

Notice that the upper righthand corner of the control panel informs you that you are entering a value, and that the cursor is precisely in the position into which you are about to enter the range to sum. Now we can draw the range into the formula following these steps:

1. Press the up-arrow key 11 times. The mode indicator changes to POINT, and as the cell pointer moves up the column, it places each column's value into the formula on the control panel. After 11 key presses, the cursor is in cell A1, and the formula in the control panel reads @SUM(A1, as Fig. 4-2 shows.

2. Now press the period key to begin typing in the rest of the range in the sum. Now the formula in the control panel looks like this:

A1   **POINT**
@SUM(A1..A1

3. Now, press the down arrow key 9 times. With each press of the down-arrow key, the cell pointer expands downward, and the second value in the control panel changes accordingly. When you reach cell A10, the control panel formula reads @SUM(A1..A10, and the worksheet looks like Fig. 4-3.

4. Now, to finish the formula, type in a closing parenthesis [ )]. The completed formula, @SUM(A1..A10), appears in the control panel and the cell pointer returns to its normal size.

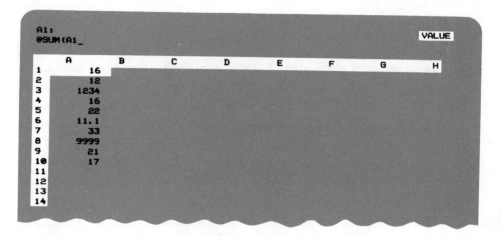

Fig. 4-2

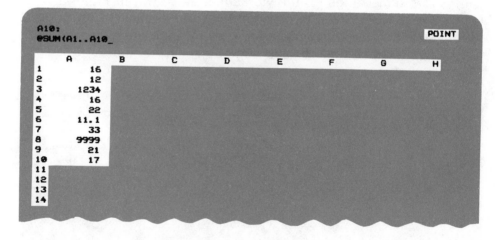

Fig. 4-3

5. Pressing the RETURN key enters the formula into the cell, and the sum of the values in the drawn range appears in the cell A12.

This way of entering formulas into the worksheet has the advantage of allowing you to see the contents of the formula. It is also a great way to enter information if you are not a good typist.

RANGES IN COMMANDS

Drawing ranges on the screen works just as well with menu commands as with formulas. Let's try out another example. Let's format the numbers in Fig. 4-3 to two fixed decimal places using the /RFF (Range Format Fixed) command.

1. Position the cursor to the top of the range to be formatted (cell A1 in this example). Type in /RFF (Range Format Fixed). Then the worksheet looks like Fig. 4-4. Press RETURN to select the two decimal places option.

2. 1-2-3 asks you to:

   Enter range to format: A1 . .A1

   Press the down-arrow key until the pointer gets to cell A12. The control panel range becomes A1..A12, and 1-2-3 draws this same range on the worksheet as shown in Fig. 4-5.

3. Press RETURN. The cell pointer shrinks back to its original size, and the numbers in the drawn range are formatted with two fixed decimal places (Fig. 4-6).

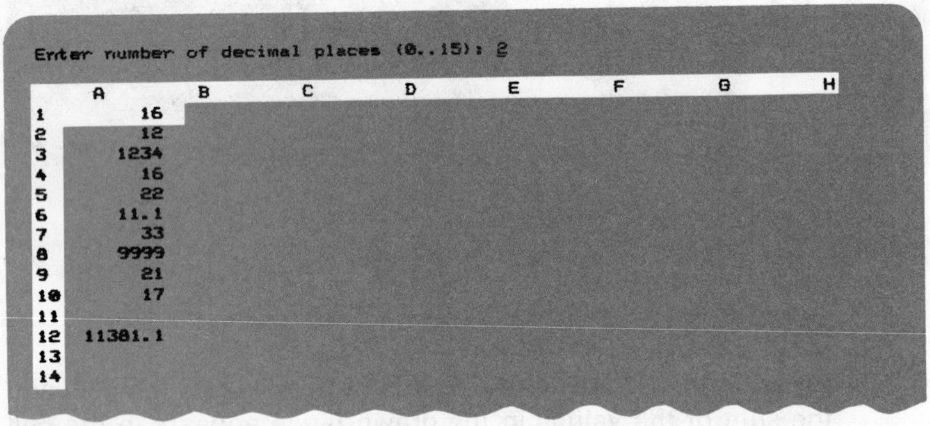

Fig.   4-4

When drawing ranges, one cell is always the *anchor* cell, simply because it does not move. The cell diagonally across from the anchor cell is the *free cell,* because we can move it anywhere on the screen. In the control panel, the anchor cell is the first cell displayed in the range, the free cell is the second cell in the range, like this:

Enter range to format: A1..A12

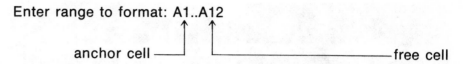

anchor cell ———————┘   └————————————————————————free cell

The arrow keys move the free cell to draw the range. You can use other keys with ranges too, mostly for anchoring and unanchoring cells. The way in which these keys behave depends upon whether or not a cell is already anchored.

If a cell is not already anchored, 1-2-3 displays only one cell address in the control panel, like this:

Enter (start of range): A1

The following keys have these effects on the unanchored cell:

(Period)	Anchors the cell named in the control panel (A1 in this example), and allows you to draw the range with arrow keys. Also, changes the single cell address to a range (A1..A1 in this example).
(Any Arrow Key)	Moves the cell pointer, and changes the cell address in the control panel, but does not draw a range. Useful for moving to the beginning cell in a range you wish to create.
Esc (Escape)	Eliminates the entire prompt from the control panel, and moves to the previous prompt. That is, cancels the entire command.

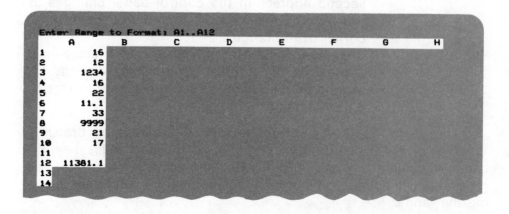

Fig.   4-5

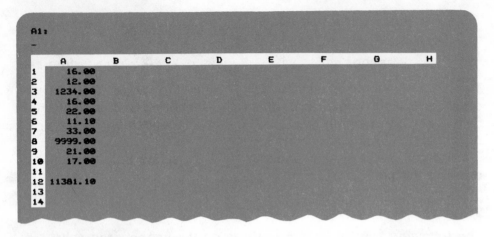

Fig.   4-6

If a cell is already anchored, these keys have a much different effect. You can tell that a cell is already anchored if it is displayed in the control panel with two coordinates, like this:

Enter (start of range) :A1..A1

Now these keys will have these effects:

(Period)   Moves the anchor to the nearest corner in a clockwise direction.

(Any Arrow Key) Expands the cell pointer in the direction of the arrow, thereby drawing the range on the screen. The second address in the control panel changes as the pointer expands, to match the lower right corner of the range.

Esc (Escape)   Unanchors the cell, and returns to a single cell address in the control panel. This is handy for moving the beginning cell address in the range to a new location.

The backspace key also affects ranges you may be drawing. Whether or not a cell is already anchored, the backspace key will cancel the range you are currently drawing on the screen and will return the cell pointer to its original position before you began drawing the range.

You can also use the End key on the numeric keypad to draw a range. For example, when the control panel asks:

Enter range to copy TO:A1..A1

pressing the End key, followed by pressing the down-arrow key, will extend the cell pointer to the last nonblank cell in the range. Any time you press the End key, followed by a press on an arrow key, the cell pointer will move to the last nonblank cell in the direction of the arrow key. If the cell pointer is already anchored, it will expand accordingly. If the cell pointer is not already within an active range when you press an End-key, arrow-key combination, the cell pointer will travel to the far corner of the worksheet in the direction specified.

Once you have practiced a bit, drawing (and undrawing) ranges is as simple as 1-2-3! If you should get lost while drawing a range on the screen, you can use the usual escape procedure to get back to more familiar territory. Just keep in mind our now familiar platitude:

If in doubt, Escape key out!

NAMING RANGES

Creating cell ranges by pointing is an efficient way to get the task done. The procedure is quite simple. We'll use the grade book example again, but one that has only data, not formulas in it yet.

Suppose you want to make each individual column of scores in the grade book worksheet into a range. Using the pointing method, you could follow these steps:

1. Position the cell pointer to the first score in the column for Test 1 as shown in Fig. 4-7.
2. Select the /RNC (Range Name Create) command. 1-2-3 will ask you to

   Enter name:

   For this example, type in the name TEST1 <RET>.
3. The screen will ask that you specify a range. Press the End key followed by pressing the down-arrow key. This will draw the entire range as shown in Fig. 4-8.
4. Now press the RETURN key. The cell pointer returns to its original position. Although you may think nothing much has happened, follow through with us here.
5. Position the cell pointer to cell B11.
6. Type in the formula @AVG(TEST1) and press the RETURN key. The worksheet now looks like Fig. 4-9.

	A	B	C	D	E	F	G	H
1	Name	Test 1	Test 2	Test 3	Test 4			
2								
3	Adams	90	100	88	70			
4	Bovee	80	90	78	68			
5	Carlson	90	100	80	80			
6	Davidson	88	90	90	80			
7	Edwards	90	70	100	100			
8	Fernandez	100	80	78	80			
9	Gomez	90	100	88	70			
10								
11								
12								
20								

Fig.   4-7

	A	B	C	D	E	F	G	H
1	Name	Test 1	Test 2	Test 3	Test 4			
2								
3	Adams	90	100	88	70			
4	Bovee	80	90	78	68			
5	Carlson	90	100	80	80			
6	Davidson	88	90	90	80			
7	Edwards	90	100	100	100			
8	Fernandez	100	80	78	80			
9	Gomez	90	100	88	70			
10								
11								
12								
20								

Fig.   4-8

	A	B	C	D	E	F	G	H
1	Name	Test 1	Test 2	Test 3	Test 4			
2								
3	Adams	90	100	88	70			
4	Bovee	80	90	78	68			
5	Carlson	90	100	80	80			
6	Davidson	88	90	90	80			
7	Edwards	90	100	100	100			
8	Fernandez	100	80	78	80			
9	Gomez	90	100	88	70			
10								
11		89.71428						
12								
20								

Fig.   4-9

We specified that the content of cell B11 is to be the average of all test scores for TEST1, and therefore, that quantity is displayed in the cell. So now you can refer to all the scores for the first test using the name TEST1 rather than remembering the range. You can use TEST1 in any formula as well as with most Range, Move, Worksheet, and Copy command options that require you to specify a range. Remembering the name TEST1 is much easier and more convenient than remembering the range coordinates.

You can use the same procedure to make a range out of the remaining test scores on the worksheet, and name these TEST2, TEST3 and TEST4 accordingly.

A range name can be up to 15 characters long, and should not contain any special punctuation marks (other than the underline character) or spaces. Though 1-2-3 will allow spaces and punctuation marks, you should avoid them because they may cause problems later if used in formulas.

Once you have created several ranges, you might later forget their names. In this example, they are easy to remember, but this is a small worksheet. But in a larger worksheet, you may need reminders. Pressing special function key F3 whenever 1-2-3 is asking for a range specification will automatically display all named ranges (Fig. 4-10).

```
A1:B1                                                              READY
Enter range to format:_
TEST1     TEST2     TEST3     TEST4
      A          B          C          D          E        F        G        H
 1   Name      Test 1    Test 2     Test 3    Test 4
 2
 3   Adams        90        100        88        70
 4   Bovee        80         90        78        68
 5   Carlson      90        100        80        80
 6   Davidson     88         90        90        80
 7   Edwards      90        100       100       100
 8   Fernandez   100         80        78        80
 9   Gomez        90        100        88        70
10
11            89.71428
12
20
```

Fig.   4-10

The real beauty of this menu is not only that it helps your memory, but you can now also refer to ranges by pointing to their names. This is helpful if you are a poor typist.

You can "undo" ranges in two ways. If you wish to get rid of a single range (by name, not its content), select the /RND (Range Name

Delete) command. In this example we'll eliminate the range named TEST1. The steps are:

1. Select the /RND command. 1-2-3 asks you to

   Enter name to delete: _____

   and displays all existing range names.
2. Move the menu pointer to the range name you wish to delete, or type in the name (TEST1).
3. Press the RETURN key.

The actual contents of the cells in the range remain unchanged. Now, do you have a problem with the formula in cell A11? After all, you told it to AVG the contents of range TEST1, but you have just eliminated TEST1 as range name. If you move the cell pointer to cell A11, you can see in the control panel that the formula there now looks like this:

@SUM(B3..B9)

1-2-3 was clever enough to rewrite the formula so that it still works correctly even though the TEST1 range name no longer exists. How's that for convenience?

You can "undo" all the ranges ever created in a worksheet with a single command. The command is /RNR (Range Name Reset). Just type in the command, press RETURN, and all range names are eliminated. And, all formulas are rewritten so they still work, just as in the example above.

In summary, the whole purpose of ranges is to simplify the use of the worksheet. 1-2-3 allows you to quickly identify groups of cells in a visual manner. It also allows us to name these groups of cells, and use them directly in formulas. The real power of working with ranges, however, is in copying groups of cells, as we shall discuss in the next chapter.

Chapter 5

COPYING RANGES

One of the greatest advantages to using ranges is that you can copy parts of the worksheet to other locations, which saves a great deal of typing effort. To demonstrate, we'll fill in a large number of cells by copying the contents of a single cell.

COPYING DATA

Fig. 5-1 shows a worksheet with only one cell filled.

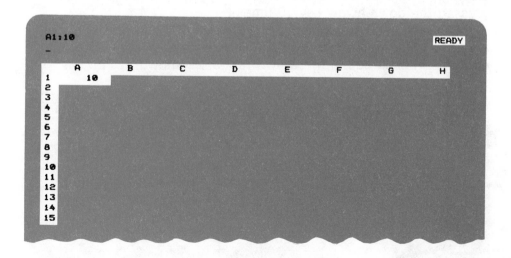

Fig. 5-1

To place this same value in some more cells, use the /C (Copy) option.

First, select the /C option. The control panel requests that you:

Enter range to copy FROM: A1..A1

Since the cell pointer is already in cell A1, the A1 also appears in the control panel. That is, 1-2-3 "assumes" that the cell to copy from is the range A1..A1 (a single cell). Press RETURN to indicate that this is indeed the cell to copy from. The control panel then requests that you:

Enter range to copy TO:A1

Now you can determine as large an area as you wish. First, press the period key, which changes the control panel to this:

Enter range to copy TO:A1..A1

Now, press the right-arrow key six times, expanding the cell pointer to cell G1 as shown in Fig. 5-2.

Enter Range to Copy FROM: A1..A1 Enter range to copy TO:A1..G1

Now expand the cell pointer downward by pressing the down-arrow key. The cell pointer will expand to include the rows, and the range specified in the control panel will extend to the lower-right corner of the highlighted range (G11) as shown in Fig. 5-3 (assuming you've pressed the down-arrow key 10 times).

The range you are copying to is the size of the entire highlighted area. So if you now press RETURN, you will see a copy of cell A1's contents in each cell in the drawn range, as shown in Fig. 5-4.

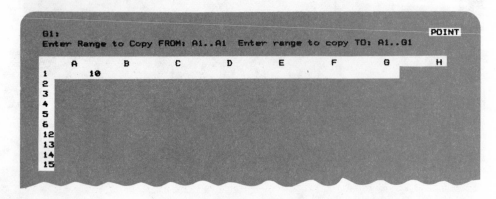

Fig. 5-2

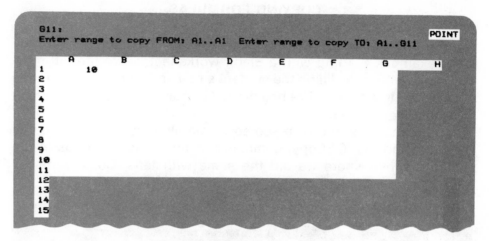

Fig. 5-3

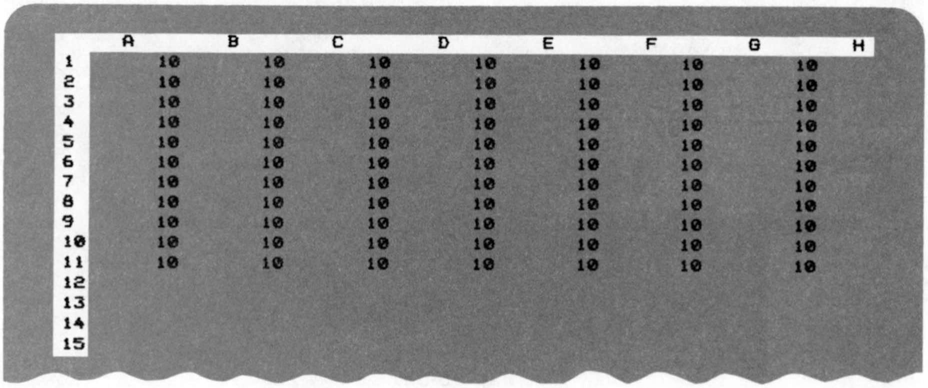

Fig. 5-4

This is a quick and easy method for filling a lot of cells (as long as all the cells need the same contents).

Using the pointing method is not necessary however. You could just as easily type in the /C command, press the RETURN key when the control panel asks for the range to copy FROM. Then, rather than pointing, just type in A1..G11 to indicate the lower right corner of the copy-to-range, then press the RETURN key.

Copying ranges of labels is exactly the same as copying numbers. Simply position the cell pointer to the cell you want to copy, select the /C (Copy) command, and define the FROM and TO copy ranges. Copying formulas, however, is a bit different, and we will discuss that now.

COPYING FORMULAS

For our example of copying formulas, we'll use the familiar grade book example. Starting with a blank worksheet, leave the left-most column available for filling the student's names. Then, create a range of zeros for test scores. The beginnings of our grade book worksheet will look like Fig. 5-5.

You can create the zero scores by simply placing a zero in cell B2 and using the /C (Copy) command to fill in the range, as in the example above where we did the same with tens. Copy from cell B2..B2 to cells B2..E12.

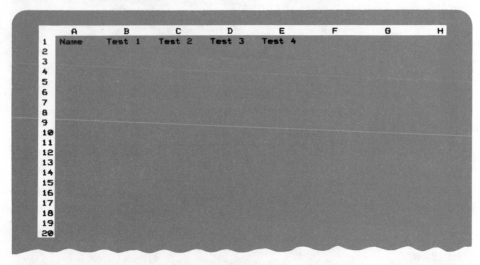

	A	B	C	D	E	F	G	H
1	Name	Test 1	Test 2	Test 3	Test 4			
2								
3								
4								
5								
6								
7								
8								
9								
10								
11								
12								
13								
14								
15								
16								
17								
18								
19								
20								

Fig.   5-5

Assume you want averages across each student, and down each test. You could fill in the necessary formulas one at a time, but there is a better method. First, put the formula @AVG(B2..E2) in cell F2 as shown in Fig. 5-6.

You can use the /WGFT (Worksheet Global Format Text) command to have the worksheet display the actual formula, rather than its calculated results. Next, rather than typing the appropriate formula into each cell, just copy this one into the appropriate range. Here's how to do so:

1. With the cell pointer still in cell F3, select the /C (Copy) command. The control panel asks:

   Enter range to copy FROM: F2..F2

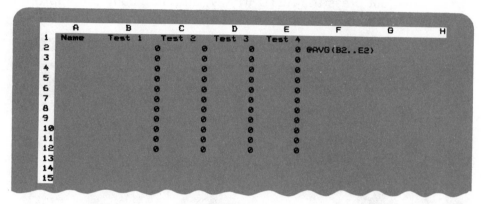

Fig. 5-6

Since the cell pointer is already in cell F2, just press RETURN, since this is the formula we wish to replicate. The control panel then requests you to:

Enter range to copy TO: F2

2. Press the down-arrow key to move the cell pointer down to cell F3. The control panel reads:

Enter range to copy TO: F3

3. To replicate the formula, press the period (.) key, so that the control panel reads:

Enter range to copy TO: F3..F3

4. Now stretch out the cell pointer to cell F12 by pressing the down-arrow key, until the expanded cell pointer looks like Fig. 5-7.

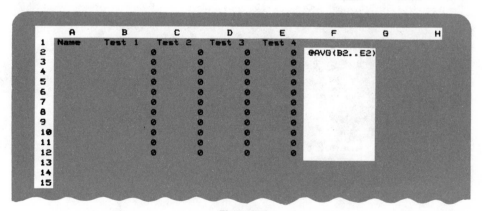

Fig. 5-7

5. Now just press the RETURN key, and magically the appropriate formulas are displayed in this column as shown in Fig. 5-8.

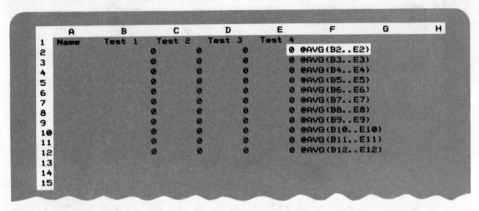

Fig. 5-8

Notice that the formula in each row has been properly corrected to perform an average for its particular row. That is, the original formula is still @AVG(B2..E2), while the formula in row 3 has automatically been corrected to @AVG(B3..E3). Also, the formula in row four has been corrected to @AVG(B4..E4), and so forth.

Try it again with the columns for average scores on each exam. Position the cell pointer to B14 and type in the formula @AVG(B2..B12), so the worksheet looks like Fig. 5-9.

Now spread the formula across all columns using the /C command. Specify cell B14 as the cell to copy FROM when prompted.

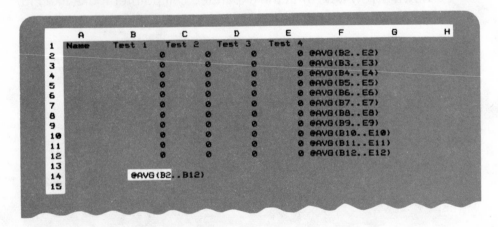

Fig. 5-9

Then specify the range C14..D14 as the range to copy TO. The result is shown in Fig. 5-10.

You may want to use the /WGC (Worksheet Global Column-width) command to widen the columns so that the entire formula can be seen in its cell.

So now you have a general *template* for a grade book. The word "template" in electronic spreadsheet jargon means a worksheet pre-formatted for a specific purpose. That is, the grade book template is much the same as a blank page in a typical grade book. The advantage of the worksheet's template, of course, is that it does the calculations automatically. Mere paper cannot compete wth this.

What is particularly important to learn from this exercise is the concept of *relative cell reference*. When you originally typed in the formula @AVG(B2..E2) into cell F2, you told 1-2-3 to display the average of all cells from four positions to the left of this point to one position to the left. So when you copied the formula, each new copy assumed you meant the average of the appropriate number of cells to the left. That is, 1-2-3 wisely decided that you did not want it to show the average score for the first student in each row. Rather, you wanted to show each student's average in the appropriate place. Therefore, 1-2-3 adjusted accordingly.

However, you may not always want 1-2-3 to make this kind of assumption. You can easily tell 1-2-3 when it should not make such an assumption, by referencing *absolute* cells. For this example, we'll set up a worksheet that calculates the monthly payment on a loan with a fixed principal and interest rate and varying terms as shown in Fig. 5-11. In the upper lefthand portion of the screen, you can type in the principal and interest. Then the spreadsheet calculates the

	A	B	C	D	E	F	G	H
1	Name	Test 1	Test 2	Test 3	Test 4			
2		0	0	0	0	0 @AVG(B2..E2)		
3		0	0	0	0	0 @AVG(B3..E3)		
4		0	0	0	0	0 @AVG(B4..E4)		
5		0	0	0	0	0 @AVG(B5..E5)		
6		0	0	0	0	0 @AVG(B6..E6)		
7		0	0	0	0	0 @AVG(B7..E7)		
8		0	0	0	0	0 @AVG(B8..E8)		
9		0	0	0	0	0 @AVG(B9..E9)		
10		0	0	0	0	0 @AVG(B10..E10)		
11		0	0	0	0	0 @AVG(B11..E11)		
12		0	0	0	0	0 @AVG(B12..E12)		
13								
14		@AVG(B2..B12)	@AVG(C2..C12)	@AVG(D2..D12)				
15								

Fig. 5-10

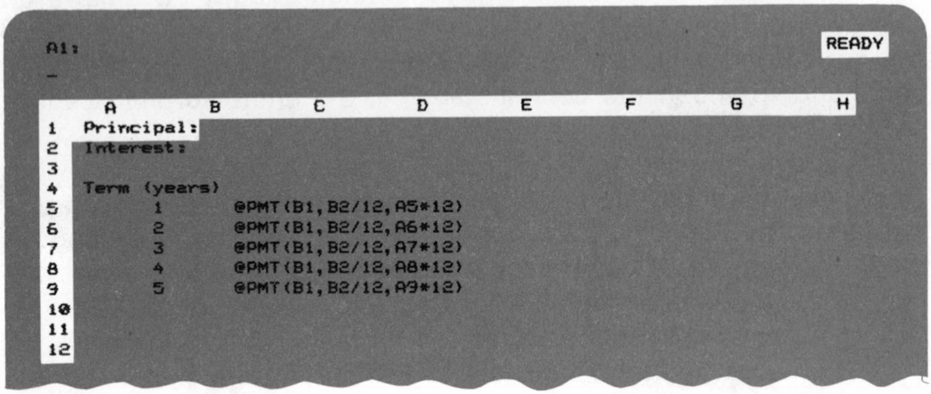

```
A1:                                                              READY
─
          A         B         C         D         E       F       G       H
 1   Principal:
 2   Interest:
 3
 4   Term (years)
 5          1        @PMT(B1,B2/12,A5*12)
 6          2        @PMT(B1,B2/12,A6*12)
 7          3        @PMT(B1,B2/12,A7*12)
 8          4        @PMT(B1,B2/12,A8*12)
 9          5        @PMT(B1,B2/12,A9*12)
10
11
12
```

Fig. 5-11

monthly payment for various terms, and displays them in the table near the middle of the screen.

You'll be interested to see how quickly you can build such a spreadsheet using ranges and copying. In cells A1 and A2, simply type in the labels Principal and Interest. In cell A4, type in the label ^Term (years). In cells A5 through A9 type in the numbers 1 through 5.

Now to calculate the payment for a 12-month loan you need to type into cell C5 the formula:

@PMT(B1,B2/12,A5*12)

Because cell B1 will contain the principal, cell B2 will hold the interest, and cell A5 holds the term. Fig. 5-12 displays the worksheet with the labels and a formula typed in.

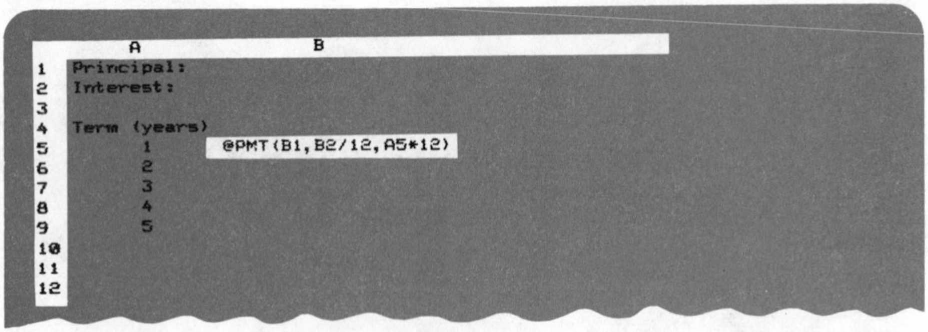

```
          A                    B
 1   Principal:
 2   Interest:
 3
 4   Term (years)
 5          1        @PMT(B1,B2/12,A5*12)
 6          2
 7          3
 8          4
 9          5
10
11
12
```

Fig. 5-12

The appropriate formulas for all cells are displayed below.

@PMT(B1,B2/12,A5*12)
@PMT(B1,B2/12,A6*12)
@PMT(B1,B2/12,A7*12)
@PMT(B1,B2/12,A8*12)
@PMT(B1,B2/12,A9*12)

However, if you use the /C (Copy) command to copy the formulas into their cells, we end up with this set of formulas:

@PMT(B1,B2/12,A5*12)
@PMT(B2,B3/12,A6*12)
@PMT(B3,B4/12,A7*12)
@PMT(B4,B5/12,A8*12)
@PMT(B5,B6/12,A9*12)

1-2-3 automatically corrects the formulas for *all* cells, yet only the last argument in the formulas actually needed to vary. The principal and interest need to remain constant, since they are stored in cells B1 and B2 only. You need to make these cell addresses *absolute,* so that when you copy the formula, only the term varies in each formula. Use the $ symbol to make a cell "absolute" (constant) rather than "relative" (variable) when you copy cells in this fashion. Let's work through the problem step by step.

1. First, position the cell pointer to cell B5 and type in this formula:

   @PMT($B$1,$B$2/12,A5*12)

   This assures that when you make copies of the formula, references to cells B1 and B2 remain constant, and only the reference to cell A5 varies in each row. Leave the cell pointer in cell B5.

2. Type in the /C (Copy) command. The control panel asks:

   Enter range to copy FROM: B5..B5

   Since this is the cell we want to copy, just press RETURN.

3. The control panel asks:

   Enter range to copy TO: B5

   Press the down arrow, so that the cell pointer moves to cell B6, and the control panel reads:

   Enter range to copy TO: B6

4. Press the period (.) key to anchor the cell. The control panel reads:

Enter range to copy TO: B6..B6

5. Press the down-arrow key three times, so that the cell pointer extends to cell B9 and the control panel reads:

Enter range to copy TO: B6..B9

6. Now press RETURN, and 1-2-3 properly fills all the cells, as Fig. 5-13 shows.

Notice that the $B$1 and $B$2 cell addresses are unchanged, yet the cell A5 address is properly adjusted for each row. That is, cells B1 and B2 are absolute (they don't change), and the A5 cell is relative (it varies properly with each row).

To recap: There are two ways to copy formulas. In one method cell addresses are relative. When you copy the formulas, the cell addresses are automatically updated in the cells you copy to. This method preserves the "meaning" of the formula (e.g., sum across a row). In the second method, cell references are absolute. That is, when you copy the formulas, the cell references do not adjust to their new cell locations. You create absolute references placing a $ in front of cell addresses that must remain constant. You can mix these relative and absolute cell addresses in a formula, as in the example above. You can even make a cell address half relative, half absolute (e.g., B$1) in which case the column address (B) will vary, but the row (1) will remain constant. Similarly, the cell address $B1 will remain constant in terms of column (B), but the row (1) will vary in the copied cells. This last type of address is referred to as a *mixed* address, because it contains one relative and one absolute coordinate.

```
              A              B
1  Principal:
2  Interest:
3
4  Term (years)
5      1        @PMT($B$1,$B$2/12,A5*12)
6      2        @PMT($B$1,$B$2/12,A6*12)
7      3        @PMT($B$1,$B$2/12,A7*12)
8      4        @PMT($B$1,$B$2/12,A8*12)
9      5        @PMT($B$1,$B$2/12,A9*12)
10
11
12
```

Fig. 5-13

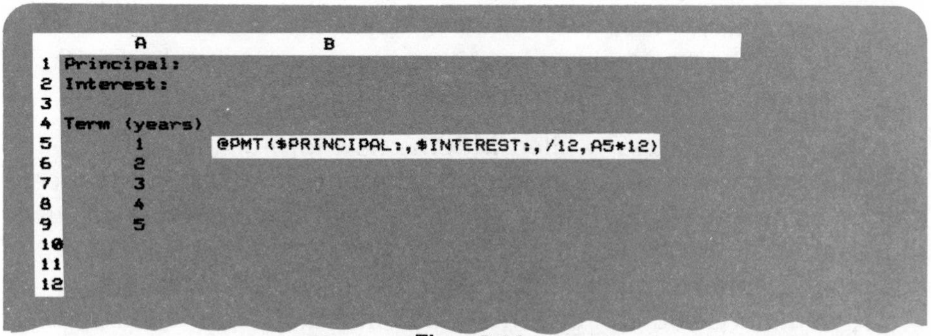

```
            A                 B
1  Principal:
2  Interest:
3
4  Term (years)
5          1     @PMT($PRINCIPAL:,$INTEREST:,/12,A5*12)
6          2
7          3
8          4
9          5
10
11
12
```

Fig. 5-14

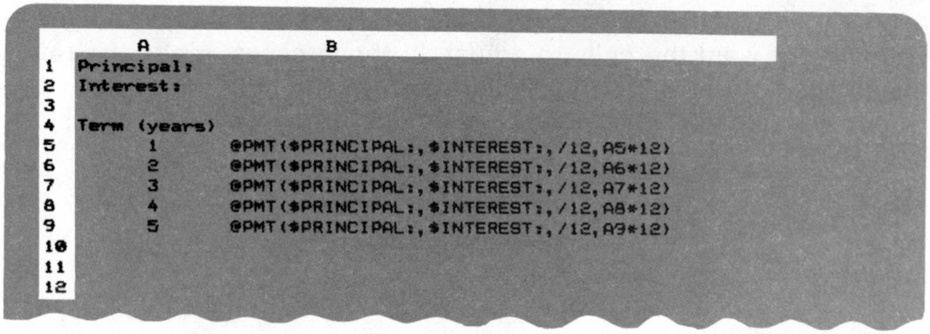

```
            A                 B
1  Principal:
2  Interest:
3
4  Term (years)
5          1     @PMT($PRINCIPAL:,$INTEREST:,/12,A5*12)
6          2     @PMT($PRINCIPAL:,$INTEREST:,/12,A6*12)
7          3     @PMT($PRINCIPAL:,$INTEREST:,/12,A7*12)
8          4     @PMT($PRINCIPAL:,$INTEREST:,/12,A8*12)
9          5     @PMT($PRINCIPAL:,$INTEREST:,/12,A9*12)
10
11
12
```

Fig. 5-15

CELL LABELS

You can use cell names rather than addresses in formulas also. These too may be either relative or absolute. Here is a procedure to do so using the same worksheet as above.

1. Position the cell pointer to cell A1 (Principal).
2. Select /RNL (Range Name Label). When the options Right, Down, Left, Up appear, select Right. When it asks to Enter label range: A1..A1, just press the RETURN key. This causes the value in cell A2 to acquire the name "Principal."
3. Position the cell pointer to cell B1. Select /RNLR (Range Name Label Right) again, and A2..A2 as the range. This gives cell B2 the name "Interest."
4. Type the formula @PMT($PRINCIPAL:,$INTEREST:/12,A5*12) into cell B5 as shown in Fig. 5-14.
5. Select /C, and B5 as the range to copy FROM:. Press RETURN.

6. Move the cell pointer down one to cell C6 with the down-arrow key. Press the period (.) key.
7. Press the down-arrow key three times to extend the COPY TO range to cell B9, then press RETURN.

The cells are properly filled with the new formula, as in Fig. 5-15.

In this example we've used given the principal and interest cells names using the /RNL (Range Name Labels) option. Then we used those labels in the formulas themselves. We included the $ in front of the range names to make these absolute in copied formulas.

In summary, you can use the Copy commands to make copies of individual cell contents. When formulas are involved, they will be properly adjusted to their new locations. In some cases, however, you will not want the cells to adjust. In those cases, make the references absolute by including dollar signs in the cell addresses.

Chapter 6

EDITING THE WORKSHEET

When developing a worksheet, there is often the need to change, or *edit*, its contents. There may be several reasons for doing so. We all make typographical errors from time to time that need to be corrected. Sometimes we put the right data in the wrong place, or the wrong formula in the right place, and so forth. And sometimes, we just change our minds about how we want the worksheet to look on the screen, so we move things around or add and delete rows and columns. In this chapter, we'll discuss 1-2-3's many editing capabilities.

THE EDIT MODE

Whenever you type something into a cell that 1-2-3 can't digest, 1-2-3 automatically goes into its *edit mode.* You can also enter the edit mode yourself by positioning the cell pointer to the cell whose content you wish to edit, and pressing Edit (F2) key. When you're in the Edit mode, the upper-right corner of the screen displays the word Edit. You can use many keys in this mode to change a cell's contents. These keys and their effects are:

⟨ (backspace)	Moves the cursor back one space, and erases a character in the entry as it moves.
Del	Erases the character above the cursor.
Esc	Erases the entire entry in the cell and stays in the Edit mode so you can try again.
Home	Moves the cursor to the first character in the entry.
End	Moves the cursor to the last character in the entry.

← (left-arrow)	Moves the cursor to the left one character without erasing anything.
→ (right-arrow)	Moves the cursor to the right one character without erasing.
⊢	Moves the cursor 5 characters to the left.
→⊣	Moves the cursor 5 characters to the right.
↵ (return)	Completes the editing of the entry and goes back to previous mode.

To practice with this, position the cell pointer to any cell, and type in the formula:

@SUM(A1..A51)

Now suppose you realize that there is an error in this formula. It was supposed to be @SUM(A1..A15). Here is a quick way to fix it.

1. Move the cell pointer to the cell with the erroneous contents. Press the F2 (Edit) key. The cell's contents appear in the control panel, along with the cursor, like this:

   @SUM(A1..A51)__

2. Use the left-arrow key to back up to the 5 in A51, like this:

   @SUM(A1..A5̲1)

3. Press the 1 key. This inserts the one in front of the present 5, as below:

   @SUM(A1..A1̲51)

4. Move the cursor to the right one place so that it is under the second one in the formula, like this:

   @SUM(A1..A151̲)

5. Now press the Del at the bottom of the numeric keypad. This deletes the character over the cursor, like this:

   @SUM(A1..A15)

6. Press the RETURN key, and the corrected formula goes back to its original cell.

You can use the F2 Edit key to change numbers, labels, or formulas.

MOVING BACKWARD THROUGH COMMANDS

Whenever you type in a series of commands, 1-2-3 always remembers each command. Once in a while, you may find that you've typed in the wrong commands and gotten yourself lost. For example, suppose you mean to type in the command /WGFT (Worksheet Global Format Text). By accident, you type in /GFT. This places you in the graph menu, and the mysterious prompt:

Enter sixth data range: B1

appears on the control panel. What to do? Escape key out! Just keep pressing the escape key until you get back to familiar territory, such as the Ready mode, and try again. That's all there is to it.

You can undo an entire series of commands with the Break key. When you discover you've taken a wrong path in a series of commands, simply hold down the Ctrl key and press the Scroll Lock key. This will send you back to the Ready mode immediately. 1-2-3 will forget the whole series of commands that led you down the wrong path.

EDITING ROWS AND COLUMNS

Sometimes we need to edit the actual worksheet, not just a single entry or a series of commands. There are several options from the Range and Worksheet modes that allow you to do so. Fig. 6-1

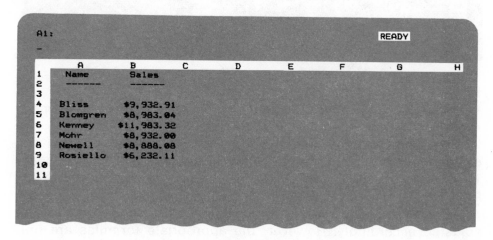

Fig. 6-1

shows a simple worksheet with some names in alphabetical order and some sales figures.

Suppose you wish to add the name Clement to the list, and keep it in alphabetical order. The /WI (Worksheet Insert) command allows you to do so. Here are the steps:

1. Position the cell pointer to the left-most cell of the new row's position. In this case, we would place the pointer in cell A5, Kenney.
2. Select the /WI (Worksheet Insert) command. It asks if you wish to insert a column or a row. Select Row.
3. 1-2-3 then asks:

   Enter row insert range: A5..A5

This is precisely where we wish to insert a row, so just press RETURN. All rows below A5 move down one to make room for the new row as shown in Fig. 6-2.

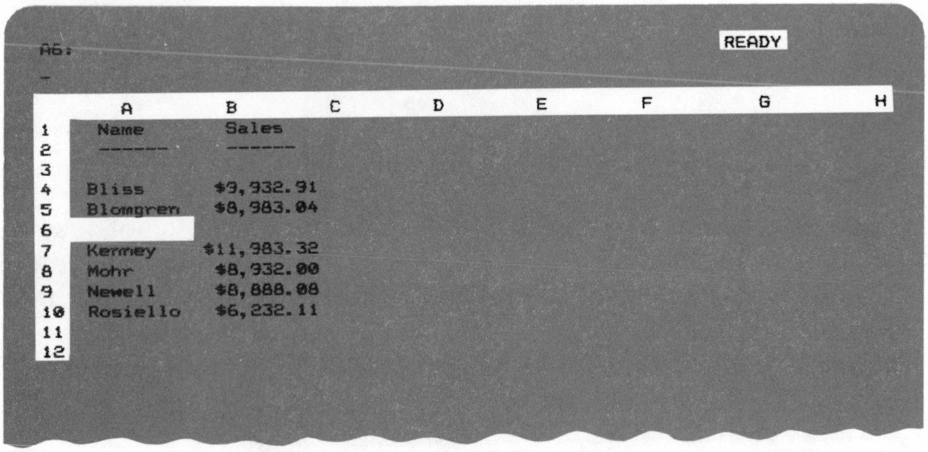

Fig.   6-2

Now you can just type Clement, and his sales figure, into the new row.

The Column option works in the same way. Simply position the cell pointer to the top of where you want the new column to appear. Then, select the /WIC (Worksheet Insert Column) option, and press RETURN. All columns to the right of the new one move over a space.

When you insert a new row or column, all existing formulas are adjusted accordingly. However, the appropriate formulas are not automatically placed in the new rows or columns. Use the /C copy command to fill in formulas when appropriate.

The /WD (Worksheet Delete) option is used to eliminate rows or columns from the worksheet. Suppose you decide to eliminate Blomgren from the list of names. To do so, simply position the pointer to her name in cell A4. Select the /WD (Worksheet Delete) command. It again asks if you wish to delete a column or a row. Select row. When it asks for the range to delete, you can simply press the RETURN key, since the cell pointer is already positioned in the appropriate row. All rows below Blomgren's name will move up a row to fill in the blank space.

CLEANING UP

Sometimes a worksheet just needs some cleaning up. Use the /RE (Range Erase) command for this. For example, suppose we wanted to erase all sales figures but wanted to keep the column there for future use. Select /RE (Range Erase), and specify the range, either by typing or drawing. In this example, the range will be B4 to B9. Press RETURN, and the cell entries are replaced with blanks (Fig. 6-3).

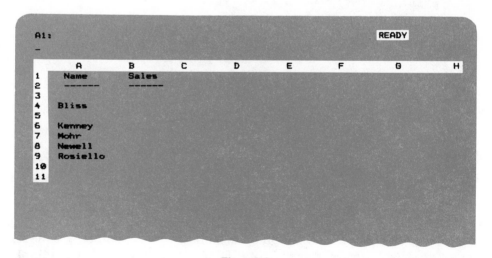

Fig. 6-3

If any of the cells in the specified range are protected, and the protection is on, then 1-2-3 will beep at you and ignore your request. To override, we need to type in the /WGP (Worksheet Global Protection) option, and select Disable. Then again type in the Range Erase command and specify the range.

You can erase the entire worksheet's contents, changing all cells to blanks. The /WE (Worksheet Erase) command provides this capability. However, it also sets all column widths back to their original 9 spaces. Column formats and protection fences are also set back to their original widths. The /WE command is usually used when you've created and saved one worksheet, and want to start building another one from scratch. Be careful. Once the worksheet is from the screen, it is erased permanently. If you have a copy of the worksheet on disk, however, the /WE will not affect the disk file.

MOVING SECTIONS OF THE WORKSHEET

Another method for redesigning a worksheet is to move a range of cells from one location on the spreadsheet to another. For example, suppose you had a long list of names and numbers as shown in Fig. 6-4.

	A	B	C	D	E	F	G	H
12	Kenney	$91,007						
13	Macallister	$93,321						
14	Mohr	$23,632						
15	Morrison	$32,434						
16	Newell	$53,234						
17	Padilla	$45,343						
18	Peterson	$54,456						
29	Rodinsky	$76,543						
20	Rodriguez	$53,345						
21	Rosiello	$34,453						
22	Rowley	$87,565						
23	Ruby	$65,385						
24	Russell	$43,645						
25	Sefing	$65,375						
26	Snyder	$83,243						
27	Sprague	$65,386						
28	Wallace	$65,423						
29	Yokem	$99,987						
30	Zalta	$43,543						
31	Total	@SUM(B1..B30)						

Fig. 6-4

Notice that only rows 12 through 31 are on the screen, since we must scroll down this far to see the total in row 31. There are additional names above in rows one through 11.

This worksheet would be better displayed in four columns rather than two. You can easily move this half of the list so that it appears next to top half of the list. Use the /M (Move) command to do so. Here are the steps:

1. Position the cell pointer to the top left corner of the range to be moved. Since there are thirty rows in this example, we'll split them into two columns of 15 rows each, so move the cell pointer to cell A16.

2. Select the /M (Move option). The control panel asks:

   Enter range to move FROM: A16..A16

   Press the right arrow key once to expand the cell pointer to cell B16, then press the End key followed by the down-arrow key to quickly expand the cell pointer to the entire range to be moved. The control panel now specifies the entire range of cells to move, A16..B31. Press RETURN.

3. The control panel then requests:

   Enter range to move TO: A16

   Move the cell pointer up to cell C1, which causes the prompt to read:

   Enter range to move TO:C1

4. Press the period key and the right arrow key to expand the cell pointer and prompt to C1..D1.

5. Press RETURN. The named range is moved over to columns C1 and D1, as shown in Fig. 6-5.

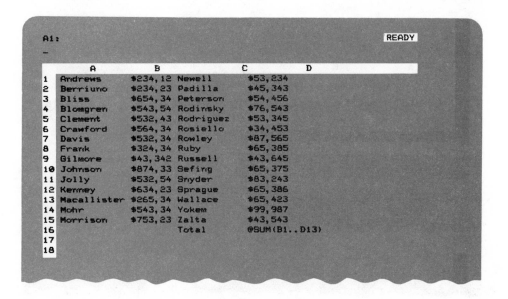

Fig. 6-5

Notice that the second argument in the @SUM formula has adjusted itself accordingly. The /M (Move) command usually makes the correct adjustment for a formula, however what 1-2-3 views as the correct adjustment and what you feel is the correct adjustment might not always match. After moving a range, check your formulas to make sure they still contain the appropriate references.

CHANGING CALCULATION PROCEDURES

1-2-3 automatically recalculates all formulas on the worksheet any time you change or add data to a single cell on the worksheet. This is great for immediate feedback, and is especially wonderful for projections and playing with "What-if" questions. However, if there are many calculations to be performed in the worksheet, and it takes a long time to perform them all, then it is suddenly not so pleasant. It means that each time you add or change data in a cell, you have to wait for all the recalculations to take place. You can change this so that recalculations only take place when you want them to.

Fig. 6-6 shows a worksheet which calculates some basc statistics on a range of numbers (A1 to A20). The numbers do not exist yet. As you type each number in, the cells with formulas in them will recalcu-

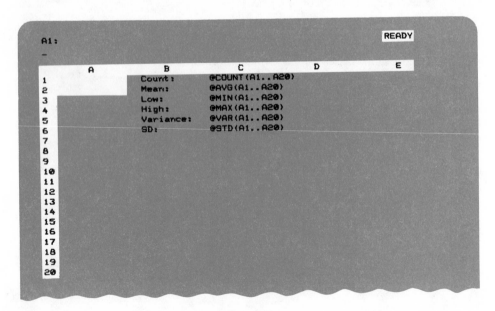

Fig. 6-6

late and display the results each time you add another number to the list. This can be somewhat bothersome, and also meaningless if you are only concerned with the statistics on the entire set of numbers. You can change the recalculation procedure from automatic to manual using the /WGR (Worksheet Global Recalculation) command.

The formulas are displayed in the worksheet because the /WGFT (Worksheet Global Format Text) command is in effect. Use the /WGFG (Worksheet Global Format General) command to make the formulas display their results, which is all zeros and ERRs until there are some data in the A1..A20 range.

Now, select /WGR (Worksheet Global Recalculation). This presents a menu of subcommands:

Natural Columnwise Row Wise Automatic Manual Iteration

Select Manual.

Now when you add numbers to the range (as in Fig. 6-7), the calculations remain zeros and ERRs even though the numbers are typed in. The CALC symbol is displayed in the lower right portion of the sceen. This is to remind you that these data have not been calculated yet.

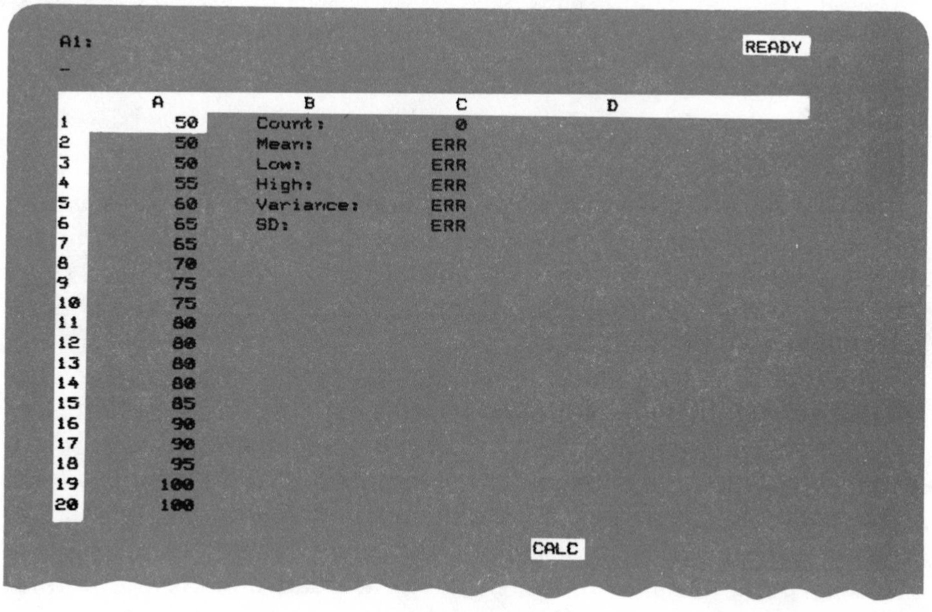

Fig. 6-7

Once you have typed some numbers into column A, you can have 1-2-3 do the calculations by pressing the Calc key (Function key F9). 1-2-3 then does all the calculations, and displays the results as shown in Fig. 6-8. Furthermore, the CALC reminder is no longer displayed in the lower righthand portion of the screen, because there is no need to recalculate.

	A	B	C	D
1	50	Count:	20	
2	50	Mean:	74.75	
3	50	Low:	50	
4	55	High:	100	
5	60	Variance:	251.1875	
6	65	SD:	15.8488958606	
7	65			
8	70			
9	75			
10	75			
11	80			
12	80			
13	80			
14	80			
15	85			
16	90			
17	90			
18	95			
19	100			
20	100			

Fig.   6-8

If you were to change any of the values in column A, there would not be an automatic recalculation. However, the CALC reminder would immediately reappear on the screen, reminding you once again that a change has occurred in the date, and to see that change you must press the Calc key.

To return to Automatic recalculation mode, simply select the /WGR command again, and choose Automatic from the options.

The /WGR command also allows you to change the order in which calculations take place. In its "natural" state, 1-2-3 calculates all formulas exactly as they should be calculated. For example, if calculation "A" requires information from calculation "B," 1-2-3 will naturally perform calculation "B" first. You can change the natural setting to either Column-Wise or Row-Wise by selecting these options from the /WGR menu. However, there is very rarely a need to do so, and unless a peculiar application absolutely demands it, it's best not to stray from the Natural calculation procedure.

STATUS OF THE WORKSHEET

When you start making many changes to the worksheet, it sometimes becomes difficult to remember all that you've done. To help your memory with this task, 1-2-3 has a built-in command that will display the status of various parameters of a worksheet. Simply type in the /WS (Worksheet Status) command and press RETURN. The top lines of the screen will display parameters and their current settings.

Parameter	Normal Setting	Optional Settings
RECALCULATION	AUTO NATURAL	MANUAL COLUMN or ROW
FORMAT	(G) General	Options from the /WGF (Worksheet Global Format) command: Fixed, Scientific, Currency, ,comma, +/−, Percent, various dates, or Text.
LABEL PREFIX	' Left-justified	" or ^ Set by /RLP (Range Labels Prefix) command.
COLUMN WIDTH	9	1 − 72 Set by /WGF command.
AVAILABLE MEMORY	(varies)	depends on RAM capacity of your computer.
PROTECTION	OFF	ON Set by /WGP (Worksheet Global Protection) command.

The worksheet status will be displayed across the top of the screen as shown in Fig. 6-9. To turn off the status display, just press any key on the keyboard.

The AVAILABLE MEMORY parameter is a good one to check with once in a while if your worksheet is large. As the worksheet grows and consumes more memory, this value shrinks. If it looks like you are going to be running out of memory soon, and want to squeeze some more work into the worksheet, see if you can get rid of any excess baggage. That is, if there are blank rows or columns on the

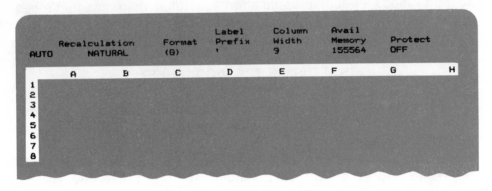

Fig. 6-9

screen that are just for formatting purposes, use the /WD (Worksheet Delete) command to delete them. The closer you can get the lower right corner of the worksheet to cell A1, the less memory you'll consume. After deleting unnecessary rows and columns, use the /FS (File Save) command to save the worksheet, then immediately retrieve the worksheet with the /FR (File Retrieve) command. Check the AVAILABLE MEMORY parameter again with the /WS command, and you'll probably see some savings.

If running out of memory is a constant problem, you will need more RAM in your computer. Most computers are expandable to 500K (half a megabyte) of RAM, which should be plenty for just about any worksheet. Expanding your computer's RAM capability will require that you purchase additional hardware, and may even require that you leave your computer in the shop for a couple of days. Check with your dealer.

In summary, 1-2-3 provides many commands for changing data that exist on the worksheet. In the next chapter, we'll discuss techniques for printing worksheets on the printer.

Chapter 7

DISPLAYING WORKSHEETS ON THE PRINTER

If you have a printer, you will probably want to display your worksheets on paper (hardcopy) from time to time. 1-2-3 has many commands for sending worksheets to the printer, and many options for formatting the hardcopy of the worksheet. You can also send a worksheet to a special disk file, called a print file, which allows you to print the worksheet at a more convenient time, or even make some changes to the printed worksheet prior to printing it.

THE STANDARD PRINTED REPORT

To print a copy of a worksheet, you first need to have the worksheet displayed on the screen. Then select the /P (Print) command. A series of print options appears in the control panel. The first one looks like this:

Printer   File
Send print output directly to the printer

To immediately print an exact copy of the worksheet as it appears on the screen, select the Printer option. Selecting the File stores a special copy of the worksheet on a disk file, which can be printed out at a later time. Once you've selected one of these options, another menu appears, which looks like this:

Range Line Page Options Clear Align Go Quit

To print a worksheet, first select the Range option, which will ask:

Enter Print Range: A1

Then you can type in or draw the range that you wish to print (usually the range of all cells in the worksheet). Then, select the go option to send the worksheet to the printer.

If nothing happens, either (1) the printer is not on, (2) the printer is not on-line, (3) the printer is not physically connected to the computer with a cable or, (4) the printer is not properly configured. If any of either 1, 2, or 3 is the problem, then 1-2-3 will beep at you and display a message indicating that it cannot find the printer. Just press the Escape (Esc) key, and you will be returned to the print menu. Make sure the printer is properly hooked up, and try again. If none of these is the problem, then see the section on "Configuring the Printer" in Appendix A.

Whenever you type in the /P command, you need to specify a range to print. However, 1-2-3 will remember the last range you used, and display it on the screen. If that range is still acceptable, you need not reenter the range. However, if you should ever select the Go option from the print menu, and only get a beep from 1-2-3, that could mean you have not specified the range yet. Select the range option again, specify a range, then select the Go option again.

HEADINGS AND FOOTINGS ON PRINTED WORKSHEETS

If you want additional headings or footings on your printed worksheet, you can select the Option choice from the print menu. When you select Options, the following menu appears on the screen:

Header Footer Margins Borders Setup Page-Length Other Quit

Select the Header option to create a heading for a worksheet, select Footer to create a footing. When you do so, 1-2-3 will ask you to type in the heading or the footing. Headings are always printed two lines above the printed worksheet, footings two lines below.

You can left-justify, center, or right-justify headings and footings. The symbol 1 is used to specify justification. Suppose you want your heading to be "Grades for Computer Science 101." You can enter in any one of three formats, with these results:

Typed in as. . .	Result
Grades for Computer Science 101	Since there is no ¦ character, this heading will be left-justified.
¦ Grades for Computer Science 101	Since there is one ¦ character, this heading will be centered.
¦¦ Grades for Computer Science 101	With two ¦ characters, this heading will be right-justified

You can get fancy and include page numbers and today's date in headings. Use the symbol # to stand for a page number and the symbol @ to stand for today's date. For example, if we type in the heading as:

@ ¦ Grades for Computer Science 101 ¦ #

it will appear with the date left-justified, the heading centered, and the page number right-justified as shown in Fig. 7-1.

```
03-Mar-84      Grades for Computer Science 101                    1



Name           Test 1      Test 2    Test 3    Test 4
-----------------------------------------------------------------
Adams              90         100        88        70
Bovee              80          90        78       100
Carlson            90          90        95        90
```

Fig. 7-1

If the printed worksheet is more than one page long, the heading (and footing) will be displayed on each page. And of course, the page number will be correct.

PRINTING THE ACTUAL CONTENTS

The Printer commands generally display the worksheet as it appears on the screen. In some circumstances, however, you might prefer to see a printed copy of the worksheet's actual contents (including formulas) rather than its output. To do so, select Options from the Print menu of choices. From the next menu of options, select Other. This displays yet another menu of options:

As Displayed Cell-Formulas Formatted Unformatted

Select Cell-formulas. Then select Quit from the Other menu, and select Go from the Print Menu. The Printer will display a listing of all active cells in the worksheet and their contents as shown in Fig. 7-2.

```
A1:  U 'Principal
B1:  U 60000
A2:  U 'Interest
B2:  U 0.17
A5:  U 'Term
B5:  U 'Payment
A6:  I 1
B6:  @PMT($B$1,$B$2/12,A6*12)
A7:  I 2
B7:  @PMT($B$1,$B$2/12,A7*12)
A8:  I 3
B8:  @PMT($B$1,$B$2/12,A8*12)
A9:  I 4
B9:  @PMT($B$1,$B$2/12,A9*12)
A10: I 5
B10: @PMT($B$1,$B$2/12,A10*12)
```

Fig.   7-2

This display shows the contents of the loan analysis worksheet we created earlier. Most of the cells have the letter U in front of them. This indicates that these are "Unprotected" cells. The formula cells, however, do not have a U in front of them. That is because the last time we used this worksheet in an example, we set up the worksheet so that the formula cells would be protected and unmodifiable.

Another way to view the actual contents of the worksheet rather than the output is to first use the /WGFT (Worksheet Global Formal Text) command to have the actual formulas rather than their outputs displayed on the screen. Then, select the /P option, specify the range of the entire worksheet, and print the file. The output will be displayed exactly as it appeared on the screen (Fig. 7-3).

```
Principal    60000
Interest      0.16

Term         Payment

   1         @PMT($B$1,$B$2/12,A6*12)
   2         @PMT($B$1,$B$2/12,A7*12)
   3         @PMT($B$1,$B$2/12,A8*12)
   4         @PMT($B$1,$B$2/12,A9*12)
   5         @PMT($B$1,$B$2/12,A10*12)
```

Fig.   7-3

You may want to make such printouts of all the worksheets you create. If some minor disaster should ever destroy a prized worksheet, a printout such as this can help you key it back in from scratch. You may have to use the /WC (Worksheet Column-width) command to make the columns extra wide to accommodate the formulas. Do so before you select the /P command.

COMPRESSED AND EXPANDED PRINT

Most dot matrix printers have commands for switching to compressed or expanded print. 1-2-3 can send special codes to such printers through the Options Setup option. Of course, you must know what special characters to send to a particular printer to achieve a desired result. You'll need to check your printer manual for that.

Once you have determined what special characters your printer requires for various print sizes, select Options from the print menu. From the menu of subcommands, select Setup. 1-2-3 will ask that you:

Enter Setup String:

Now you need to type in the appropriate code. The code is typically a number below 26 (the "control key" range of the ASCII standard character set used by most computers). It is necessary to precede the code with a backslash, and extend it to three characters. For example, the Epson printer uses ASCII character 15 to go into compressed print mode. So, the actual code you type onto the screen is:

\ø15

After typing in the code, press RETURN. Select Quit from the menu of subcommands, then Go from the Print menu. The worksheet will be printed in compressed print.

When printing worksheets with compressed or expanded print, you will probably want to adjust the margins accordingly. The "Option Margins" option will allow you to adjust the left and right margins of your printed worksheet. To do so, select Options from the Print menu, and select Margins. This allows you to further select from the left, right, top, and bottom margins. If you are changing the print size, you probably want to alter the right margin accordingly.

Select R for right margin, and type in a new value for the right margin (the standard right margin is 76). You may have to experiment a bit to get just the report you want, since the printer may not always produce exactly what you had expected.

Changing the right-margin setting is also useful if you use wide paper in your printer. To take advantage of the full width of the paper, set the right margin to 120 or so.

You can also change the number of lines printed on each page by adjusting the page length. 1-2-3 assumes a standard 8½ by 11 inch page size, and prints 66 lines to a page. If you are using other than standard size paper, or you set your printer to print 8 lines to the inch (rather than the standard 6 lines), you can change the page length. Type in the /P command, select Options from the Print menu, select Page-length from the next menu. 1-2-3 will ask that you:

Enter Lines per Page: 66

Type in the new page length. For example, if you are printing 8 lines to the inch, you'll want the page length to be 88 (8 lines times 11 inches). Type in 88 and press RETURN. Your worksheet will be formatted accordingly.

DISPLAYING BORDERS IN PRINTED REPORTS

In an earlier chapter, we used the /WT (Worksheet Titles) command to "freeze" titles on the screen so that they would remain in position as we scrolled about the worksheet. You can achieve the same effects on printed worksheets using the Borders choice from the Options menu. From the Print menu, select Options, and select Borders from the Options menu. 1-2-3 will ask if you want Rows or Columns as borders. After you select one, specify the range of the "frozen" border. You can freeze both column and a row by selecting one option, defining the border, then selecting the other option, and defining its border. When you actually print the report with the Go option, each page of the report will include the frozen borders.

The other options from the /P menu include Lines, Page, Align, Clear, and Quit. The Line option advances the paper in the printer one line each time you press the L key or RETURN. The Page option advances the paper in the printer to the top of the next page. The Align option re-aligns the paper in the printer, in case you forget to properly set the top of the page before turning on the printer. To use it, set a page perforation just above the print head on the printer, and select this option. The Clear option clears the Range, headings, footings, Margins, Page-length, and Setup characters back to their original 8½ by 11 standard format. The Quit option returns to the 1-2-3 Ready mode.

INTERFACING WORKSHEETS WITH WORD PROCESSORS

We mentioned earlier that printed worksheets could be sent to disk files rather than directly to the printer. This allows you to send a worksheet to a disk file, then pull it into a word processor (such as the WordStar™ program) for additional editing or for inclusion in a formal document. You can use all of the various options described in this chapter with worksheets sent to disk files as well as with printed worksheets. To send worksheets to disk files for printing, you should:

1. Select File rather than Printer from the first /P menu.
2. Specify a file name to store the worksheet on when asked. The file name can be up to eight characters in length, and may not include spaces, periods, or commas.

Your worksheet will be "printed" on the named disk file rather than on the printer. 1-2-3 will add the extension .PRN to your file name, so if you call your file LOANS, it will be stored on disk as LOANS.PRN. You can specify which disk drive to use by preceding the file name with the letter of the drive and a colon. Hence, if you name the file B:LOANS, the disk in drive B will have the LOANS.PRN file on it.

Now suppose you have a 10-page report that you've created with the WordStar™ program stored on a disk. You want to include the LOANS worksheet in the report, but you don't want to do any cut and paste (Heaven forbid!). You can read the disk-file version of the worksheet into your report by following these steps.

1. Remove the 1-2-3 disk from drive A, and put in the WordStar disk that also has the 10 page report in it. Call up Wordstar™, and use the Document mode to edit the 10 page report, so the report appears on the screen ready for editing.
2. Position the cursor to the place in the report that you want the worksheet to appear.
3. Type in the command ^KR (hold down the CTRL key and type the letters KR). WordStar™ asks for the NAME OF FILE TO READ? Type in B:LOANS.PRN <RET>. (Don't forget the .PRN, because 1-2-3 always adds this extension.)

The worksheet appears just where you want it to in your report. Word processing systems other than WordStar™ may require different commands for reading in the worksheet file, but the procedures will be basically the same.

If the worksheet you are sending to a disk file is large, you may want to ensure that no extraneous "page breaks" or headings and footings get sent to the disk file. You can do so by selecting Options from the Print menu. From there, select Other, and then select Un-formatted. When you select the Go option, the worksheet will be sent to the named disk file without any extraneous print characters (such as page breaks). This gives you more control over formatting the report through a word processing system.

In summary, 1-2-3 provides many options for displaying work-sheets on paper through the /PP command. The same options are available for sending worksheets to special print files on disk. You can use print files on a disk as you would any standard word process-ing file.

In the next chapter, we'll discuss techniques for managing work-sheet files on disk.

Chapter 8

MANAGING WORKSHEET FILES

We have already discussed two basic commands for managing worksheets files; /FS (File Save) and /FR (File Retrieve). 1-2-3 has several additional commands for managing disk files. These allow you to extract parts of worksheets, combine worksheets, and create files that are compatible with other software systems. In this chapter, we will discuss the various file commands.

SAVING WORKSHEETS TO DISK FILES

Whenever you are creating a new worksheet or editing an existing one, it is a good idea to save the worksheet on a disk file from time to time. If you forget to save a worksheet before exiting 1-2-3, the worksheet is lost for good. Also, a sudden power shortage or accidentally typed command can wipe out a worksheet. This can be most unpleasant, especially if you've been working on the worksheet for several hours. If you remember to save a worksheet every fifteen minutes or so, the most you could possibly lose is fifteen minutes of labor. It only takes a few seconds to save a worksheet on disk. It could take much longer to recreate a lost one.

To save a file, select the /FS (File Save) option. The names of all existing files on the presently logged disk drive will show on the screen, as follows:

Enter save file name:

LOANS   GRADES   STATS   TAXES   FIG1_1   FIG1_2

If the worksheet you are currently saving has been saved previously, its name will appear along with the prompt, like this:

Enter save file name:TAXES

<u>**LOANS**</u>   **GRADES**   **STATS**   **TAXES**   **FIG1_1**   **FIG1_2**

If this is a new worksheet, then you'll need to come up with a new name for the file. (Remember, 8 letters maximum, no spaces or punctuation.) Type in the new file name and press the RETURN key. The file will be saved on disk, and will also remain on the screen for you to work with.

If this is not a new worksheet, you can just press RETURN to reuse the present file name. 1-2-3 asks:

<u>**Cancel**</u> **Replace**

If you select cancel, the present worksheet will not be saved. If you select replace, the worksheet currently displayed on the screen will replace the disk file that has this file name.

When you save a worksheet to a disk file, 1-2-3 also stores all the format characteristics of the worksheet. It remembers column widths, label prefixes, number displays, ranges, printer settings; anything that affects the way in which the worksheet is to be displayed. This is so that when you later retrieve the worksheet for future use, it looks exactly the same on the screen as it did when you saved it.

If you try to save a worksheet to a file, and there is not enough room on the disk to store the file, 1-2-3 will display the message "disk full." This unhappy message can create problems if you don't have any other formatted disk handy. If you do have another disk handy, you can press the Esc key when you see the error message, put a new disk in drive B. Then use the /FS command again to save the worksheet on the new diskette. You can also erase some files on the existing disk to make room for the new worksheet. We discuss this under "Erasing Files" later in this chapter.

RETRIEVING FILES FROM DISK

The /FR (File Retrieve) command pulls copies of worksheets from disk files onto the screen. To use it, simply select the /FR command. All existing worksheet files on the logged disk drive appear on the screen. Either type in the name of the file you want to work with, or highlight it with the menu pointer and press RETURN. The worksheet will appear on the screen, and completely erase the presently displayed worksheet from the screen.

Note that when you retrieve a file, you only bring up a copy of the worksheet. The disk file remains intact. Any changes you make to the worksheet on the screen do NOT affect the disk file. This can be both a curse and a blessing. For example, suppose you are editing a worksheet on the screen, and accidentally make a complete mess of it. If you just use the /FR command to retrieve the worksheet again, it will come back in its original form; so all you have lost is some editing time. You need not go back and try to "undo" the accidental mess you've created. On the other hand, if you spend a couple of hours editing a worksheet, and you make some great improvements, then you accidentally retrieve the same file again, the original comes onto the screen, and the newly edited version is lost for good.

Again, you can avoid risky situations by just remembering to save the worksheet from time to time. If you do so every fifteen minutes, the most you can lose is 15 minutes labor.

DISPLAYING FILES AND STORAGE SPACE

1-2-3 can display file names of all 1-2-3 files stored on disk. The /FL (File List) command shows all file names of a particular type, and also displays the amount of available space left on the disk. When you select the command, it asks which type of files you wish to see:

Worksheet Print Graph

Worksheet (.WKS) files are stored worksheets, Print (.PRN) files are those created with the /PF (Print File) command. Graph (.PIC) files, which we have not discussed yet, are special files for printing graphs. Select which types of files you want to display the names of. The file names will be displayed, and will temporarily overwrite any worksheet that is displayed on the screen, as such:

Available disk space (bytes): 40960

LOANS	**TAXES**	**GRADES**	**TENYEAR**
STATS	**NAMES**	**FIG_1**	**FIG1_2**
FIG1_3			

After viewing the file names, just press any key to return to the READY mode. The current worksheet will appear on the screen unchanged. If there are no files of the type you've selected to display on the disk, then 1-2-3 beeps and displays a message. Press RETURN or the Esc key to return to the Ready mode.

You can use the /FD (File Directory) command to change the currently logged disk drive prior to doing a /FS to see file names in a particular disk drive.

ERASING FILES

It is not unusual to get a bit of junk cluttering up a disk. Old letters to friends, old backup (.BAK) files, and the like really don't need to be stored forever. 1-2-3 has a built-in command to erase a file from disk. This can come in handy when you try to save a worksheet and get an error message saying that the disk is full. Often, if you just erase an unwanted file or two, and try to save again, you'll have enough disk space. (The /FL command displays available disk space.)

To erase files, first select the /FE (File Erase) command. 1-2-3 will ask which type of file you want to erase, Worksheet, Print, or Graph. Select one of these, then indicate a file name and press RETURN. The file is erased permanently from the disk, and the space it was using up becomes available for storage.

You can also use "wild cards" in file names to erase entire groups of files. There are two wild card characters for file names. One is the question mark (?), which matches any single character in a file name. The other is an asterisk, which matches any group of characters in a file name. Hence, if you ask to erase file name GRADE?, you'll erase GRADE1, GRADE2, GRADE3, GRADE4, GRADE5, etc. If you elect to erase G*, you'll erase any file on the disk that begins with the letter G, such as GRADES, GOOSE, GENLEDGE, etc.

Do keep in mind that you are *permanently* erasing the files you select, so do be very careful with these wild cards. For example, if you select Worksheet from the File Erase menu, then just type in an*, you will erase *all* the worksheet files from the disk. This is one command you do not want to type in by accident. 1-2-3 always double-checks before erasing a file. When it asks for confirmation, always make sure you have typed in what you meant to prior to confirming the erase.

SAVING PARTS OF WORKSHEETS

At some point, you may create a worksheet that is too large to store on a single floppy diskette. When this happens, you will get the message "disk full" when you attempt to save the worksheet, even if the diskette has no previously saved files on it. When there are no existing files to erase to make more room, you'll need to break the worksheet into two or more parts, and store the separate pieces on separate diskettes. The /FX (File extract) option allows you to do this.

Suppose you have a gigantic worksheet that extends from cell A1 to cell HH500. You attempt to save it on an empty disk in drive B with the /FS command, but get a disk full error. You will need to split up the worksheet. Here's how to do it. Leave the blank disk in drive B, and select the /FX (File eXtract) command. This brings up two choices:

Formulas   Values

Select Formulas. Then, provide a file name, such as GIANT1, and press RETURN. 1-2-3 will ask for the range to store. To store the top half of this worksheet type in the range A1..HH250 <RET>. The top half of the worksheet is stored on this diskette.

Now, remove the disk from drive B, and put in another blank, formatted diskette. Again, select the /FX option, select Formulas, and enter a file name. GIANT2 would be good in this example, because it reminds us that this is part two of the giant worksheet. When 1-2-3 asks for the range, specify the bottom half, A251..HH500, and press RETURN. At this point, the giant worksheet is safely stored on two separate diskettes, and is still on the screen.

One of the options that the /FX command allows is to store the partial worksheet either with the formula (Formula), or just the results of the formulas (Values). If you choose the latter option, Values, the formulas are lost forever in the stored file. Unless you are absolutely sure that results of calculations will not change in future use of the extracted portion of the worksheet, select the Formulas option from this menu.

COMBINING FILES INTO A SINGLE WORKSHEET

Let's discuss methods for getting GIANT1 and GIANT2 back to the screen now. First, you want to load up 1-2-3 in the usual fashion, and put the disk with GIANT1 in drive B. Then use the /FR (File Retrieve) command to load B:GIANT1 onto the screen. Next, press the End and down-arrow keys to get down to the last cell in the worksheet, positioning the pointer to cell A256. Next, put the diskette with GIANT2 on it in drive B. Select the /FC (File Combine) command. 1-2-3 will ask if you wish to Copy, Add, or Subtract. Select Copy for this example. Next 1-2-3 will ask if you want to combine the Entire file, or a Named range. Select Entire, press RETURN, then type in the file name GIANT2 <RET>. The rest of the giant worksheet is displayed on the screen starting at the cell pointer's position.

In chapter 15, we'll see how we can use the /FX and /FC commands to help with the task of managing year-to-date totals.

ADDITIONAL TECHNIQUES FOR MANAGING FILES

The Lotus Access System has additional capabilities for managing disk files. Recall that when you first call up LOTUS from the A>, it displays these options:

Lotus Access System V.1A (C) 1983 Lotus Development Corp.

1-2-3 File-Manager   Disk-Manager   PrintGraph   Translates Exit

===

Both the File-Manager and the Disk-Manager options provide additional tools for managing files. If you select the File-Manager option, it asks that you:

Select source disk.

A   B

===

Most likely you've been storing worksheet files on the disk in drive B, so select B. The screen then displays a number of new options as well as information on all the files stored on the disk in drive B, as below:

Copy Erase Rename Archive Disk-Drive Sort Quit
Copy selected files from the current disk to another.

===

FILENAME	EXT	DATE	TIME	SIZE	
LOANS	WKS	03-Mar-83	3:12pm	12880	
GRADES	WKS	31-Mar-83	12:00am	14080	
TAXES	WKS	01-Apr-83	1:31pm	13040	
MAIL	WKS	03-Apr-83	3:46pm	12880	Current Drive: B
PIC1	PRN	04-Apr-83	4:46pm	760	Number of files: 98
PIC2	PRN	11-Jun-83	3:31pm	348	Total Bytes Used: 53988
					Total Bytes Free: 28160

The Copy option allows you to make backups of disk files to a separate diskette. When you select this option, 1-2-3 asks that you select files for backing up, and displays instructions for doing so (along with the file names), like this:

Press [Space] to toggle mark.
Press [Enter] to process.
Press [Esc] to return to menu.

Use the up- and down-arrow keys to highlight various names in the list of file names. To mark a file for copying, press the space bar while it is highlighted. This places a # symbol next to the file name. You can mark as many file names as you wish. When you are done marking files for copying, press the RETURN key. 1-2-3 will then display the message:

A
Use disk A as destination.

Press the RETURN key, and 1-2-3 will double-check with the options:

No   Yes   Quit

Select Yes, and 1-2-3 will take copies of the selected files from the disk in drive B, and store them on the disk in drive A.

This procedure for marking files is also used with other file-management capabilities. They are:

Erase   Erases marked files.
Rename Allows you to change the names of marked files.
Archive Creates identical copies of marked files on the same disk with new names that you provide.

The Disk-Drive option allows you to change the drive used as the source. The Sort option allows you to sort the displayed file names into a new order. When you select the Sort option, it provides the options below:

Primary Key   Secondary Key   Reset   Go   Quit

The Primary Key allows you to select the main criterion for sorting the file names, as such:

Name **Extension** **Date/Time** **Size**

If you select Name, files will be sorted alphabetically by name. If you select Extension, files will be sorted alphabetically by extension (i.e., .WKS, .PIC, .PRN, etc.). The Date/Time option will sort files chronologically, and size will sort by size. Once you select an option, 1-2-3 will ask if you want the sort performed in Ascending (smallest-to-largest) or Descending (largest-to-smallest) order. Once you select an option, the Sort menu will reappear.

The Secondary key option provides for a sort-within-a-sort. For instance, if you select Name as the Primary Key, and Extension as the Secondary Key, file names will be sorted in alphabetical order by file name, and multiple files with the same name will be sorted alphabetically by extension, such as:

```
LOANS.PIC
LOANS.PRN
LOANS.WKS
```

The Go option performs the sort. The Quit option returns you to the Lotus Access System menu.

The Disk-Manager option from the Lotus Access System provides tools for managing entire disks, rather than individual files. Its options appear as below:

Disk-Copy **Compare** **Prepare** **Status** **Quit**

These options will require that you use the 1-2-3 Utilities disk. When you select an option, 1-2-3 will ask that you insert the Utilities into drive A first, and will pause to allow you to do so. Each Disk-Manager option is summarized as follows:

Disk-Copy   Copies all the files from one disk to another. Have a blank disk prepared to use before selecting this option. Disk-Copy always copies from disk drive A to drive B. It uses the DOS DISK-COPY program from the 1-2-3 Utilities disk.

Compare   Compares two diskettes to see if they are identical, using the DOS DISKCOMP program.

Prepare   Formats a blank disk, fresh out of the box, for use on your computer. Uses the DOS FORMAT program.

Status   Reports available disk space using the DOS CHKDSK program.

Quit   Returns to the Lotus Access System Menu.

These options are useful for making backup copies of disks with important worksheet data on them. Use the Prepare option to format a new diskette, then use the Disk-Copy option to transfer copies of all files from the worksheet disk to the new disk.

INTERFACING 1-2-3 WITH OTHER SOFTWARE SYSTEMS

You can read files from other software products into 1-2-3, and send 1-2-3 worksheet files to other software products too. 1-2-3 provides two options for this: The /FI (File Import) option from the 1-2-3 worksheet, and the Translate option from the Lotus Access System menu.

The /FI option reads standard ASCII text files from disk into RAM. An ASCII file is one that is typically created by a word processing system or a BASIC sequential data file. However, it is possible to use this capability a bit more creatively. For example, if you have a Supercalc™ spreadsheet that you would like to send to 1-2-3, you can create an ASCII data file of the Supercalc spreadsheet, then read it into 1-2-3 using the /FI command. Here is the procedure:

1. Run Supercalc and load the spreadsheet you wish to transfer using the Supercalc /L command. Use the /GB (Global Border) command to eliminate the borders. Select the /O (Output) command, and the D (Display) option from the Supercalc menu. Tell Supercalc the range you wish to output (e.g., A1:E25). A prompt will ask if you want to output to the screen, printer, or disk. Select disk. When Supercalc asks for a file name, supply one (we'll use the file name SC123 for this example). When done, Quit Supercalc. The name of the file you've just created will be SC123.PRN (Supercalc adds the .PRN extension).

2. Next, if possible, put quotation marks around all labels in the SC123.PRN file. This can easily be accomplished by using a

word processing system and editing the SC123.PRN file. Use the Nondocument mode if your word processor has one. After placing all labels in quotation marks, save the SC123.PRN file.

3. Load up 1-2-3, and when a blank worksheet appears on the screen, select the /FI (File Import) option. 1-2-3 will ask if you want Text or Numbers. Select numbers. 1-2-3 will ask for the name of the file to import. In this example, the file name is SC123.PRN. (The /FI command requires that the file being imported have the extension .PRN).

1-2-3 will read the SC123.PRN file and display it on the screen. It will treat any data surrounded by quotation marks as a label, and all numeric characters as numbers. The worksheet may require some additional formatting and work after being read into the 1-2-3 worksheet. File transfers are tricky business for a computer, and sometimes they do not happen the way you might expect.

The Lotus Access System menu also provides an option to *Translate*. This option allows you to transfer 1-2-3 worksheets to and from various microcomputer software products. When you select the Transfer option, you will be prompted to insert the Lotus Utility disk into drive A. Then this menu appears on the screen:

VC to WKS   DIF to WKS   WKS to DIF   DBF to WKS   WKS to DBF   Quit

===

The abbreviations used in the menu are actually file name extensions, which can be summarized as follows:

.VC   VisiCalc™ spreadsheet file.
.WKS   1-2-3 worksheet file.
.DIF   Data Interchange Format file, used primarily in spreadsheet programs.
.DBF   A dBASE II™ database file.

Before you can transfer files to and from 1-2-3, file names must have the appropriate extensions. You can use the Lotus File-Manager program to check existing file names and rename files if necessary.

Once you select an option from the menu, 1-2-3 will ask which drive to look for requested files on, A or B. Provide the appropriate drive. Then 1-2-3 will display the names of all files on that disk that are available for the option you've selected. Select files to be translated by highlighting with the pointer and marking, as in the examples with the File-Manager option described previously.

Next, 1-2-3 will ask which disk drive to store the translated files on, A or B. Select a drive, 1-2-3 will display the translation you have requested, and ask for confirmation, as follows:

Translate B:CHECKS.DBF to B:CHECKS.WKS

No **Yes** **Quit**

===

If this is indeed the translation you wish, select Yes, and 1-2-3 will create a translated copy of the file selected. When the translation is complete, the Lotus Access System menu reappears on the screen.

To get back to the 1-2-3 worksheet, select Exit from the Lotus Access System menu. The screen will double check for confirmation, then prompt you to insert the 1-2-3 System disk into drive A. From there, you can go back to working with the worksheet on the screen.

In the next chapter, we will develop and discuss some practical 1-2-3 worksheets.

Chapter 9

Some Practical Examples

It is time to start putting our new knowledge to work. In this chapter, we'll explore some practical applications of 1-2-3, and discuss the techniques used in creating them. We'll discuss and demonstrate a number of worksheets which use a variety of 1-2-3's capabilities.

THE CHECK REGISTER

We'll design the check register worksheet to look like the check register in a checkbook. However, rather than figuring out the balance ourselves, we'll have 1-2-3 do it for us. Fig. 9-1 shows a partially filled checkbook worksheet. This worksheet has the following characteristics:

```
      A       B    C      D            E         F        G
1                          Check Register
2
3     Date    No.       Description    Deposit    Check    Balance
4     ======  ===       ============   ========   =====    =======
5     01-Jan          Bal. Forward    $2500.00             $2500.00
6     02-Jan   101    Rent                        $500.00  $2000.00
7     02-Jan   102    Utilities                   $50.00   $1950.00
8     03-Jan   103    Car Payment                 $152.00  $1798.00
9     04-Jan   104    Deposit         $500.00              $2298.00
10                                                         NA
11                                                         NA
12                                                         NA
```

Fig. 9-1

Formats

Column A is seven spaces wide, column B is five spaces wide. Column C is three spaces wide, and left blank as a gap between columns B and D. Column D is 20 spaces wide. Columns E, F, and G are each 12 columns wide. Each was set using the /WCS (Worksheet Column-width Set) command. All other columns are the standard nine character width.

Column A was set to Date 2 format using the /RFD2 (Range Format Date 2) command, the specified range was A5..A100. Columns E, F, and G are Currency format, formatted with the command, /RFC2 (Range Format Currency 2 decimal places). The specified range is E5 to G100.

Labels

All labels are centered in their cells. Use the /WGLC (Worksheet Global Label-prefix Center) prior to entering labels so that they will all be centered. Underlining labels were created by positioning the cell pointer to the appropriate cell and entering a \= <RET>. The \= causes the equal sign character to fill the entire cell.

Formulas

Only column G contains formulas. Cell G5 contains this formula:

@IF(E5>0#OR#F5>0,G4+E5−F5,@NA)

In English, this translates to "If there is either a deposit or a check entered in this row, display the current balance, otherwise display the message NA." The current balance is calculated by adding the previous balance to the deposit amount in the current row, and subtracting the check amount in the current row. Once this formula is entered into cell G5, it can easily be replicated in all rows using the /C command. Select /C, indicate G5..G5 as the range to copy FROM, and G6..G100 as the range to copy TO. In the /WGFT (Worksheet Global Format Text) format, Column G looks like Fig. 9-2 after the completed copy command.

The formulas extend to row 100, so there is room for 100 checks on the register. You could make the register extend all the way down to row 2048, but each time you enter a new check or deposit, the recalculation procedure could take a good deal of time. Of course, you could simply change the recalculation procedure to manual

```
                    G                                           H
1
2
3      Balance
4      ========
5      @IF(E5)0#OR#F5)0,G4+E5-F5,@NA)
6      @IF(E6)0#OR#F6)0,G5+E6-F6,@NA)
7      @IF(E7)0#OR#F7)0,G6+E7-F7,@NA)
8      @IF(E8)0#OR#F8)0,G7+E8-F8,@NA)
9      @IF(E9)0#OR#F9)0,G8+E9-F9,@NA)
10     @IF(E10)0#OR#F10)0,G9+E10-F10,@NA)
11     @IF(E11)0#OR#F11)0,G10+E11-F11,@NA)
12     @IF(E12)0#OR#F12)0,G11+E12-F12,@NA)
```

Fig. 9-2

using the /WGRM (Worksheet Global Recalculation Manual) option. Then you could enter a group of checks quickly, and press the F9 (Calc) key to calculate the balances.

Data

The first item of data entered into the worksheet should be a beginning balance entered as a deposit in cell E5. Then, the date, check number, description of payee, and amount for each check or deposit can be entered in a row. Do not skip any rows, however, since the worksheet uses the balance from the row immediately above to calculate the balance in the current row.

STOCK PORTFOLIO

1-2-3 can be used to quickly analyze a stock portfolio. In the example below, the worksheet calculates the amount and percent of gain or loss and the yield. The worksheet is displayed in Fig. 9-3.

Format

Column widths vary; each was set using the /WCS (Worksheet Column-width Set) command.

Labels

All labels are centered using the /WGLC (Worksheet Global Label-prefix Center) command. Column C values are displayed in the

```
      A     B      C       D        E       F        G         H
 1  Stock Portfolio
 2
 3                        Purchase  Current Market    Dollar    Percent
 4  Stock Sym  Shares     Price     Price   Value     Gain      Gain
 5--------------------------------------------------------------------
 6                  500    24.50     19.70   9850.00  -2400.00   -0.24
 7                 1000    17.11     23.13  23130.00   6020.00    0.26
 8                  500    54.25     61.55  30775.00   3650.00    0.12
 9                 1000    48.33     46.44  41440.00  -1890.00   -0.04
10
11                                         110195.00  5380.00
12
20
```

Fig. 9-3

general format. Columns D through H are displayed with two fixed decimal places by using the command /RFF2 (Range Format Fixed 2 decimal places) command, and specifying D6..H11 as the range to format.

Formulas

Formulas are in columns F, G, and H, and appear as in Fig. 9-4 in Text format.

The formulas across the top row (row 6) were typed in exactly as they appear. Then, the entire row of formulas was copied to rows seven, eight, and nine using the /C command. The range F6..H6 was the range copied from; range F7..H9 was the range copied to. Hence, only one copy command was used to fill in remaining rows after the first row of formulas was typed in. The formulas in cells F11 and F12 were typed in as they appear.

```
      E              F           G             H
 1
 2
 3  Current      Market      Dollar        Percent
 4  Price        Value       Gain          Gain
 5--------------------------------------------------------------------
 6   19.70       +E6*C6      (E6*C6)+(D6*C6)   +G6/(E6*C6)
 7   23.13       +E7*C7      (E7*C7)+(D7*C7)   +G7/(E7*C7)
 8   61.55       +E8*C8      (E8*C8)+(D8*C8)   +G8/(E8*C8)
 9   46.44       +E9*C9      (E9*C9)+(D9*C9)   +G9/(E9*C9)
10               --------    --------
11               @SUM(F6..F9) @SUM(G6..G9)
12
13
```

Fig. 9-4

Data

Data for a new stock can be added by insetting a new row in the worksheet, using the /WIR (Worksheet Insert Row) command. For each new stock acquired, enter the name, ticker symbol, number of shares, and purchase price. To evaluate the status of existing stocks, enter the current prices into column E. The worksheet performs all other calculations as soon as the current price is entered or changed.

LOAN AMORTIZATION SCHEDULE

This one may look somewhat familiar to you. It is similar to the loan analysis worksheet in the Lotus Tutorial; except that this worksheet allows you to enter any term between 2 and 30 years, and calculates the amortization accordingly. Of course, you can also adjust the principal and rate as well. For example, Fig. 9-5 displays the amortization schedule for a $50,000 loan at 16% interest for five years.

The worksheet extends to row 36 to allow a maximum term of 30 years. Years that extend beyond the term of the loan being analyzed are filled with the Not Available (NA) symbol. If you were to change the term in the above example, the worksheet would look like Fig. 9-6. Here is how this worksheet was created.

	A	B	C	D	E
1		Principal	$50,000.00		
2		Rate	16.00%		
3		Years	5		
4		Payment	$1,215.90		
5					
6	Year	Beg. Bal.	End Bal.	Total Pd.	Interest
7	1	$50,000.00	$42,903.70	$14,590.83	$7,494.53
8	2	$42,903.70	$34,584.91	$14,590.83	$6,272.05
9	3	$34,584.91	$24,833.04	$14,590.83	$4,838.96
10	4	$24,833.04	$13,401.21	$14,590.83	$3,159.00
11	5	$13,401.21	$0.00	$14,590.83	$1,189.63
12	6	NA	NA	NA	NA
13	7	NA	NA	NA	NA
14	8	NA	NA	NA	NA
15	9	NA	NA	NA	NA
16	10	NA	NA	NA	NA
17	11	NA	NA	NA	NA
18	12	NA	NA	NA	NA
19	13	NA	NA	NA	NA
20	14	NA	NA	NA	NA

Fig. 9-5

```
          A        B            C            D           E
 1               Principal  $50,000.00
 2               Rate           16.00%
 3               Years              10
 4               Payment      $837.56
 5
 6     Year      Beg. Bal.    End Bal.      Total Pd.    Interest
 7      1        $50,000.00   $47,791.93    $10,050.79   $7,842.72
 8      2        $47,791.93   $45,203.48    $10,050.79   $7,462.33
 9      3        $45,203.48   $42,169.11    $10,050.79   $7,016.42
10      4        $42,169.11   $38,612.01    $10,050.79   $6,493.69
11      5        $38,612.01   $34,442.13    $10,050.79   $5,880.90
12      6        $34,442.13   $29,553.89    $10,050.79   $5,162.55
13      7        $29,553.89   $23,823.56    $10,050.79   $4,320.45
14      8        $23,823.56   $17,106.05    $10,050.79   $3,333.28
15      9        $17,106.05    $9,231.32    $10,050.79   $2,176.05
16     10         $9,231.32       $0.00     $10,050.79     $819.47
17     11              NA           NA            NA           NA
18     12              NA           NA            NA           NA
19     13              NA           NA            NA           NA
20     14              NA           NA            NA           NA
```

Fig. 9-6

Format

Column A is six spaces wide, all others are 10 spaces wide. Use the /WGC (Worksheet Global Column-width) command to set all columns to a width of 10, then use /WC (Worksheet Column-width) to narrow column A to five spaces. Cells C1 and C4 are in currency format, using the /RFC2 (Range Format Currency 2 decimal places) command. Cell C2 is in percent format, using the /RFP2 (Range Format Percent 2 decimal places) command. Cell C3 is in general format. Column A is in general format. Cells in the range B7..E36 are in currency format.

Labels

All labels are left-justified.

Formulas

Cell C4 calculates the payment on the loan using this formula:

@PMT(C1,C2/12,C3*12)

Cell B7 has the simple formula:

+C1

since the beginning balance for the first year is the principal amount of the loan.

Cell C7, which calculates the ending balance for the term, uses the present value function, but first checks to make sure that the calculation is necessary. The formula in cell C7 looks like this:

@IF(A7<=$C$3,@PV($C$4,$C$2/12,12*($C$3−A7)),@NA)

In English, this formula says, "If the present year is less than or equal to the term of the loan, display the present value of the loan, otherwise display the 'not available' message, NA." The dollar sign symbols are used to make the cell references absolute, so that when the formula is copied it will still refer to the amounts in the assumptions area of the spreadsheet. This formula was copied from cell C7 down to cell C36 using the /C (copy) command.

Cell D7 calculates the total paid to term. It also checks to make sure that the current year is within the term specified. The formula looks like this:

@IF(A7<=$C$3,+$C$4*12,@NA)

In English, this formula says, "If the current term is less than or equal to the term specified in the assumptions, display the payment times 12 months, otherwise display the not available symbol." The total paid in each term of the loan is always the same. This formula was copied into the range D8 to D36 using the Copy command.

The interest paid in a given term is calculated by subtracting the beginning balance for the term (column B) and the ending balance for the term (column C) from the total paid (column D), so the formula reads:

+D7−(B7−C7)

Once again, the formula was entered into cell E7, and copied to the range E8..E36 using the copy command.

Cell B8 contains the formula:

@IF(A8<=$C$3,C7,@NA)

Which states: "If the current year is within the term, display the ending balance from the last year; otherwise display the not available symbol." This formula was copied to the range B9..B36 using the copy command.

Data

Data for this worksheet are Principal, typed into cell C1, Interest rate, typed into cell C2, and Term in Years, typed into cell C3. 1-2-3 performs all remaining calculations on the worksheet.

This is a very useful worksheet for either personal or business use. It provides full flexibility in playing "What-if" scenarios with potential loan schedules.

TEN YEAR PROJECTION WITH
INTERNAL RATE OF RETURN

Fig. 9-7 shows a ten-year projection worksheet for a real estate concern. Column B contains assumptions about increase rates, column C holds assumptions on first year amounts. Columns D through M display projected amounts for ten years. Rows 7 through 10 display rental income for four tenants, rows 12 through 15 display various expense items. Row 17 displays the cash flow. Cell B19 requests a guess for the internal rate of return (IRR), and cell B20 displays the actual internal rate of return. Only columns A through G are presently visible, but the projection extends to 1994, at which time the cash flow is $13,168 in this example. Here are the details of the financial projection worksheet.

	A	B	C	D	E	F
1	Ten Year Projection for Commercial Real Estate					
2	With Internal Rate of Return					
3	==					
4		Increase				
5	Description	Rate %	1984	1985	1986	1987
6						
7	Tenant 1	0.12	$15,000	$16,800	$18,816	$21,074
8	Tenant 2	0.15	$10,000	$11,500	$13,225	$15,209
9	Tenant 3	0.16	$5,000	$5,800	$6,782	$7,804
10	Tenant 4	0.18	$5,000	$5,900	$6,962	$8,125
11						
12	Maintenance	0.13	$11,000	$12,430	$14,046	$15,872
13	Insurance	0.13	$7,500	$8,475	$9,577	$10,822
14	Debt	0.10	$10,000	$10,000	$12,100	$13,310
15	Mngmt Fee	0.14	$9,000	$10,260	$11,696	$13,334
16						
17	Cash Flow		($2,500)	($2,165)	($1,688)	($1,035)
18						
19	IRR Guess:	0.16				
20	IRR Actual: 0.24255					

Fig. 9-7

Format

All dollar amounts are Currency format with zero decimal places. Use the /RFC0 (Range Format Currency 0 decimal places) command, and specify the range C7..M17. All other numeric amounts are displayed in General format. Column A is 11 characters wide, all others are the standard nine characters wide.

Labels

All labels are left-justified.

Formulas

Column formulas were placed into column D as in Fig. 9-8. Then the formulas were copied to the cells for the remaining years in the

```
        A           B          C         D          E         F
1  Ten Year Projection for Commercial Real Estate
2  With Internal Rate of Return
3  ========================================================
4               Increase
5  Description   Rate %     1984      1985       1986      1987
6  ------------------------------------------------------------
7  Tenant 1                           +C7+(C7*$B$7)
8  Tenant 2                           +C8+(C8*$B$8)
9  Tenant 3                           +C9+(C9*$B$9)
10 Tenant 4                           +C10+(C10*$B$10)
11 ------------------------------------------------------------
12 Maintenance                        +C12+(C12*$B$12)
13 Insurance                          +C13+(C13*$B$13)
14 Debt                               +C14+(C14*$B$14)
15 Mngmt Fee                          +C15+(C15*$B$15)
16 ------------------------------------------------------------
17 Cash Flow                          @SUM(D7..D10)-@SUM(D12..D15)
18
19 IRR Guess:
20 IRR Actual: @IRR(B19,C17..M17)
```

Fig. 9-8

projection. Use the /C (Copy) command, specify D7..D15 as the range to copy from, and E7..M15 as the range to copy to. All formulas for the ten year projection will be filled in accordingly. Notice that all formulas look similar to the one in column D7, like so:

+C7+(C7*$B$7)

In English, this formula says: "The contents of this cell are the contents of the previous cell plus the percent increase rate times the value in the previous cell." In other words, the numbers increase by the percentage amount throughout all ten years.

The cash flow for each year is determined by subtracting the total expenses for the year from the total income. The formula is expressed in column D as:

@SUM(D7..D10)−@SUM(D12..D15)

This formula was spread across all ten years using the Copy command. Finally, the internal rate of return is calculated in cell B20 with this formula:

@IRR(B19,C17..M17)

The guess for the IRR is entered into cell B19, and the IRR is calculated from the cash flows, cells in the range C17..M17.

Data

Without any data, the worksheet looks like Fig. 9-9. To use the worksheet, fill in estimated increase rates into column B. Then, fill in first year income and expenses for 1984 (column C). The worksheet automatically calculates all the remaining cells on the worksheet.

To determine internal rate of return, enter a guess into cell B19. If 1-2-3 does not reach convergence after 20 tries, it will display ERR. You may have to make a few guesses before you get a value.

```
         A            B        C        D        E        F
 1  Ten Year Projection for Commercial Real Estate
 2  With Internal Rate of Return
 3  ==============================================================
 4              Increase
 5  Description    Rate %   1984     1985     1986     1987
 6  --------------------------------------------------------------
 7  Tenant 1                         $0       $0       $0
 8  Tenant 2                         $0       $0       $0
 9  Tenant 3                         $0       $0       $0
10  Tenant 4                         $0       $0       $0
11  --------------------------------------------------------------
12  Maintenance                      $0       $0       $0
13  Insurance                        $0       $0       $0
14  Debt                             $0       $0       $0
15  Mngmt Fee                        $0       $0       $0
16  --------------------------------------------------------------
17  Cash Flow               $0       $0       $0       $0
18
19  IRR Guess:
20  IRR Actual: ERR
```

Fig. 9-9

ACCOUNTS RECEIVABLE AGING REPORT

Here is a useful worksheet for keeping track of accounts receivable, and also one which provides some practice with 1-2-3's serial date arithmetic. It is an accounts receivable aging report. It allows you to enter today's date into some cells, then it automatically shifts billings into appropriate columns, current billing, over 30 days, over

60 days, over 90 days. Also, for each invoice sent, you can record the date it was sent, the amount, and the customer's name. The worksheet is displayed in Fig. 9-10. The details on this report are:

```
A1:                                                          READY
-

   A  B  C   D        E         F         G       H        I
 1 Today's Date                 A/R Ageing Report
 2 Mo:10
 3 Da:15
 4 Yr:83
 5
 6 Due Date
 7 MM DD YY    Amount Customer  Current Over 30 Over 60 Over 90
 8 ============================================================
 9 10  2 83  $500.00   Jose's     500       0       0       0
10  8 15 83 $1000.00    Petco       0       0    1000       0
11  7 30 83  $900.00   Valdox       0       0     900       0
12  6 30 83  $450.00   ABC Co.      0       0       0     450
13 10 30 83  $550.00   Bos Co.    550       0       0       0
14  9  1 83  $459.00   Zep Co.      0     459       0       0
15                     ----------                  ----------
16          $3,859.00              1050    459    1900     450
19
20
```

Fig. 9-10

Format

Columns A, B, and C are each three spaces wide. All others are 10 spaces wide. Column D is in currency format with two decimal places, all other numbers are in general format.

Labels

All labels are right-justified.

Formulas

Formulas appear in columns F, G, H, and I. Cell F9 contains this formula:

@iF(@DATE($B$4,$B$2,$B$3)−@DATE($C9,$A9,$B9)<=30,$D9,0)

In English this formula says: "If the serial value of today's date minus the serial value of the due date is less than or equal to 30, then display the amount owed in this column, otherwise display a zero." There are several absolute references in the formula, particularly those which refer to today's date ($B$4,$B$2,$B$3), since that date is stationary. Use the Copy command to copy the formula downward, filling in the range F9..F14.

The formulas for determining if a bill is over 30 days due are in column G. Cell G9 contains this formula:

@IF(@DATE($B$4,$B$2,$B$3)−@DATE($C9,$A9,$B9)>30#AND#
@DATE($B$4,$B$2,$B$3)−@DATE($C9,$A9,$B9)<=60,$D9,0)

The formula is displayed on two lines here, but in the cell it is simply one long formula. In English, this formula says: "If the serial today's date minus the serial due date is greater than thirty, and the serial today's date minus the serial due date is less than or equal to sixty, then display the amount due in this column, otherwise display a zero."

The formula for determining bills due over 60 days is similar, and is used in column H. Column H9 contains this formula:

@IF(@DATE($B$4,$B$2,$B$3)−@DATE($C9,$A9,$B9)>60#AND#
@DATE($B$4,$B$2,$B$3)−@DATE($C9,$A9,$B9)<=90,$D9,0)

Create this formula by copying the formula in cell G9 to cell H9. Then, with the cell pointer in cell H9, press the Edit key (F2). this will bring a copy of the formula to the control panel, where you can use the arrow keys to move about and change the 30 (days) to 60, and the 60 (days) to 90. This formula has the same English translation as the previous formula, but checks to see if the due date is between 60 and 90 days over today's date.

Column I contains this formula:

@IF(@DATE($B$4,$B$2,$B$3)−@DATE($C9,$A9,$B9)>90,$D9,0)

This is identical to the formula in cell F9, except that it checks to see if the due date is greater than 90 days, rather than less than 30. Copy the formula in cell F9 to cell I9, and use the F2 Edit key to change the <=30 day figure to >90.

Once all formulas have been placed in row 9, use the Copy command to fill in the range F9 to I14 (though you may extend the formulas much farther down the worksheet if you prefer). They will all show the message ERR (error) until some dates are filled in on the worksheet.

Row 16 also contains formulas, but these are simple @SUMs of the columns above them. Cells in row 16 contain these formulas:

Cell	Formula
D16	@SUM(D9..D14)
F16	@SUM(F9..F14)
G16	@SUM(G9..G14)
H16	@SUM(H9..H14)
I16	@SUM(I9..I14)

Data

When using the accounts receivable worksheet, start by filling in today's date in cells B2, B3, and B4. Then, fill in the date for an individual invoice in columns A, B, and C below the Due Date prompt (the first bill goes in row 9). Fill in the amount of the bill in column D, and the customer's name in column E. All other cells are calculated by 1-2-3.

If you run out of space, use the /WIR (Worksheet Insert Row) command to make more room. Don't forget to copy the formulas into the new rows however, using the Copy command. To delete a bill that has been paid, use the /WDR (Worksheet Delete Row) command. Everything on the worksheet will adjust accordingly.

Now that we've covered just about everything there is to know about the worksheet, let's discuss another powerful feature of 1-2-3, graphics.

1-2-3 GRAPHICS

Chapter 10

CREATING GRAPHS

In this chapter we will discuss the commands and techniques to display 1-2-3 data on the various types of graphs. The techniques for plotting graphs vary somewhat from computer to computer, and are especially dependent upon which type of CRT (screen) your computer uses. Your computer may have any one of the three following screens (1) monochrome, which is the standard screen used for general computing purposes, (2) graphics screen, which allows high-resolution graphics in black and white, and (3) RGB color monitor, which allows color graphics. 1-2-3 treats each somewhat differently, as summarized below:

1. Monochrome Screen: If you have only the monochrome display, 1-2-3 cannot display graphs on the screen at all. However, you can still print graphs on the printer.

2. Graphics Monitor: 1-2-3 can display graphs on both the screen and the printer. Where multiple sets of data are displayed in a graph, 1-2-3 will use various shadings (cross hatching) to identify various data items.

3. Color Monitor: If your computer has a color monitor, 1-2-3 can display graphs in black and white and two additional colors.

4. Multiple Monitors: If your computer happens to have both a standard monochrome screen and a graphics screen, 1-2-3 can display a worksheet and graph simultaneously. This is an especially powerful feature, as it allows you to try out various combinations of data on the worksheet in a "what-if" fashion, and see the results displayed immediately on the graph on the other screen.

WHAT IS "GRAPHABLE"?

You can graph any range of numbers, be it a row or a column on a worksheet. On some displays, such as stacked-bar, side-by-side bar, and line graphs, you can plot up to six entire ranges of numbers. Each range in a graph must be assigned a letter, A through F. For example, look at the worksheet shown in Fig. 10-1.

To plot the performance of a single product for a single season on a graph, you need to specify the range to plot. To plot the sales performance in Spring, you would need to specify B6..B9 as the graph's A range. To plot the performance of multiple products over all four seasons, such as with a stacked-bar graph, you would have to specify all four ranges. Range B6 to E6 would be range "A" for plotting purposes. Range B7 to E7 would be range B, and so forth.

```
         A            B            C            D           E
 1
 2                         ABC Company
 3                       Seasonal Sales
 4   Product           Spring      Summer       Fall        Winter
 5   ----------
 6   Golf              42,000      47,000       37,000       32,000
 7   Tennis            47,000      60,000       45,000       33,000
 8   Surfing           30,000      82,000       44,000       41,000
 9   Skiing            29,000      29,000       41,000       76,000
10   ----------
11   Total            $148,000    $218,000     $167,000     $182,000
12
13
```

Fig. 10-1

DEFINING DATA TO BE PLOTTED

All of the commands for plotting graphs on the screen are under the /G (Graph) option from the 1-2-3 Main Menu. When you select this option, 1-2-3 displays the Graph menu of options:

Type X A B C D E F Reset View Save Options Name Quit

To define a range to be plotted, select a name for the range from options A–F. Then type in the range which will represent range A for plotting purposes. In Fig. 10-2, we have selected A from the Graph menu, and drawn in the range B6..E6 <RET>.

Enter first data range: B6..E6

	A	B	C	D	E
1					
2			ABC Company		
3			Seasonal Sales		
4	Product	Spring	Summer	Fall	Winter
5	-------				
6	Golf	42,000	47,000	37,000	32,000
7	Tennis	47,000	60,000	45,000	33,000
8	Surfing	30,000	82,000	44,000	41,000
9	Skiing	29,000	29,000	41,000	76,000
10		-------			
11	Total	$148,000	$218,000	$167,000	$182,000
12					
13					

Fig. 10-2

Once you have done that, 1-2-3 returns to the Graph Menu. Now that you have named a range to plot, you need to tell 1-2-3 what Type of graph you want these data plotted on. So select Type from the Graph menu, and a submenu of graph types appears on the screen like this:

Line Bar XY Stacked-bar Pie

For this example, select Pie. Again, the Graph menu reappears. Now to see the graph, select View from the Graph menu, and lo and behold, a pie chart appears on the screen as shown in Fig. 10-3.

If you have only a monochrome display, you do not see anything. Instead, you hear only a beep. However, you can save the graph and print it later, as we discuss shortly. If you have two monitors hooked up, you still see the worksheet on the monochrome display, and the pie

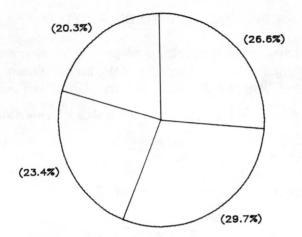

Fig.   10-3

chart on the graphics display. If you have a graphics screen (only) hooked up, the graph overwrites the worksheet on the screen.

When you have finished looking at the graph, simply press any key and the worksheet will be displayed on the screen, along with the Graph menu.

Take another look at these data in a bar graph form. You have already defined the A range to plot, so now just need to select another graph Type. So select option Type, and specify Bar. Next, select View, and voila!, the same data appear plotted on a bar graph, as shown in Fig. 10-4.

Fig.   10-4

Press any key to make the present graph clear and the worksheet and Graph menu to reappear. This time select four ranges, A through D, to plot on the screen. Select B from the Graph menu, and define the range as B7..E7 <RET>. Select option C, and type in the range B8..D8 <RET>. Select option D, and type in the range B9..E9 <RET>. Now select the Type menu option, and specify Bar. Then select View, and watch a side-by-side bar graph appear on the screen, as in Fig. 10-5.

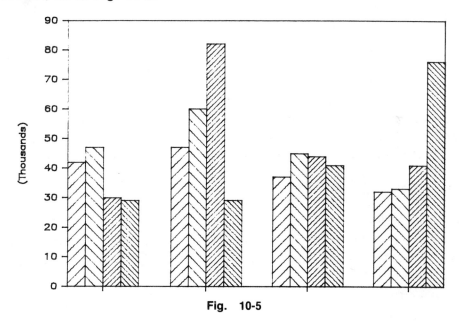

Fig.   10-5

You can view this as a Stacked-bar bar chart by pressing any key to bring the worksheet and Graph menu back to the screen. Then, select graph Type again, and select Stacked-bar from the options. Select View again, and the data are displayed as in Fig. 10-6.

To view these data on a Line Graph, press any key to redisplay the worksheet and Graph Menu. Select Type, and from its options, select Line. Now, select a format for the Line graph. From the Graph Menu, select the Options option. From its menu select Format. From the next menu, select Graph (to specify a format for the entire graph or certain ranges). The next menu to appear looks like this:

<u>Lines</u> Symbols Both Neither

For this example, select B for both lines and symbols. Once you have defined an option for the line graph, select Quit from the two sub-menus to get back to the Graph menu. Select View once again, and

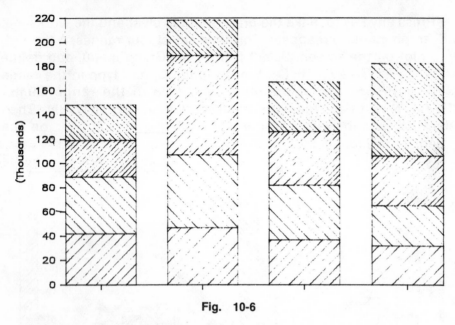

Fig.   10-6

the data are plotted accordingly. Fig. 10-7 shows the data displayed
with both symbols and lines.

As you can see, displaying various types of graphs is an easy
process. However, none of these graphs has very descriptive labels.
You need to use some other options to put labels into the graphs.

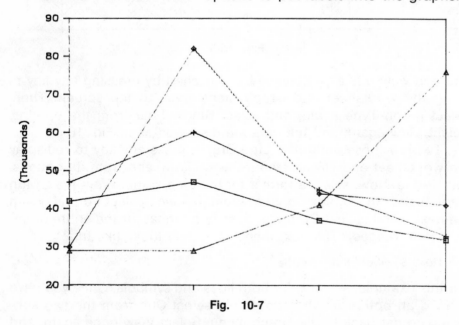

Fig.   10-7

PUTTING LABELS ON GRAPHS

1-2-3 allows three types of labels for graphs: (1) Axis labels which are displayed beneath each column on the graph, or alongside pie slices. (2) Overall labels, which are actually titles or headings for the graph, and (3) Legends, which tell what set of data various shadings or colors in the graph refer to.

Let's begin with some X-axis titles. Note in Fig. 10-8 that a range of titles is built right into the worksheet. Range B4..E4 contains the titles Winter, Spring, Summer, Fall.

	A	B	C	D	E
1					
2			ABC Company		
3			Seasonal Sales		
4	Product	Spring	Summer	Fall	Winter
5	————————	———————	———————	———————	———————
6	Golf	42,000	47,000	37,000	32,000
7	Tennis	47,000	60,000	45,000	33,000
8	Surfing	30,000	82,000	44,000	41,000
9	Skiing	29,000	29,000	41,000	76,000
10		———————	———————	———————	———————
11	Total	$148,000	$218,000	$167,000	$182,000
12					
13					

Fig. 10-8

To include these on the graph itself. select the X option from the Graph menu. Type in the range of labels, B4..E4 <RET>. Since you have already defined all other aspects of the graph, just select View, and the graph is redisplayed as in Fig. 10-9.

On the pie chart, these labels are printed next to the individual slices. If we keep all these parameters the same, and select Pie from the Type options, and view the graph again, we see the graph displayed in Fig. 10-10.

Notice that only the A-range is displayed in the pie chart. Since the pie chart is only capable of plotting one range of figures, it always plots range A, regardless of what other ranges have already been defined.

You can also display overall titles in any graph. The Options Titles command provides many options for this. When you select Options, this menu appears:

Legend Format Titles Grid Scale Color B&W Data-Labels Quit

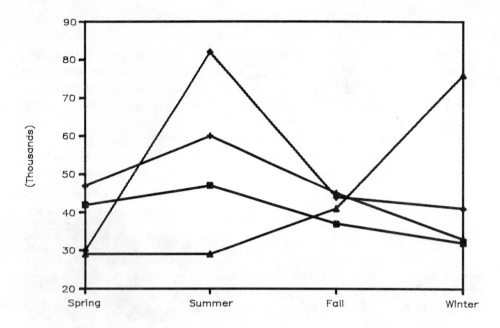

Fig.   10-9

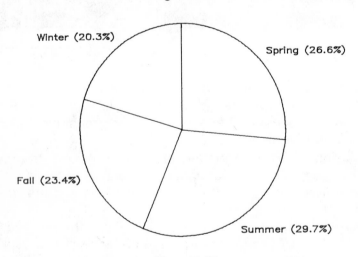

Fig.   10-10

Select Titles. Another menu appears on the screen:

First Second X-axis Y-axis

From here you can select a First and/or Second line title, as well as titles for the X and Y axes. Select option First, and type in the title

"ABC Company Product Sales" <RET> (leave out the quotation marks). Next, select Titles again, then Second. Type in "By Season", <RET>. Next, select Titles again and choose X for an X-axis title. Type in "Season" <RET>. Finally, select Titles Y-Axis and type in the title "Sales" <RET>. Whenever you type in a title, 1-2-3 goes into Edit mode, so you can backspace to make corrections or use the Esc key to erase a title. When you are finished creating titles, select Quit from the options menu to get back to the Graph menu.

Select Type from the Graph menu, and opt to print a Bar chart. Then select View to see the data. The result is displayed in Fig. 10-11. The First line title is displayed at the top of the graph, centered and in enlarged print. The Second line title is also centered, but in normal size print. The X axis title appears below the X axis, centered, and the Y axis title is printed sideways next to the Y axis.

For the finishing touches, add some legends that describe which bar goes with which product. The one catch with legend names is that they have to be brief. For example, if six ranges are displayed on the graph, then each legend name can only be one character long. 1-2-3 allows you to use legend names that are up to 19 characters long. But for neatness' sake, keep them abbreviated.

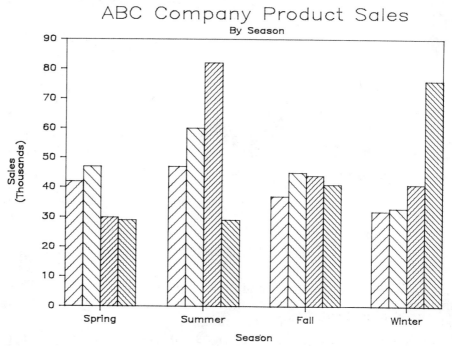

Fig. 10-11

First, select Options, and from the options menu select Legends. It displays a menu of data ranges for creating legends:

A B C D E F

Our example bar graph contains ranges A–D. So select A, and type in the legend name Golf <RET>. Select Legend again, then select B, and type in the abbreviated legend name, Tenn <RET>. Type in names Surf and Ski for ranges C and D using the same procedure. Then Quit the options menu to return to the Graph menu. Select View. The graph appears with the legends shown at the bottom of the graph as shown in Fig. 10-12.

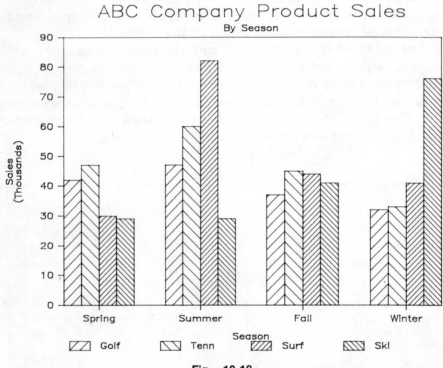

Fig.   10-12

FORMATTING GRAPHS

1-2-3 allows even more options for formatting our graphs. These are also displayed on the Options menu. Rather than go into elaborate detail in their use, we'll just summarize them here.

The Grid option provides choices for displaying grid lines on graphs. Its menu asks if you want Horizontal, Vertical, Both, or to

Clear grid lines displayed on the graph. If we select Both, then a graph is displayed as seen in Fig. 10-13.

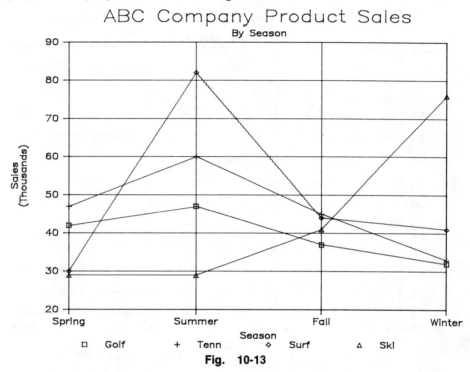

Fig. 10-13

This option, of course, has no effect on pie charts. Selecting Horizontal will place horizontal grid lines on the graph, Vertical prints only vertical grid lines. The Clear option clears grid lines from the graph.

The Scale option allows you to manually set both the X and Y axis range. If you don't specify a scale, 1-2-3 automatically figures out the best scale and plots accordingly. The Scale command allows you to override the automatic settings and put in your own. When selected, it gives these options:

Y Scale   X Scale   Skip

The graph displayed in Fig. 10-13 uses a Y-axis range of 20 to 90,000. You can change this by selecting the Y option from this menu, and selecting Manual from the two options displayed. Next you need to type in a new Y-axis range, such as 0 to 120,000. So, select Lower scale limit, type in 0 <RET>. Then select Upper scale limit and type in 120000 <RET>. When done changing these options select Quit to return to the Graph menu.

Next select View to once again look at the graph, and it will appear as in Fig. 10-14. You can see that the Y-axis range has indeed changed.

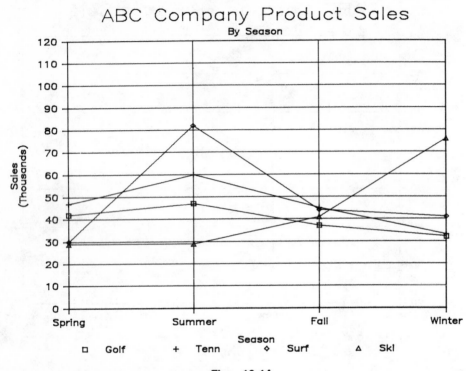

Fig.   10-14

You can alter the format in which the numbers are displayed along the axes. For example, the Y-axis values in the graph in Fig. 10-14 are dollar amounts. You can switch these to the currency format using the Format option from the Options menu. From the Graph menu, select Options Scale. From the next submenu to appear, select Y scale. From the next menu, select Format. Specify a format from the options provided:

Fixed, Scientific, Currency, ,(comma), General, Percent, Date

We discussed these formats in Chapter 3. For our present example, select the Currency option. When you View the graph, the values along the Y axis will be in currency format, as shown in Fig. 10-15.

Finally, you can specify that the graph be displayed in color using the Color choice from the Options menu. If you have a black-

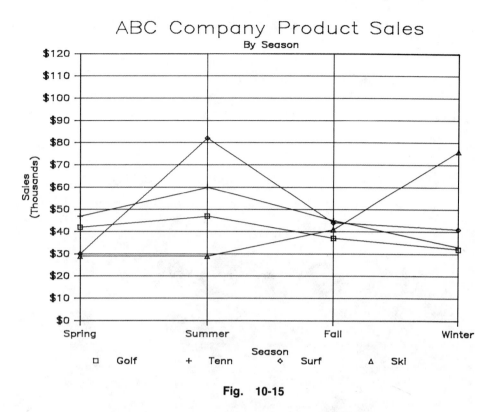

ABC Company Product Sales
By Season

Fig.   10-15

and-white monitor, graphs will be displayed in different shadings rather than with hatch marks.

If you have a color monitor, the data ranges are displayed in three different colors. Only graph bars, lines, and symbols are displayed in color, the titles, scale numbers, axes, and any grid lines are still displayed in white (on the screen). The ranges displayed will be in these colors on the screen:

A White
B Red
C Blue
D White
E Red
F Blue

These do not necessarily affect the way in which the graphs will be displayed on the printer. We'll deal with that in the next chapter.

"WHAT-IF" ANALYSES WITH GRAPHS

Once you have created a graph, you can quickly jump back and forth between the worksheet and the graph using the Graph (F10) key. This is very helpful if you want to get an immediate visual display of the effects of a change in assumptions on the worksheet. For example, Fig. 10-16 shows the Real Estate projection worksheet we developed in Chapter 9.

	A	B	C	D	E	F
1	Ten Year Projection For Commercial Real Estate					
2	With Internal Rate of Return					
3	==					
4		Increase				
5	Description	Rate %	1984	1985	1986	1987
6						
7	Tenant 1	.15	$8,000	$9,200	$10,580	$12,167
8	Tenant 2	.11	$7,500	$8,325	$9,241	$11,386
9	Tenant 3	.09	$8,500	$9,265	$10,099	$11,008
10	Tenant 4	.11	$4,500	$4,995	$5,544	$6,154
11						
12	Maintenance	.11	$9,000	$9,990	$11,089	$12,309
13	Insurance	.11	$7,500	$8,325	$9,241	$10,257
14	Debt Service	-.05	$10,000	$9,500	$9,025	$8,574
15	Mngmt. Fee	.15	$3,500	$3,500	$4,025	$4,550
16						
17	Cash Flow		($1,500)	$470	$2,084	$3,897
18						
19						
20						

Fig.   10-16

Plotting the cash flows on a bar graph produces the graph shown in Fig. 10-17. Pressing any key after viewing the graph will redisplay the worksheet on the screen. Now we can change an assumption. In Fig. 10-18, we've changed the −.05 increase rate for the debt service to +.05. The quantities adjust accordingly on the worksheet.

Pressing the F10 key redisplays the graph on the screen, and it too has adjusted to the new assumption, as in Fig. 10-19.

This easy to use feature is one of 1-2-3's best. If you are used to using other spreadsheets for "What-if" modeling, but have never had this immediate graphics capability, you'll soon wonder how you ever got along without it.

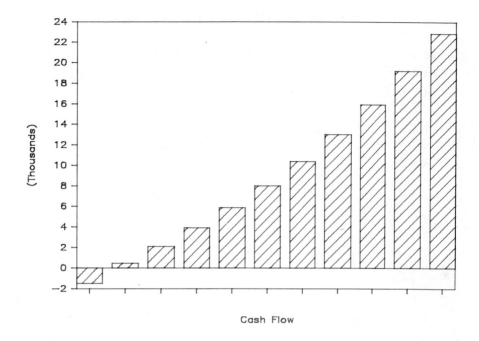

Fig.   10-17

	A	B	C	D	E	F
1	Ten Year Projection For Commercial Real Estate					
2	With Internal Rate of Return					
3	===					
4		Increase				
5	Description	Rate %	1984	1985	1986	1987
6						
7	Tenant 1	.15	$8,000	$9,200	$10,580	$12,167
8	Tenant 2	.11	$7,500	$8,325	$9,241	$11,386
9	Tenant 3	.09	$8,500	$9,265	$10,099	$11,008
10	Tenant 4	.11	$4,500	$4,995	$5,544	$6,154
11						
12	Maintenance	.11	$9,000	$9,990	$11,089	$12,309
13	Insurance	.11	$7,500	$8,325	$9,241	$10,257
14	Debt Service	.05	$10,000	$10,000	$10,500	$11,025
15	Mngmt. Fee	.15	$3,500	$3,500	$4,025	$4,550
16						
17	Cash Flow		($1,500)	($530)	$84	$894
18						
19						
20						

Fig.   10-18

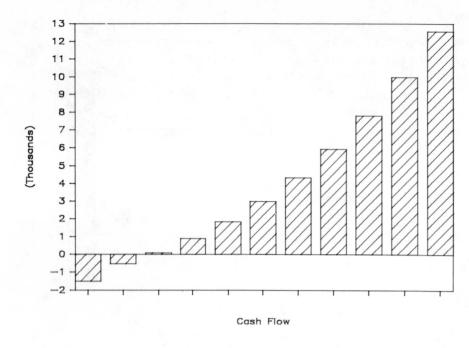

Cash Flow

Fig.   10-19

SAVING GRAPHS

For any given worksheet, chances are you will want to be able to use several different graphs. 1-2-3 can only work with one graph at a time, so if you have just created one graph and want to start creating another, you might want to give the first graph a name so you can use it again later. The /GNC (Graph Name Create) option provides this capability. Once you have a graph designed to your liking, select the NC (Name Create) option from the Graph menu, and type in a name, up to fourteen letters long.

If you have created and saved several graphs, you can use the /GNU (Graph Name Use) option to view or modify a previously saved graph. The /GNU command displays the names of all existing graphs for a worksheet, and you can select any graph from the list of names by typing in the name or pointing.

To get rid of a graph from the list of saved graphs, use the /GND (Graph Name Delete). If you want to get rid of all named graphs, use the /GNR (Graph Name Reset) command. But be careful, since this command quickly erases all graphs that have ever been created for a worksheet from the list of saved graphs, leaving you with no graphs.

A common error made by 1-2-3 users is to forget to name graphs that they wish to reuse. This is indeed unfortunate because it means that the entire graph will have to be reconstructed from scratch. And always, always, save the entire worksheet again with the /FS (File Save) command after naming graphs, because 1-2-3 will forget the named graphs as soon as you exit the worksheet if you don't.

Chapter 11

PRINTING GRAPHS

Before you can print a graph, you need to store a special version of the graph on a disk file. Each graph you wish to print must have its own unique first name (up to eight letters long). 1-2-3 will add the extension .PIC (picture) to your file name. Use the /GS (Graph Save) command to create these special files.

SAVING GRAPHS FOR PRINTING

Let's assume that for a given worksheet you have created and named 5 graphs: GRAPH1, GRAPH2, GRAPH3, GRAPH4, and GRAPH5. Now you want to make printed copies of all five graphs. First, call up the worksheet that has the five graphs with the /FR (File Retrieve) command. Next, use the /GNU (Graph Name Use) command to select one of the graphs for printing. (You may want to use the View option to make sure you have the right one.) Now, select Save from the Graph menu, and type in a name for the file. The name can be up to eight characters long with (you guessed it), no spaces or punctuation. If you have previously used the /GS command to save graphs for printing, the names of these graphs will be displayed on the screen. You can select a name from this list by pointing, but be careful. By doing so, you completely erase the graph that was originally stored under that file name.

To save additional graphs for printing, follow the same series of steps for each graph. That is, select /GNU (Graph Name Use), and pick a graph. Then, use /GS (Graph Save) to save the graph to a .PIC file. When you have finished storing graphs for printing, return to the

READY mode (by Quitting the Graph menu). If you've made any changes to the worksheet, or named any new graphs while saving them to PIC files, be sure to save the worksheet with the /FS (File Save) command. Then, Exit 1-2-3 by selecting the /Q (Quit) option from the main menu.

This returns control to the Lotus Access System menu which looks like this:

1-2-3 File-Manager Disk-Manager PrintGraph Translate Quit

From this menu, you want to select the PrintGraph option. Lotus will display this message:

Insert the PrintGraph disk in drive A and press [Enter]; press [Esc] to quit.

Your PrintGraph disk is probably in the jacket at the back of the Lotus manual. This is where it was when you first bought Lotus anyway. If it isn't there now, well, I can't help you find it. But it looks just like the other Lotus diskettes and says PrintGraph on the label. Once you find it, put it in drive A and press the RETURN key. As you may have guessed, this now brings up yet another display full of options, like this:

Select   Options   Go   Configure   Align   Page   Quit

You will see additional options below the menu. We will get to those in a moment.

Your first move will be to make sure that PrintGraph is properly configured to your printer. You only need to go through this step once. PrintGraph will remember your printer's characteristics after you define and save them.

CONFIGURING PRINTGRAPH TO YOUR PRINTER

To configure PrintGraph, select the Configure option from the menu by pointing or just typing in the letter C (you don't need to use slashes with the PrintGraph program). A new menu appears, that looks like this:

File   Device   Page   Interface   Save   Reset   Quit

From this menu, select Device <RET>. This shows a list of printers you can easily configure PrintGraph to, like this:

> Anadex 9620A Silent Scribe Printer
> # Single Density Epson FX-80
> Double Density Epson FX-80
> Quad Density Epson FX-80
> HP 7470A Plotter
> Okidata 92A or 93A Printer
> Single Density Prism 132
> Single Density Prism 80
> Double Density Prism 80
> Strobe 100 Plotter
> Sweet P Plotter

The exact list you see may be somewhat different, because Lotus Development Corp. continually adds new printers to the list.

Notice that the Epson printer has a # symbol next to it. This means that this is the printer the PrintGraph is currently configured for. To change to another printer, use the up- and down-arrow keys to highlight the various printer names. For example, if you're using an Okidata printer, move the highlight mark to Okidata, then press the Space Bar key to move the marker to the highlighted printer as shown:

> Anadex 9620A Silent Scribe Printer
> Single Density Epson FX-80
> Double Density Epson FX-80
> Quad Density Epson FX-80
> HP 7470A Plotter
> # Okidata 92A or 93A Printer
> Single Density Prism 132
> Single Density Prism 80
> Double Density Prism 80
> Strobe 100 Plotter
> Sweet P Plotter

Then press the return key.

When the PrintGraph menu of options reappears, the newly selected printer will appear on the screen under GRAPHICS DEVICE in the right column of the screen display, like the following:

===

SELECTED
GRAPHS

COLORS		SIZE Half		DRIVES
Grid:	Black	Left Margin:	.785	Pictures
A Range:	Black	Top Margin:	.5ØØ	B:\
B Range:	Black	Width:	6.922	Fonts
C Range:	Black	Height:	5.ØØØ	A:\
D Range:	Black	Rotation:	.ØØØ	
E Range:	Black			**GRAPHICS DEVICE**
F Range:	Black			

	MODES		GRAPHICS DEVICE
			Okidata 93A
Eject:	No		Parallel
Pause:	No		

FONTS		PAGE SIZE	
1. BLOCK1		Length:	11.ØØ
2: BLOCK2		Width:	8.ØØ

Selecting the proper Graph Device is essential to avoid printing a lot of meaningless nonsense on your printer. The other options displayed on the screen above are not so pressing, but are worthy of discussion.

Other choices from the Configure menu are:

File   Page   Interface   Save   Reset   Quit

The File option effects this portion of the PrintGraph display:

Pictures
B:\
Fonts
A: \

This display informs you that PrintGraph assumes that the graphs to be printed are stored on the disk in drive B, and fonts used for printing are stored on the disk in drive A. If your computer has A and B drives, you probably won't want to change these. If, however, you are using a system with a hard disk, you may want to change the disk drive for Pictures to drive C. To do so, select File from the menu, and specify drive C for Pictures.

The Page option refers to this portion of the display:

PAGE SIZE

Length:	**11.000**
Width:	**8.000**

If you are using standard 8½ by 11 inch paper, you won't want to change these. If you are using extra-wide paper (130 columns), you might want to change the Width to 14.000. You can do so by selecting the Page option and typing in the new width.

The Interface option is a bit technical, and refers to the type of cable and which port you are using to connect your computer to your printer. This option effects this display on the screen:

GRAPHICS DEVICE

Okidata 93A
Parallel   ←

The Parallel option is usually used for connecting to a printer. However, some printers use a serial communications cable. If you are not sure which type of interface your computer has, you will need to check with either your computer dealer, your printer manual, or the printer manufacturer. Once you've found out, select the appropriate interface from the options that PrintGraph displays:

1 Parallel Interface from the standard IBM Monochrome Display and Printer Adapter.
2 Optional Serial Interface from the IBM Asynchronous Communications Adapter (RS-232-C).
3 Optional Parallel Interface
4 Optional Serial Interface

Chances are, you have the standard parallel interface, and will not have to be concerned with this.

Once you get these configuration matters squared away, you can use the Save option from the Configure menu to make them the default values. That is, every time you call up PrintGraph, it will automatically assume these values so you don't have to go through the configuration process again. The Reset option from the Configure menu "undoes" the Saved options, and returns PrintGraph to its natural state. The Quit option redisplays the main PrintGraph menu.

SELECTING GRAPHS FOR PRINTING

If you choose the Select option from the main PrintGraph menu, the screen will display all existing graphs that are ready for printing like so:

PICTURE	DATE	TIME	SIZE
GRAPH1	Ø6/11/84	12:ØØ	896
GRAPH2	Ø6/11/84	12:1Ø	942
GRAPH3	Ø6/11/84	12:2Ø	11Ø7
GRAPH4	Ø6/11/84	12:3Ø	899
GRAPH5	Ø6/11/84	12:4Ø	968

You can opt to print one graph or several graphs. To select graphs for printing, use the up- and down-arrow keys to highlight the various file names, and press the space bar to mark a highlighted graph for printing. The graphs you select to be printed will be marked with the # symbol, as follows:

	PICTURE	DATE	TIME	SIZE
#	GRAPH1	Ø6/11/84	12:ØØ	896
#	GRAPH2	Ø6/11/84	12:1Ø	942
#	GRAPH3	Ø6/11/84	12:2Ø	11Ø7
#	GRAPH4	Ø6/11/84	12:3Ø	899
	GRAPH5	Ø6/11/84	12:4Ø	968

In this example, we've selected graphs 1 through 4 for printing by pressing the space bar while each was highlighted on the screen. If you are not sure whether or not you want to print a graph from the options listed, press the F10 (Graph) function key to get a quick glimpse of the graph on the screen prior to selecting it.

Once you have marked graphs for printing, you can just press the RETURN key to go back to the main PrintGraph menu. The graphs you have selected to print will appear on the screen as follows:

Select Options Go Configure Align Page Quit
Select Pictures
==

SELECTED
GRAPHS

		COLORS	SIZE Half		DRIVES
GRAPH1	Grid:	Black	Left Margin:	.785	Pictures
GRAPH2	A Range:	Black	Top Margin:	.500	B:\
GRAPH3	B Range:	Black	Width:	6.922	Fonts
GRAPH4	C Range:	Black	Height:	5.000	A:\
	D Range:	Black	Rotation:	.000	
	E Range:	Black			**GRAPHICS DEVICE**
	F Range:	Black			

	MODES		Okidata 93A
Eject:	No		Parallel
Pause:	No		

	FONTS		PAGE SIZE	
1:	BLOCK1	Length:		11.00
2:	BLOCK2	Width:		8.00

To print all the selected graphs, just select Go from the PrintGraph menu of choices. The printer will print all of the selected graphs. Be patient, getting a graph out to the printer takes a little time.

DESIGNING PRINTED GRAPHS

The PrintGraph program allows you to be pretty creative with printed graphs. Use the Options selection from the PrintGraph menu to design your printed graph. The Options choice provides yet another menu of choices which looks like this:

Color   Font   Size   Pause   Eject   Quit

The first option, Color, effects this portion of the PrintGraph display:

COLORS

Grid:	Black
A:Range:	Black

B:Range:	Black
C:Range:	Black
D:Range:	Black
E:Range:	Black
F:Range:	Black

If you do not select the Colors option, all lines on the graph will be printed in black. However, if you choose to print in color, you can specify a color for each range in the graph, as well as for the background grid. Of course, the color option will only work if your printer can print in color. The colors available for color printers are:

Red
Orange
Yellow
Blue
Purple
Brown
Black

Depending on the color you choose for the various ranges, the COLORS portion of the PrintGraph display will show the selected colors, like this:

COLORS

Grid:	Black
A:Range:	Blue
B:Range:	Red
C:Range:	Brown
D:Range:	Yellow
E:Range:	Purple
F:Range:	Black

When you select Go from the PrintGraph menu, the graphs will be printed using this color scheme.

The Font option from the Options menu allows you to select various fonts for displaying titles and legends on the printed graph. The selected fonts always appear at the lower left of the PrintGraph display under the title FONTS, in this fashion:

FONTS

1:   BLOCK1
2:   BLOCK2

Font 1 is the print font used for the main title of the graph; font 2 is used for all other titles. If you do not select a font, PrintGraph will use BLOCK1. If you want to change the font, select the Fonts option from the menu, and it will display your other options, like this:

BLOCK1
BLOCK2
ITALIC1
ITALIC2
ROMAN1
ROMAN2
SCRIPT1
SCRIPT2

Examples of the various fonts are displayed in Fig. 11-1.
Select fonts by pointing and highlighting, in the same fashion as selecting graphs for printing.

The Size option from the menu of choices allows you to define the dimensions of your printed graph. This is especially useful if you are going to be including the graphs in a written document. When you select the Size option, you are given three alternatives:

Full
Half
Manual

The Full option will print the graph horizontally across a full 8½ by 11 inch sheet of paper. The Half option will print the graph vertically on an 8½ by 11 inch sheet of paper, using the full width and about half the page height. The Manual option allows you to specify the dimensions of your graph, and provides the options listed in Table 11-1.

Table 11-1. Manual Options

Manual Option	Description
Height	Determines the height of the graph in inches.
Width	Determines the width of the graph in inches.
Left	Determines the size of the left margin, in inches.
Top	Determines the top margin on the graph, in inches.
Rotation	Determines the number of degrees of clockwise rotation. Zero degrees prints the graph vertically, 90 degrees prints it horizontally.

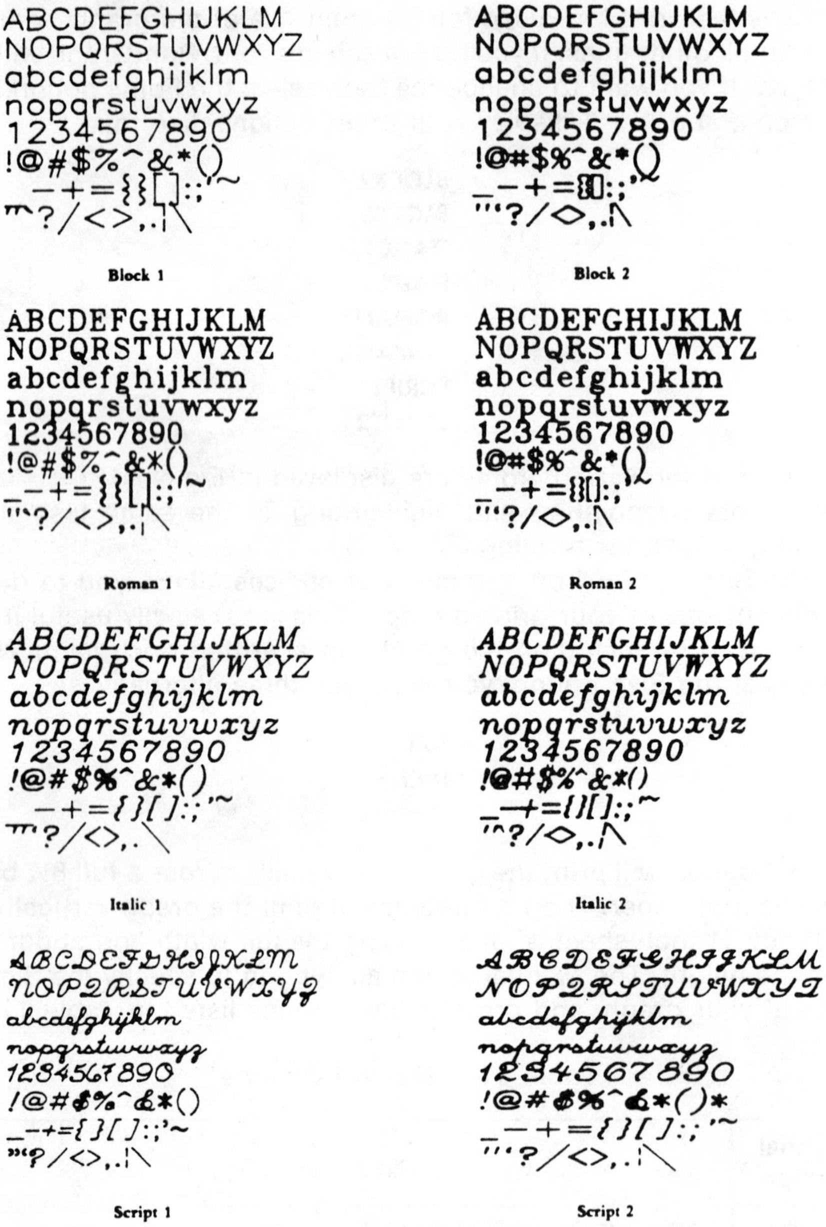

ABCDEFGHIJKLM
NOPQRSTUVWXYZ
abcdefghijklm
nopqrstuvwxyz
1234567890
!@#$%^&*()
 _−+={}[]:;'~
¨´?/<>,.\

Block 1

ABCDEFGHIJKLM
NOPQRSTUVWXYZ
abcdefghijklm
nopqrstuvwxyz
1234567890
!@#$%^&*()
 _−+={}[]:;'~
¨´?/◇,.\

Block 2

ABCDEFGHIJKLM
NOPQRSTUVWXYZ
abcdefghijklm
nopqrstuvwxyz
1234567890
!@#$%^&*()
 _−+={}[]:;~
¨´?/<>,.⌐

Roman 1

ABCDEFGHIJKLM
NOPQRSTUVWXYZ
abcdefghijklm
nopqrstuvwxyz
1234567890
!@#$%^&*()
 _−+={}[]:;
¨´?/◇,.\

Roman 2

ABCDEFGHIJKLM
NOPQRSTUVWXYZ
abcdefghijklm
nopqrstuvwxyz
1234567890
!@#$%^&()*
 _−+={}[]:;'~
¨´?/<>,.

Italic 1

ABCDEFGHIJKLM
NOPQRSTUVWXYZ
abcdefghijklm
nopqrstuvwxyz
1234567890
!@#$%^&()*
 _−+={}[]:;'~
¨´?/◇,.

Italic 2

𝒜ℬ𝒞𝒟ℰℱ𝒢ℋℐ𝒥𝒦ℒℳ
𝒩𝒪𝒫𝒬ℛ𝒮𝒯𝒰𝒱𝒲𝒳𝒴𝒵
abcdefghijklm
nopqrstuvwxyz
1234567890
!@#$%^&*()
 _−+={}[]:;'~
¨´?/<>,.\

Script 1

𝒜ℬ𝒞𝒟ℰℱ𝒢ℋℐ𝒥𝒦ℒℳ
𝒩𝒪𝒫𝒬ℛ𝒮𝒯𝒰𝒱𝒲𝒳𝒴ℐ
abcdefghijklm
nopqrstuvwxyz
1234567890
!@#$%^&*()*
 _−+={}[]:;'~
¨´?/<>,.\

Script 2

Fig.   11-1

Chances are, either the Full or Half option will be suitable for your needs. But the Manual options are fun to experiment with when time permits. The Manual Rotation option can produce some especially interesting results.

The size options always appear on the PrintGraph display under the heading SIZE, like this:

SIZE	HALF
Left Margin:	.785
Top Margin:	.395
Width:	6.5∅∅
Height:	4.691
Rotation:	.∅∅∅

The Pause option of the Options menu determines whether or not the printer will pause between graphs. The Eject option assures that each graph will be printed on a separate page, and should be set to Yes if you plan on printing many graphs at once. These choices always appear under the heading MODES on the PrintGraph display, which is near the center, bottom of the screen. It looks like this:

MODES	
Eject:	No
Pause:	No

EXITING PRINTGRAPH

When you have finished printing graphs, select the Quit option from the PrintGraph menu. The screen will prompt you to reinsert the Lotus System Disk back into drive A, and from there you can go back to the worksheet or terminate your session with 1-2-3.

The following pages show several graphs that were printed with a Sweet P Plotter. As with many aspects of 1-2-3, the best way to learn is by experimenting. Remember, you need to save each graph that you develop with 1-2-3 prior to calling up the PrintGraph program to print them. And don't forget to save the worksheet too, so that any named graphs associated with the worksheet will be accessible in the future.

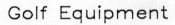

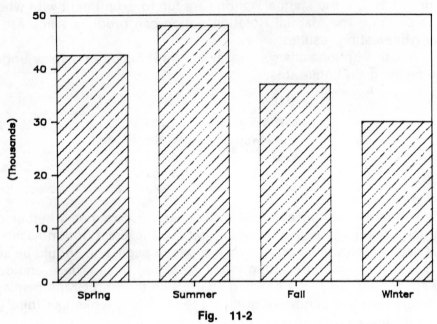

Fig.   11-2

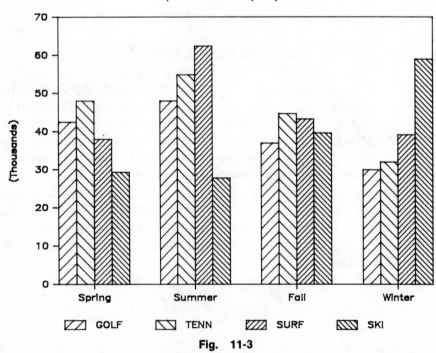

Fig.   11-3

Sports Equipment

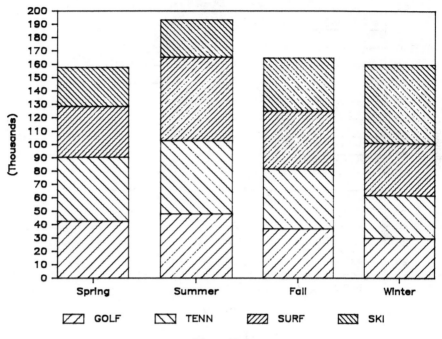

Fig.   11-4

Sports Equipment

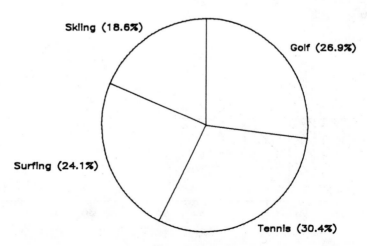

Fig.   11-5

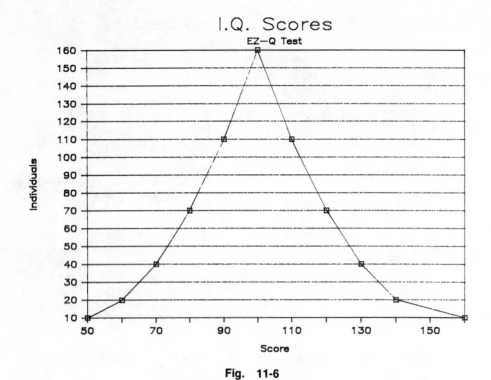

Fig.   11-6

Fig.   11-7

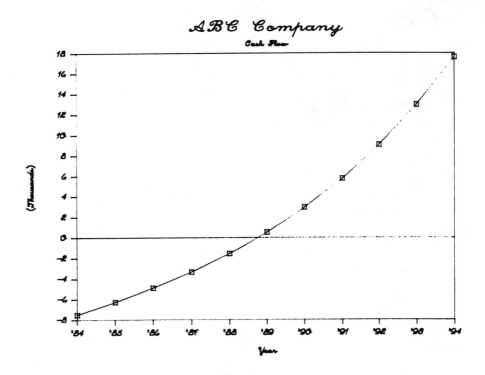

Fig.   11-8

DATABASE MANAGEMENT

Chapter 12

DATABASE MANAGEMENT

As if the spreadsheet and graphics capabilities alone are not enough, 1-2-3 also includes a built-in database management system. A database management system is used to store and manage general information, such as a mailing list or inventory data. With 1-2-3's database capabilities, you can store, retrieve, sort, look up, and isolate important items of information quickly, and still perform all the standard worksheet operations with them!

WHAT IS A DATABASE?

Few people realize that they have probably worked with databases many times before they ever laid a finger on the computer keyboard. For example, a shoe box filled with index cards that have names and addresses on them is a database. Lists of sales leads, customers, phone numbers, library card catalogs, accounts receivable—just about anything that forms a list or a pile of index cards is actually a database.

Every time you look up information in your "shoe box" database, you are managing it. Most day to day database management is quite simple, such as looking up a phone number or a client's billing status. But some tasks are not so simple or pleasant. Sorting all the index cards into alphabetical order, then resorting them into zip code order for bulk mailing is tedious and time consuming with index cards. Or finding all the individuals who have outstanding invoices due, or making copies of certain individuals' cards takes a good deal of time. But with 1-2-3's database management capabilities, these tasks are a breeze.

Let's take a look at a shoe box filled with 5 × 7 inch index cards as an example of a database as shown in Fig. 12-1. Each index card presumably has on it the name, address, city, state, and zip code of one individual, as in the card displayed in Fig. 12-1.

Fig.   12-1

If you were to take all of the information from the shoe box, and type it onto a list, you may end up with a sheet of paper that looks like this:

LNAME	FNAME	ADDRESS	CITY	STATE	ZIP
Adams	Andy	123 A St.	San Diego	CA	92123
Smith	Sandy	234 B St.	Los Angeles	CA	91234
Jones	Janet	333 C St.	New York	NY	12345
Zeppo	Zeke	1142 Oak St.	Newark	NJ	01234
Kenney	Clark	007 Bond St.	Malibu	CA	91111

FIELD NAMES

Of course there could be hundreds or even thousands of individuals on the list.

Computers store data on databases in exactly the same format as this list. There are some very specific terms that we use with computer databases, and it's a good idea to get familiar with these terms, since it will make matters much easier in the long run.

First, you can see that the above list has five individuals in it. In computer lingo, each one of these individuals occupies one *record*. Therefore, the list (or database) above has five records in it, one record for each individual.

Second, you can see that for each individual (or record), there are six items of information: Last name, first name, address, city, state, and zip code. Each of these individual items of information is called a *field* in computer argot. So the database above consists of five records, each record containing six fields.

In addition to the actual data in the database, there is also a line which describes what each column contains (LNAME, FNAME, ADDRESS, CITY, STATE, ZIP). These column headings are called *field names,* and are essential for database management. Each field must have a unique name associated with it, hence our database above has six field names.

Typically, managing a database such as this requires that you perform certain routine tasks from time to time. These tasks can be summarized as:

1. ADD new data to the database.
2. EDIT and DELETE data from the database.
3. SEARCH for an item or group of items.
4. SORT the data into some meaningful order.

How can 1-2-3 help with these tasks? In many ways which will probably make you throw away your index cards once and for all (though you may be wise to save them for a backup, just in case . . .). But before you can manage a database with 1-2-3, you need to create one.

CREATING A 1-2-3 DATABASE

Creating a 1-2-3 database is essentially the same as creating a 1-2-3 worksheet. The only major difference is that you must make absolutely certain to include the field names. We'll use our mailing list example above to illustrate.

The first step is to do a little preplanning. You need to determine the maximum width for each field in each record. For example, the LNAME field, which holds the last name should be at least 15 characters long, so the field width should be 15. The FNAME field (first name) may have to be 25 characters long, just in case you get a first name like Mr. and Mrs. Theodore, or one even longer. We certainly can't skimp on the street address, so it will have to allow up to about 30 characters. The city field should be about 15 long. The state field can be two if you happen to know the 2-letter codes for every state in the nation, but five just in case (Mass.). The new hyphenated zip codes are 10 characters long (12345-6789), so reserve 10 characters for these. Summarizing, the field names and widths will be:

Field Name	Field Width
LNAME	20
FNAME	25
ADDRESS	30
CITY	15
STATE	5
ZIP	10

Now you have to inform 1-2-3 of this decision.

To begin, load up 1-2-3 in the usual fashion so that a blank worksheet appears. The first step will be to format the column widths so that they are the proper width for each field. Each field will occupy one column. Use the /WC command to specify the width of each column. To put LNAME in the first column, give 1-2-3 the command to adjust this column to a width of 20. We use the /WC command as usual for this. That is, type in /WC, then select S to set the new column width, type in the number 20 <RET>. Now type in the field name LNAME into cell A1. The field names must always be placed into the top row of each column.

Next, you need to move the pointer to cell B1, and use the /WC command to set its width to 25. Then again, put the field name FNAME into the top row (B1), then set the column widths and field names for the remaining fields in this same fashion. When finished, the worksheet should look like Fig. 12-2.

ADDING DATA TO THE DATABASE

Adding data to the database is the same as filling cells in the worksheet. The simplest method for entering a record is to position the cell pointer to the next record to be filled in the database (the

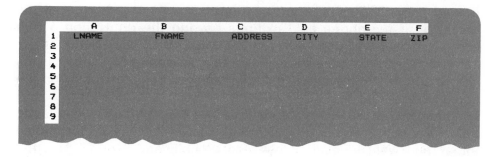

Fig. 12-2

first blank record at the bottom), and type in the new data in the usual fashion, following each entry with a right-arrow key to move the cell pointer to the next field. You will have to precede the address field's data with a label prefix (such as the apostrophe), since 1-2-3 will not be sure whether to make this a label or a number (i.e., 124 A St.).

EDITING DATA IN THE DATABASE

Editing a field in the database is the same as editing a cell in the worksheet. You simply position the cell pointer to the field that needs to be changed, and type in the new data. Or, use the Edit key (F2) to modify the existing data.

To delete data from the database, use the /WDR (Worksheet Delete Row) command, or the database delete command described in Chapter 14.

Once in a while you need to do a different kind of database edit, where you actually need to add an entirely new field to the database. For example, suppose you decide to include phone numbers in the database. In this case, just position the cell pointer to column G1 (the top of the seventh column) and define its width with the /WC command. You might want to be pretty liberal with your phone field width. For example, a phone number could actually look like this:

H:(619) 555-1212   W:(619) 555-1111

That phone number is 35 characters wide. If you want to be able to include extensions, you have to allow for even more characters. Then be sure to type in the new field name, PHONE, in the first row of the column. Then adding phone numbers is simply a straightforward editing task of filling in a phone number for each individual in the database. If the phone field extends beyond the right edge of the screen so that you can't see the LNAME and PHONE fields at the same time, you can use the split-screen command to divide up the worksheet so that the two fields are displayed simultaneously on the screen.

In some cases, you might want to insert a field between existing fields. For instance, suppose you decide to include a field for middle initial, and want to place it between LNAME and FNAME. Use the /WIC (Worksheet Insert Column) command to add the new field. Simply position the cell pointer to cell B1. Enter the /WIC command so that all columns to the right get pushed over a notch. Then, use the /WC command to format the column to an appropriate width, and be sure to put the field name (perhaps MI for middle initial) at the top of the column. Then, fill in the middle initials for the existing names on the list.

As you have probably surmised, you can use any of the worksheet commands to add to and edit data on the database. You can use the /WTH (Worksheet Titles Horizontal) command to keep field names on the screen while scrolling through the records in the database. The /POBR (Print Option Border Row) command will display field names along the top of each page on a printed copy of the database. You can use the Worksheet and Range commands to format the database, and the Copy command to make copies. The database is, after all, just a regular worksheet with the addition of field names at the top. However, there are additional capabilities we can use, and the next chapter discusses one of them: sorting.

Chapter 13

SORTING THE DATABASE

Sorting a database is simply putting all the records into some meaningful order, such as alphabetically by last name or in zip code order. Occasionally you may just want to sort some of the records in the database, but this does not occur too often. To "pull out" records that have a certain characteristic in common (such as all Smiths), use searching techniques, which are discussed in the next chapter. For now, we'll discuss sorting all of the records in the database. First we need to discuss the basic concept of the *key field*.

THE KEY FIELD

Whenever you wish to sort a database, you need to specify a key field. That is, you need to specify which field you wish to sort by. If you want to sort by zip code, use ZIP as the key field. If you want the records sorted alphabetically by last name, specify LNAME as the key field. Sometimes you might use multiple key fields, as we'll discuss in a moment. For the moment, it is important to discuss key fields in relation to how one goes about designing a database.

You may be wondering why we used two fields for each individual's names on the database, LNAME and FNAME. Why not just NAME? The reason is that the computers cannot recognize data based upon context as we can. For example, look at these names:

John Smith
Andy Williams
Ruth Ashley

                    Clark Kenney
                    Pat Enscoe

If asked to sort these names into alphabetical order, you would probably put them into this order (unless you happen to be a computer
programmer):

                    Ruth Ashley
                    Pat Enscoe
                    Clark Kenney
                    John Smith
                    Andy Williams

The names are properly alphabetized by last name, the way we usually sort people's names. However, if we were to ask the computer to
sort these names, we'd get this list:

                    Andy Williams
                    Clark Kenney
                    John Smith
                    Pat Enscoe
                    Ruth Ashley

The names are sorted by first name. Why? Because the computer
does not understand the concept of first and last name. It does not
know that these are names and are, therefore, to be sorted by last
name. You and I know this, because we understand this rule, and
furthermore, we can spot the last name by its context and order. That
is, chances are that Smith is the last name and John is the first name.
Computers do not think this way. In fact, they don't think at all.

   In view of this, you must think about all possible key fields in a
database before you design it. If you know that you will be sorting by
last name sometimes in the future, then the last name should be in a
field all its own so it can be used as a key field for sorting. Of course,
you could use a single NAME field, and enter the names in last, first
format, as below:

                    Smith, John
                    Williams, Andy
                    Ashley, Ruth
                    Kenney, Clark
                    Enscoe, Pat

These would sort properly because the last name is out in front. But
this creates a new problem. Suppose you want to print a form letter

from this database? You could not get at the first name to print salutations and the like. All your letters would start out with a salutation such as "Dear Smith, John." The moral of the story is; break out all your records to as many meaningful fields as you can, and keep the key fields in mind while you're determining how to structure each record in the database.

GETTING THINGS IN ORDER

To sort a database, we use the 1-2-3 /DS (Data Sort) command. Let's step through an example using our mailing system, which is displayed in Fig. 13-1.

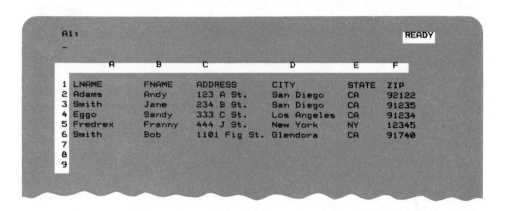

Fig.   13-1

The records are in random order. (Actually, they are in the order in which we originally entered them.) To sort them by last name, enter the /DS command, which brings up a number of options in the control panel:

Data-Range Primary-Key Secondary-Key Reset Go Quit

First, you must specify the range of data to sort. Usually, you want to sort the entire database, so position the pointer to the Data Range option on the menu, and type in the upper left and lower right cell addresses (NOT including the Field Names!). In this example, the data range would be entered as A2..F6. You can either type in or draw the range, as usual.

The next step is to specify the key field to sort on. In this example, we will sort the records alphabetically by last name (LNAME), so move the menu pointer to Primary-Key option, and select A1 as the field to sort on. 1-2-3 will ask if you want the data sorted in ascending (smallest-to-largest) or descending (largest-to-smallest) order. Typically we list things from A to Z, so select Ascending. Now, to perform the actual sort, simply select the Go menu option. Instantly, the records appear on the screen in sorted order as shown in Fig. 13-2.

	A	B	C	D	E	F
1	LNAME	FNAME	ADDRESS	CITY	STATE	ZIP
2	Adams	Andy	123 A St.	San Diego	CA	92122
3	Eggo	Sandy	333 C St.	Los Angeles	CA	91234
4	Fredrex	Franny	444 J St.	New York	NY	12345
5	Smith	Jane	234 B St.	San Diego	CA	91235
6	Smith	Bob	1101 Fig St.	Glendora	CA	91740
7						
8						
9						

Fig. 13-2

To put these into zip code order, simply specify cell address F1 as the key field by selecting the Primary-Key option from the sort menu. Select Go again, and the records will be instantly sorted into zip code order. 1-2-3 always remembers the last specified data range, so there is no need to respecify on the second sort.

Sorting is a pretty easy task in 1-2-3. Once in a while you may forget to specify a range or a primary field. If you do, 1-2-3 will beep to remind you. Press the Escape key to quiet the beeper, and select the Data-Range and Primary key options from the Sort Menu, and specify the ranges.

SORTS-WITHIN-SORTS

On large databases, sometimes a simple sort like this is not sufficient. For example, suppose you sort a database by zip code, but there are 500 people in the 92122 zip code area. In this case, you might want everyone in the 92122 zip code order to be listed alphabetically by last name. That is, within common zip codes, list last names alphabetically. Another example is sorting by last name. If you have 50 Smiths on your database, it would be helpful if these were listed alphabetically by first name rather than in haphazard order. It would certainly help us to pinpoint John Smith among a group of 50

Smiths. The telephone book sorts names this way for the obvious purpose of making names easier to locate in the book.

In everyday language, we typically call this a sort-within-a-sort, because the items appear to be sorted by one criterion first (LNAME), then sorted again by the second criterion (FNAME) without affecting the first sort. In computer argot, we call this "sorting by primary and secondary keys." The Primary key is the "major" sort order (such as LNAME), the Secondary key is the "minor" (within-sort) order. 1-2-3 can perform sorts-within-sorts if you select both a primary and secondary key from the sort menu of options.

To perform a sort-within-a-sort, use the /DS (Data Sort) command as usual. Specify the Data range as the entire database as usual. To sort by last name, and alphabetically by first name within common last names, make A1 (LNAME) the primary key, and A2 (FNAME) the secondary key. Select the Go option, and the records will be sorted instantly on the screen. Fig. 13-3 shows the database sorted by LNAME and FNAME. Notice that Bob Smith is now properly listed before Jane Smith, rather than vice versa.

	A	B	C	D	E	F
1	LNAME	FNAME	ADDRESS	CITY	STATE	ZIP
2	Adams	Andy	123 A St.	San Diego	CA	92122
3	Eggo	Sandy	333 C St.	Los Angeles	CA	91234
4	Fredrex	Franny	444 J St.	New York	NY	12345
5	Smith	Bob	1101 Fig St.	Glendora	CA	91740
6	Smith	Jane	234 B St.	San Diego	CA	91235
7						
8						
9						

Fig.   13-3

WHEN THE UNEXPECTED HAPPENS

Once in a while, the sort command does not produce quite what we had expected. One of the most common surprises is that things often appear at the top of the list which don't belong there. This is most often caused by the fact that a blank space is considered to be "less than" any letter in the alphabet by the computer. Therefore, if some of the last names in a database had (seemingly) invisible blank spaces in front of them, they would all appear at the very top of the list. That is, if we had these names in a list (I've put in quotation marks only to make the blank space stand out):

"Smith"
"Jones"
"Adams"
" Zeppo"

they'd come out in this order when sorted:

" Zeppo"
"Adams"
"Jones"
"Smith"

The leading blank in Zeppo's last name was considered to be "less than" the A at the start of Adam's name. Of course, any last names that were all blanks would appear at the very top of the list.

Also, make sure you always specify the entire database (with the field names) when selecting the data range. If you do not include all the rows, then only some of the rows will be sorted. If you do not include all the columns, then only the specified columns will be sorted, and will no longer line up properly with the unsorted columns. That is, the names may be in proper order, but the address, city, state, and zip will be in random order!

Another task we commonly perform with database is *searching*. For example, you may want to look up Jane Smith's address, or pull out all the records for people in the 92122 zip code area. Searching the database is the topic of the next chapter.

Chapter 14

SEARCHING THE DATABASE

Searching a database involves asking the computer to display all the records that meet a specific criterion or several criteria. For example, using our mailing list as an example, you may want the computer to carry out any of the following searches:

Display everyone in the 12345 zip code area.
Display everyone with the last name Smith.
Display everyone in California with the last name Jones.
Find John Smith.
Display everyone who lives in either San Diego or Los Angeles.
Display everyone in the 90000 to 99999 zip code area.

In computer jargon, we often use the term "query" rather than "search," but it means the same thing.

QUERY RANGES

We use the /DQ (Data Query) command to search for records in a database. The /DQ command requires that we first create some special search ranges:

INPUT RANGE: The Input Range is usually the entire database itself.

CRITERION RANGE: The Criterion Range is the field name(s) and the value(s) to search for. For example, to find all the people in the 92122 zip code area, ZIP is the field to search on, and 92122 is the value to search for. Both of these items need to be specified in the Criterion Range.

OUTPUT RANGE: If you want to create a new database from the selections made by a database search, you must specify this range as the location for placing the results of the search.

The Output Range is only necessary for searches that use the Extract or Unique options. We will discuss those shortly.

You need to set up these ranges while the worksheet is in the Ready mode, prior to selecting any menu options. Let's work through an example using a search on the small database shown in Fig. 14-1.

	A	B	C	D	E	F
1	LNAME	FNAME	ADDRESS	CITY	STATE	ZIP
2	Adams	Andy	123 A St.	San Diego	CA	92122
3	Smith	Bob	234 B St.	San Diego	CA	91234
4	Eggo	Sandy	333 C St.	Los Angeles	CA	91235
5	Fredrex	Frammy	444 J St.	New York	NY	12345
6	Smith	Jane	1101 Fig St.	Glendora	CA	91740
7						
8						
9						
10						
11						
12						

Fig.   14-1

The first step is always to create the Criterion Range. The easiest way to do this is to make a copy of either all the field names, or a few field names, using the Copy command. In this example, type in the /C command, specify A1..F1 as the range to copy FROM, and A9..F9 as the range to copy to. This places a list of field names outside the existing database, as shown in Fig. 14-2.

The actual location of the criterion range is unimportant, just as long as it is outside of the database. Also, the Criterion Range need not have all the field names in it, only those you wish to search on. We included all the field names here because we'll be doing several searches in this chapter, and we can just use the same criterion range over several times.

```
        A          B          C              D          E       F
  1   LNAME      FNAME      ADDRESS        CITY       STATE   ZIP
  2   Adams      Andy       123 A St.      San Diego  CA      92122
  3   Smith      Bob        234 B St.      San Diego  CA      91234
  4   Eggo       Sandy      333 C St.      Los Angeles CA     91235
  5   Fredrex    Frammy     444 J St.      New York   NY      12345
  6   Smith      Jane       1101 Fig St.   Glendora   CA      91740
  7
  8
  9   LNAME      FNAME      ADDRESS        CITY       STATE   ZIP
 10
 11
 12
 15
```

Fig.   14-2

Next, you must specify the search criterion (the value to search for). Do this by typing in the characteristic you wish to search for in the cell below the field to search on. For example, to search for all Smiths on the sample database, type the name Smith directly beneath the LNAME cell in the Criterion Range, as shown in Fig. 14-3.

Once the Criterion Range exists, and the value you wish to search for is placed under the field name you wish to search, you can use the /DQ (Data Query) command to perform the search.

```
        A          B          C              D          E       F
  1   LNAME      FNAME      ADDRESS        CITY       STATE   ZIP
  2   Adams      Andy       123 A St.      San Diego  CA      92122
  3   Smith      Bob        234 B St.      San Diego  CA      91234
  4   Eggo       Sandy      333 C St.      Los Angeles CA     91235
  5   Fredrex    Frammy     444 J St.      New York   NY      12345
  6   Smith      Jane       1101 Fig St.   Glendora   CA      91740
  7
  8
  9   LNAME      FNAME      ADDRESS        CITY       STATE   ZIP
 10   Smith
 11
```

Fig.   14-3

FINDING RECORDS ON THE DATABASE

To begin the search, type in the command /DQ (Data Query). This brings up a menu of searching options:

Input Criterion Output Find Extract Unique Delete Reset Quit

First you need to specify the Input Range, so select Input from the menu of options. Specify the Input range, which must include the field names. The Input Range is usually the entire database, so in this example it is (A1..F6). As usual, you can either type in the cell addresses for the range, or draw the range by pointing.

Next you must tell 1-2-3 where the Criterion Range is, so select the Criterion option from the menu of choices. 1-2-3 will ask for the cell coordinates for the Criterion Range. In this example, the range is A9..F10. (You really only need to specify the smaller A9..A10 here, but if you include all the field names now, you won't have to redefine the Criterion range for other types of searches later.)

Now to perform the search, select the Find option from the menu. 1-2-3 will highlight the first Smith in the database, as shown in Fig. 14-4.

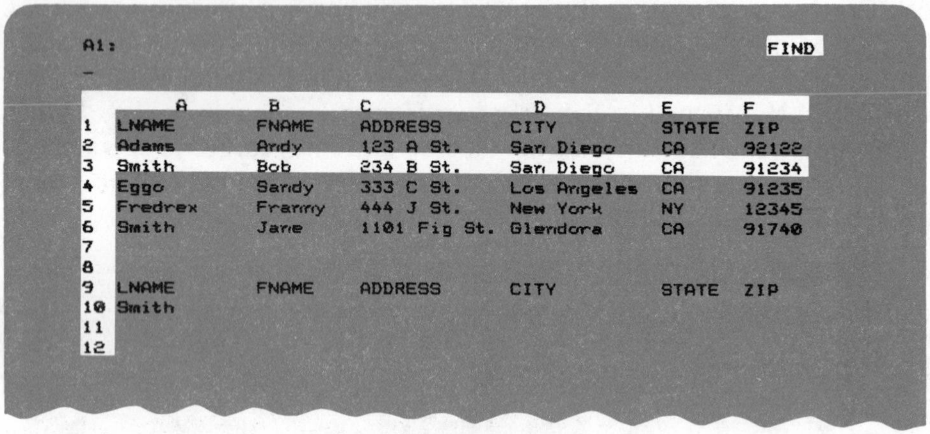

Fig.   14-4

You can use the up-arrow and down-arrow keys to move to other Smiths in the database. If there are no Smiths above or below the Smith that the pointer is highlighting, then 1-2-3 will beep at you when you try to move in that direction.

Notice that nothing else seems to work right now. That's because the Find mode (as indicated by the mode indicator, upper right of screen) only finds. It can't do anything else. Press the Esc key to return to the Data menu.

You can be more specific in your search criteria and have 1-2-3 find Jane Smith rather than Smith. In this case you need to search on two fields: LNAME and FNAME. The values to search for would be Smith and Jane, respectively. The criterion range would have to be set up to handle both criteria, as in rows nine and 10 in Fig. 14-5.

	A	B	C	D	E	F
1	LNAME	FNAME	ADDRESS	CITY	STATE	ZIP
2	Adams	Andy	123 A St.	San Diego	CA	92122
3	Smith	Bob	234 B St.	San Diego	CA	91234
4	Eggo	Sandy	333 C St.	Los Angeles	CA	91235
5	Fredrex	Frammy	444 J St.	New York	NY	12345
6	Smith	Jane	1101 Fig St.	Glendora	CA	91740
7						
8						
9	LNAME	FNAME	ADDRESS	CITY	STATE	ZIP
10	Smith	Jane				
11						
12						

Fig. 14-5

In this example the first record highlighted by the Find command will be the one that has Smith as the LNAME *and* Jane as the FNAME. The database only has one Jane Smith, so only her record would be highlighted by the search.

PULLING OUT SIMILAR RECORDS

Sometimes you may wish to pull out records from the database which have some characteristic in common, such as all the people who live in San Diego. Before pulling records out of the database, you need to have a place to put them. That is, you need to specify an Output Range. This you must do in the Ready mode. The easiest method is to copy the row with the field names in it to another location on the worksheet. Make sure that the location you copy to has plenty of blank rows under it, because 1-2-3 will fill these with the records extracted from the database in the search.

To create the Output Range by copying, select /C and specify the top row (A1..F1) as the field to copy from, and A14 to F14 as the field to copy to. The field names will move to row 14, as shown in Fig. 14-6.

Notice also that the Criterion Range now has San Diego under the City range. For this search, we want to pull out all the individuals

	A	B	C	D	E	F
1	LNAME	FNAME	ADDRESS	CITY	STATE	ZIP
2	Adams	Andy	123 A St.	San Diego	CA	92122
3	Smith	Bob	234 B St.	San Diego	CA	91234
4	Eggo	Sandy	333 C St.	Los Angeles	CA	91235
5	Fredrex	Franny	444 J St.	New York	NY	12345
6	Smith	Jane	1101 Fig St.	Glendora	CA	91740
7						
8						
9	LNAME	FNAME	ADDRESS	CITY	STATE	ZIP
10				San Diego		
11						
12						
13						
14	LNAME	FNAME	ADDRESS	CITY	STATE	ZIP
15						
16						
17						
18						
19						

Fig. 14-6

who live in San Diego, so we've set up the Criterion Range accordingly while in the worksheet Ready mode.

Now, select the /DQ command to bring up the Data Query menu, and from there select Output. 1-2-3 will ask for the coordinates of the Output Range. In this example, A14..F14 is the Output range. (If you specify only the Output Range's field names, 1-2-3 assumes that the Output Range extends to the bottom of the worksheet.)

Next, select the Extract option from the menu, and 1-2-3 copies all the records that meet the search criterion to the Output Range, as shown in Fig. 14-7. Notice that all the records in the Output Range have San Diego as their city.

If you change the search criteria in the Criterion Range, and perform another Extract search, the records meeting the new criteria will be pulled from the database, and overwrite the records presently in the Output Range.

To create a database of only the records selected from the search, use the /FX (File Xtract) command, as discussed in Chapter 8.

AND'S AND OR'S

When you search on two fields at the same time, you may want records that match both criteria. At other times, you may want records that match either criterion. For example, suppose you want a

```
           A          B          C          D              E       F
 1   LNAME      FNAME      ADDRESS      CITY           STATE   ZIP
 2   Adams      Andy       123 A St.    San Diego      CA      92122
 3   Smith      Bob        234 B St.    San Diego      CA      91234
 4   Eggo       Sandy      333 C St.    Los Angeles    CA      91235
 5   Fredrex    Frammy     444 J St.    New York       NY      12345
 6   Smith      Jane       1101 Fig St. Glendora       CA      91740
 7
 8
 9   LNAME      FNAME      ADDRESS      CITY           STATE   ZIP
10                                      San Diego
11
12
13
14   LNAME      FNAME      ADDRESS      CITY           STATE   ZIP
15   Adams      Andy       123 A St.    San Diego      CA      92122
16   Smith      Bob        234 B St.    San Diego      CA      91234
17
18
19
```

Fig. 14-7

listing of all the people whose last name is Smith and who live in California. In this case, you need to search on two fields, LNAME and STATE. And you would need two searching criteria: Smith and CA. To do so, set up the Criterion Range with the two field names at the top, and the two criteria directly beneath the field names as illustrated in Fig. 14-8.

In English, this Criterion range says, "Display the records that have Smith as the LNAME *and* CA as the state."

```
A1:                                                          FIND
 —
           A          B          C          D              E       F
 1   LNAME      FNAME      ADDRESS      CITY           STATE   ZIP
 2   Adams      Andy       123 A St.    San Diego      CA      92122
 3   Smith      Bob        234 B St.    San Diego      CA      91234
 4   Eggo       Sandy      333 C St.    Los Angeles    CA      91235
 5   Fredrex    Frammy     444 J St.    New York       NY      12345
 6   Smith      Jane       1101 Fig St. Glendora       CA      91740
 7
 8
 9   LNAME      FNAME      ADDRESS      CITY           STATE   ZIP
10   Smith                                             CA
11
12
```

Fig. 14-8

	A	B	C	D	E	F
1	LNAME	FNAME	ADDRESS	CITY	STATE	ZIP
2	Adams	Andy	123 A St.	San Diego	CA	92122
3	Smith	Bob	234 B St.	San Diego	CA	91234
4	Eggo	Sandy	333 C St.	Los Angeles	CA	91235
5	Fredrex	Frammy	444 J St.	New York	NY	12345
6	Smith	Jane	1101 Fig St.	Glendora	CA	91740
7						
8						
9	LNAME	FNAME	ADDRESS	CITY	STATE	ZIP
10					CA	
11					NY	
12						

Fig.   14-9

Some searches with multiple fields require an "or" type of logic. For example, suppose you want a listing of all the people who live in New York or in California. In this case, there is only one field to search on (STATE), but two criteria to consider (New York and California). To set up a criterion range that has an "or" capability for a single field like this, put the criteria to search for in the same column, one above the other, as shown in Fig. 14-9.

In English, once again, this Criterion Range says, "List all the people in the database who live in either New York or California."

As soon as you have two levels of criteria like this, you need to redefine the Criterion Range to include the new level. This is important to remember but easy to forget. If you forget, you won't get an error. Instead, everything will seem to work just fine, but the records that come out of the search will not be what you asked for. In this example, the Criterion range *must* be changed to A9..F11. Use the Criterion option from the Data Query menu to redefine the Criterion Range.

To search on two fields with an "or" relationship, stagger the two search criteria in this same fashion. For example, suppose you wanted a listing of all the people who live in either Los Angeles (proper) or the 91234 zip code area (a presumed suburb of Los Angeles). In this case, you have two fields to search on, STATE and ZIP, and two search criteria, so the Criterion Range would look like the one in Fig. 14-10. Notice how the search criteria are staggered onto two separate lines.

You can even combine "and" and "or" type searches if you wish to have three factors in the search. For example, suppose you want a

	A	B	C	D	E	F
1	LNAME	FNAME	ADDRESS	CITY	STATE	ZIP
2	Adams	Andy	123 A St.	San Diego	CA	92122
3	Smith	Bob	234 B St.	San Diego	CA	91234
4	Eggo	Sandy	333 C St.	Los Angeles	CA	91234
5	Fredrex	Frammy	444 J St.	New York	NY	12345
6	Smith	Jane	1101 Fig St.	Glendora	CA	91740
7						
8						
9	LNAME	FNAME	ADDRESS	CITY	STATE	ZIP
10				Los Angeles		
11						91234
12						

Fig. 14-10

listing of all the Smiths who live in either Los Angeles or San Diego. In this case, you are searching on two fields, LNAME and CITY. However, there are three search criteria involved, Smith, Los Angeles, and San Diego. The Criterion Range capable of finding all the Smiths in either Los Angeles or San Diego would look like Fig. 14-11. In English, this says: "In order to be listed, a person must have the last name Smith and live in Los Angeles, OR have the last name Smith and live in San Diego."

	A	B	C	D	E	F
7						
8						
9	LNAME	FNAME	ADDRESS	CITY	STATE	ZIP
10	Smith			Los Angeles		
11	Smith			San Diego		
12						

Fig. 14-11

SEARCHING FOR RECORDS WITHIN A RANGE OF VALUES

Sometimes you may need to perform searches on ranges of values. For example, suppose you want a listing of all the people in the 92111 to 92117 zip code area. (e.g., 92111, 92112, 92113, to 92117). You certainly would not want to do all those searches one at a time. Rather, you need to specify a range of values to search for in the Criterion range. The Criterion Range in Fig. 14-12 sets up a search for all people in the desired zip code area.

```
         A         B         C            D             E        F
  1    LNAME     FNAME     ADDRESS      CITY          STATE    ZIP
  2    Adams     Andy      123 A St.    San Diego     CA       92122
  3    Smith     Bob       234 B St.    San Diego     CA       91234
  4    Eggo      Sandy     333 C St.    Los Angeles   CA       91234
  5    Fredrex   Franny    444 J St.    New York      NY       12345
  6    Smith     Jane      1101 Fig St. Glendora      CA       91740
  7
  8
  9                                     ZIP
 10                                     +F2>=92111#AND#F2<=92117
 11
 12
```

Fig. 14-12

The search criterion, +F2>=92111#AND#F2<=92117, is actually a formula. The cell reference in the formula must refer to the first record of the database. F2 is the first zip code in this database example, so F2 is the cell reference in the formula. When you ask 1-2-3 to Find or Extract, it will test every zip code in the database to see if it fits into the criteria specified by the formula. If the zip code meets the criterion, it is selected as a match, otherwise, it is ignored.

You have to be careful with specifying ranges of numbers like this. For example, the criterion +F2>92199#OR#F2<93000 will match every record on the database. Why? The "or" condition won't knock any records out of the range. After all, 01234 is less than 92300, and therefore 1-2-3 selects it. The formula says that the zip code has to be *either* less than 92300 *or* greater than 92199, and so since only one of the conditions need be true for the or statement to find a match, this one will match. 01234 will be rejected by the +F2>92199#AND#F2<93000 formula, however, because even though it is less than 92300, it is not greater than 92199.

SEARCHING WITH WILD CARDS

There are a number of symbols that you can use in the Criterion Range to control the logic of a search in other ways. These symbols are often called "wild cards," because they can be used to represent any character, just as a wild card in a card game can be used to act as any other card. We discussed this concept under Managing Files in an earlier chapter, but we will review here.

The wild card characters are:

?	Matches any character.	A database search for FNAME = J??N will find *John*, *Jean*, and *Joan*, but not *Janet*, or Bob.
*	Matches any group of characters.	A database search for John* will find J o h n, J o h n s o n, a n d Johnathon, but not UpJohn.
˜	Does not match characters.	Finds records that have any group of characters *except* those in the Criterion Range. Therefore, ˜John will find Isaac, Betty, Joe, and Andy, but not John.

The ˜ also ignores empty cells. That is, a search for ˜John (not John) will display everybody except John *and* empty fields.

AUTOMATIC ELIMINATION OF DUPLICATES

In some cases, you may want to see what you have in a database in terms of variety instead of content. For example, if you have 500 records in a mailing list, you may want to know how many *unique* zip codes are in the database. Obviously, the database has 500 zip codes in it, but no doubt some are duplicated. The /DQ Unique option allows you to list only the unique contents within a field. To perform this kind of search, you must search the field using a blank for the search criterion, and select the Unique option from the /DQ menu. The Criterion Range specification would be F9..F10. That is, the zip field with nothing in it, like this:

```
9                              ZIP
10
```

The result of a Unique search using the mailing list is displayed in the Output Range in Fig. 14-13. In this example, the Output field contained only one field, ZIP. Therefore, only the unique zip codes are displayed in the Output Range.

	A	B	C	D	E	F
1	LNAME	FNAME	ADDRESS	CITY	STATE	ZIP
2	Adams	Andy	123 A St.	San Diego	CA	92122
3	Smith	Bob	234 B St.	San Diego	CA	91234
4	Eggo	Sandy	333 C St.	Los Angeles	CA	91234
5	Fredrex	Frammy	444 J St.	New York	NY	12345
6	Smith	Jane	1101 Fig St.	Glendora	CA	91740
7						
8						
9						ZIP
10						
11						
12						
13						ZIP
14						92122
15						91234
16						12345
17						91740
18						

Fig. 14-13

DELETING RECORDS FROM THE DATABASE

The procedure for deleting records from the database is similar to all the procedures mentioned above. Suppose the big earthquake finally hits California, and you wish to eliminate all these people from your database. You would merely need to specify CA under the field name STATE in the Criterion Range, and select Delete from the Data Query options. All records that match the criterion are eliminated from the database, and all records below deleted records move up a notch to fill in the blanks left by the deletions. The Delete option does not require an Output Range, because it does not extract any records.

OTHER OPTIONS

You have probably noticed two other options on the /DQ menu; Reset and Quit. The Quit option simply returns you to the 1-2-3 ready mode. The Reset option "undoes" the parameters of the previous search. 1-2-3 always remembers the parameter of the last search, and this is the option you can choose to make it forget. This is useful if you use the F7 function key rather than the /DQ command (though the two are identical). The F7 key will enter the /DQ command and immediately reperform the last search.

   To summarize, searching the database allows you to specify types of records to search for, and allows you to perform various functions upon the records that meet the search criterion. Searches can be on single fields or multiple fields, as well as a single criterion or several criteria. When several criteria are used, the "logic" of the search can be either both ("and") or either ("or"). This gives you a great deal of flexibility in managing a database.

Chapter 15

"WHAT IF" TABLES AND STATISTICS

One of the greatest assets of any spreadsheet program is that it allows you to set up a model, financial or otherwise, and experiment with "what if" possibilities. Usually you do this by developing the model, then substituting different values into the model and observing their effects. 1-2-3 has added a whole new twist to the "What if" type of analysis by providing the /DT (Data Table) commands. These commands let us build our model on the worksheet, then 1-2-3 tries out the various "what if?" questions automatically. (What'll they think of next?)

PROJECTING NET INCOME WITH A DATA TABLE 1

Let's look at an example of the Data Table 1 command by determining the net income for a company. For this example, we'll assume that ABC Company has a fixed overhead cost of $300,000 per year, and an additional variable cost of about 50% of gross sales. So the net income for any given amount of sales for ABC Co. can be expressed as:

NET INCOME = GROSS SALES − (50% ∗ GROSS SALES) − 300,000

ABC Company would like to find out what their net income for the year will be assuming gross sales of between two and three million dollars, in increments of $100,000. This problem can be solved by setting up a Data Table as shown in Fig. 15-1:

Notice that in cell B3, we've entered the formula:

$$+A3-300000-(.50*A3)$$

	A	B	C	D	E
1	Gross	Net			
2	Sales	Income			
3		+A3-300000-(.50*A3)			
4	$2,000,000				
5	$2,100,000				
6	$2,200,000				
7	$2,300,000				
8	$2,400,000				
9	$2,500,000				
10	$2,600,000				
11	$2,700,000				
12	$2,800,000				
13	$2,900,000				
14	$3,000,000				

Fig.   15-1

A3 refers to the cell which contains gross sales, minus 300,000 (for fixed costs) and 50% times gross sales. Cells A4 to A14 contain the projected gross sales, two to three million dollars in increments of 100,000. Cell A3 is currently empty. This is the proper format for a data table. That is, the table should look like this:

[BLANK CELL] [FORMULA FOR TEST]
[TEST 1]
[TEST 2]
[TEST 3]
[TEST 4]
     etc.

In the example, cell A3 is the blank cell, cells A4 to A14 contain the values to test, and cell B3 contains the test formula for net income. Now to perform the automated "what if," type in the /DT1 (Data Table 1) command. 1-2-3 will ask for the *table range.* The table range should extend from the blank cell in the table to the bottom right cell in the formula column. So if we were to draw the table range by pointing on the screen, it would look like Fig. 15-2. If we were to type in the table range, it would be A3..B14.

Next, 1-2-3 will ask for the *Input Cell.* The input cell is the blank one used in the formula, in this example, cell A3. Fill in the value A3, and press RETURN. And that's all there is to it.

1-2-3 will substitute each of the gross sales figures below the Input Cell into the Input Cell, and will calculate the net income for all 11 gross sales figures. It will display its results in the column to the right of each sales figure as in Fig. 15-3.

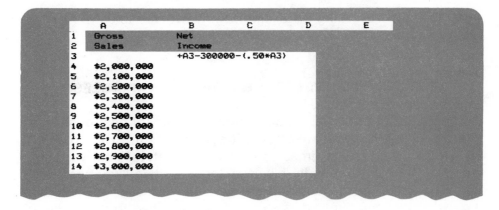

Fig.   15-2

	A	B	C	D	E
1	Gross	Net			
2	Sales	Income			
3		($300,000)			
4	$2,000,000	$700,000			
5	$2,100,000	$750,000			
6	$2,200,000	$800,000			
7	$2,300,000	$850,000			
8	$2,400,000	$900,000			
9	$2,500,000	$950,000			
10	$2,600,000	.$1,000,000			
11	$2,700,000	$1,050,000			
12	$2,800,000	$1,100,000			
13	$2,900,000	$1,150,000			
14	$3,000,000	$1,200,000			

Fig.   15-3

Let's review what we (and 1-2-3) have just done. First, we set up a data table by providing a column of "what if" data below a blank cell. Then, we created column for calculating the "what ifs" next to the blank cell. Then we selected the /DT1 command, and showed 1-2-3 where the data table was on the screen, and where the Input cell was. 1-2-3 then took over, and substituted 2,000,000 into the input cell, calculated the net income, and placed it next to the figure 2,000,000. Then it substituted the value 2,000,000, calculated the net income, and placed it in the cell to the right of the figure 2,100,000, and so forth, until it reached the last value, 3,000,000 in the left column of the data table.

This is actually a very simple example of the Data Table command's capabilities. You can appreciate the true power of the data table command by using an example with two variables /DT2 (Data Table 2) command.

PROJECTING NET INCOME WITH TWO VARIABLES

In the above example, we considered the 50% of cost of sales as a variable cost, however we treated it as a constant. ABC Co. might wish to test the various gross sales with a variety of cost variables, say from 40 to 55 percent. In this case, there are two "what ifs" to be considered, the gross sales and the percent of cost of sales. When two "what ifs" are involved in an equation, we need to use the /DT2 (Data Table 2) command. The rules here are a little different.

Fig. 15-4 shows the basic skeleton for analyzing the effects of gross sales and the variable cost of sales percentage figure in a data table.

	A	B	C	D	E
1	Sales:		Percent:		
2					
3	+B1-300000-(D1*B1)	0.4	.045	0.5	0.55%
4	$2,000,000				
5	$2,100,000				
6	$2,200,000				
7	$2,300,000				
8	$2,400,000				
9	$2,500,000				
10	$2,600,000				
11	$2,700,000				
12	$2,800,000				
13	$2,900,000				
14	$3,000,000				

Fig.   15-4

As before, the assumed gross sales figures are listed down the lefthand column of the data table. The various percentage figures for the test are in the top row. The /DT2 command requires that the formula be in the upper-left corner of the table. In this example, the formula is:

$$+B1-300,000-(D1*B1)$$

The data table is set up such that each gross sales amount is substituted into cell B1, and each of the percentage figures is substituted into cell D1. So the formula still calculates net income from gross sales minus the $300,000 fixed cost and minus the variable cost figure. The structure of the table looks like this:

[INPUT CELL]   [INPUT CELL]

[FORMULA]   [TEST 1]   [TEST 2]   [TEST 3]   [TEST 4]   etc. . .
[TEST 1]
[TEST 2]
[TEST 3]
[TEST 4]
   etc. . .

The two Input cells can be placed anywhere in the worksheet, but the table itself must adhere to this structure.

We're ready to have 1-2-3 answer the many "what ifs." Type in the command /DT2 (Data Table 2). 1-2-3 asks for the table range. The table range must extend from the upper left corner of the table (the one with the formula in it) to the lower right corner of the table. So in this example, the range must be defined as cells A3..E14, as shown in Fig. 15-5.

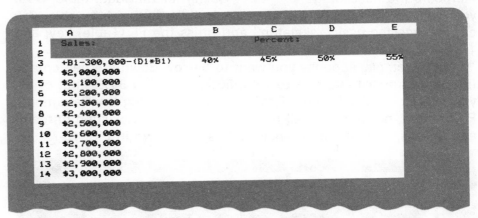

Fig. 15-5

1-2-3 will also ask for the Input Cells. These are the ones specified in the formula, cells B1 and D1. The Input Cells can be placed anywhere on the screen, but make sure that both the formula and the cells you specify as Input Cells are the same. Also, note that Input Cell 1 is for the column values, and Input Cell 2 is for the row values.

Once you specify the Input Cells, press RETURN, and 1-2-3 will calculate the net income gross sales amount and each percentage figure, as shown in Fig. 15-6.

	A	B	C	D	E
1	Sales:		Percent:		
2					
3	($300,000)	0.4	0.45	0.5	0.55
4	$2,000,000	$900,000	$800,000	$700,000	$600,000
5	$2,100,000	$960,000	$855,000	$750,000	$645,000
6	$2,200,000	$1,020,000	$910,000	$800,000	$690,000
7	$2,300,000	$1,080,000	$965,000	$850,000	$735,000
8	$2,400,000	$1,140,000	$1,020,000	$900,000	$780,000
9	$2,500,000	$1,200,000	$1,075,000	$950,000	$825,000
10	$2,600,000	$1,260,000	$1,130,000	$1,000,000	$870,000
11	$2,700,000	$1,320,000	$1,185,000	$1,050,000	$870,000
12	$2,800,000	$1,380,000	$1,240,000	$1,100,000	$915,000
13	$2,900,000	$1,440,000	$1,295,000	$1,150,000	$1,005,000
14	$3,000,000	$1,500,000	$1,350,000	$1,200,000	$1,050,000
15					

Fig. 15-6

ADJUSTING THE DATA TABLE

Once you have created and calculated a data table, 1-2-3 remembers the table range and Input Cell(s) for that data table. So if you want to change some of the assumptions in the data table, you can change the basic "skeleton" and press the F8 (Table) key, and 1-2-3 will automatically recalculate.

For example, suppose you want to narrow down the percentage figures in the last example to 48%, 50%, 52%, and 54%. First of all, you need to get back to the Ready mode by Quitting the Data menu. From there, position the cell pointer to each of the existing percentage figures, and type in the new values, as shown in Fig. 15-7.

	A	B	C	D	E
1	Sales:		Percent:		
2					
3	($300,000)	0.48	0.50	0.52	0.54
4	$2,000,000	$900,000	$800,000	$700,000	$600,000
5	$2,100,000	$960,000	$855,000	$750,000	$645,000
6	$2,200,000	$1,020,000	$910,000	$800,000	$690,000
7	$2,300,000	$1,080,000	$965,000	$850,000	$735,000
8	$2,400,000	$1,140,000	$1,020,000	$900,000	$780,000
9	$2,500,000	$1,200,000	$1,075,000	$950,000	$825,000
10	$2,600,000	$1,260,000	$1,130,000	$1,000,000	$870,000
11	$2,700,000	$1,320,000	$1,185,000	$1,050,000	$870,000
12	$2,800,000	$1,380,000	$1,240,000	$1,100,000	$915,000
13	$2,900,000	$1,440,000	$1,295,000	$1,150,000	$1,005,000
14	$3,000,000	$1,500,000	$1,350,000	$1,200,000	$1,050,000
15					

Fig. 15-7

Then, to recalculate the net incomes, simply press the F8 (Table) key, and the entire table will be recalculated with the new values.

In some cases, you may want to make more extensive changes to your data table, such as adding rows and columns or moving things about. 1-2-3 always remembers table ranges and Input Cells once they are created. To change these, you can simply redefine them when 1-2-3 asks for these values in future data table commands. You can also use the Reset option from the /DT menus to make 1-2-3 "forget" previous data table settings.

DATABASE STATISTICS

The database statistical commands are similar to the statistics functions in 1-2-3 (@VAR, @STD, @AVG, etc.). However, they include additional capabilities for using database Input and Criterion ranges. The database statistical functions are:

@DAVG(input,offset,criterion)	Database Average
@DCOUNT(input,offset,criterion)	Database Count of Items
@DMAX(input,offset,criterion)	Highest number in Database
@DMIN(input,offset,criterion)	Lowest number in database
@DSTD(input,offset,criterion)	Database Standard Deviation
@DSUM(input,offset,criterion)	Database Sum
@DVAR(input,offset,criterion)	Database Variance

The Input and Criterion arguments are ranges similar to those used with the /DQ (Data Query) commands. The Offset argument specifies the field on which to perform the calculations. If the offset is zero, 1-2-3 calculates statistics on the first field. If the offset is 1, calculations are performed on the second field, and so forth.

Fig. 15-8 shows a partial list of individuals' ages and their annual incomes (the actual list extends below the bottom of the worksheet window to row 99).

Notice that in the Criterion Range, we've placed the formula:

$$A4>39\#AND\#A4<5\emptyset$$

which makes the criteria for performing the statistics all people between the ages of 40 and 49 (inclusive). The resulting statistics show the mean, highest, and lowest incomes for individuals in this age group. The count indicates the number of persons in the group who fit this criterion, and the variance and standard deviation (SD). Look-

```
       A        B        C        D        E        F        G    H
 1  Data from Income Questionnaire
 2
 3  Age        Annual Income              Criterion
 4  57         $31,032
 5  32         $26,990                    Age
 6  29         $21,830                    +A4>39#AND#A4<50
 7  27         $19,129
 8  30         $33,000
 9  36         $41,932
10  57         $61,084                    Statistics
11  22         $17,320
12  61         $87,200                    Average : 35,258
13  43         $29,992                    Minimum : 19,000
14  32         $23,543                    Maximum : 49,000
15  34         $22,080                    Count    :     27
16  49         $43,005                    Variance:266,178
17  50         $47,500                    SD:      :11363.1
18  21         $16,040
19  22         $18,000
20  37         $34,000
```

Fig. 15-8

```
       A        B        C        D        E        F        G
 1  Data from Income Questionnaire
 2
 3  Age        Annual Income              Criterion
 4  47         $31,032
 5  32         $26,990                    Age
 6  29         $21,830                    +A4>39#AND#A4<50
 7  27         $19,129
 8  30         $33,000
 9  36         $41,932
10  57         $61,084                    Statistics
11  22         $17,320
12  61         $87,200                    Average :@DAVG(A3..B99,1,E5..E6)
13  43         $29,992                    Minimum :@DMIN(A3..B99,1,E5..E6)
14  32         $23,543                    Maximum :@DMAX(A3..B99,1,E5..E6)
15  34         $22,080                    Count   :@DCOUNT(A3,B99,1,E5..E6)
16  49         $43,005                    Variance:@DVAR(A3,B99,1,E5..E6)
17  50         $47,500                    SD:     :@DSTD(A3,B99,1,E5..E6)
18  21         $16,040
19  22         $18,000
20  37         $34,000
```

Fig. 15-9

ing at this same worksheet with the formulas displayed in text format, you see the worksheet displayed in Fig. 15-9.

Notice that for each formula, the first argument is always the range A3..B99. This is the Input Range for this database (assuming the rows extend down to 99). The second argument is always 1, which is the offset. That is, the column of interest, income, is one column to the right of the age range. The third argument, E5..E6, represents the Criterion Range, where the formula +A4>39#AND#A4<50 is displayed under the field name Age.

If you changed the criterion formula to:

+A4>29#AND#A4<4∅

then 1-2-3 would calculate the statistics on incomes in the age range of 30 to 39 (inclusive). Changing the formula into something simple, like +A4>0, would provide statistics for all age ranges (at least, everyone over the age of zero!).

FREQUENCY DISTRIBUTIONS

Another handy statistic that 1-2-3 provides is a *frequency distribution,* a table that displays how many items in a database fit into various categories. To use this capability, you first need to set up a *bin range.* Fig. 15-10 shows the age and salary data and a bin range.

```
A1:                                                              READY
─

           A        B         C        D        E         F        G    H
 1   Data from Income Questionnaire
 2
 3   Age           Annual Income         Frequency Distribution
 4   47            $31,032               (Bin Range)
 5   32            $26,990                 20
 6   29            $21,830                 30
 7   27            $19,129                 40
 8   30            $33,000                 50
 9   36            $41,932                 60
10   57            $61,084                 70
11   22            $17,320
12   61            $87,200
13   43            $29,992
14   32            $23,543
15   34            $22,080
16   49            $43,005
17   50            $47,500
18   21            $16,040
19   22            $18,000
20   37            $34,000
```

Fig. 15-10

The bin range is in cells D5..D10, and contains the ages 20, 30, 40, 50, 60, and 70. These numbers must have a range of blank cells immediately to the right for 1-2-3 to fill in, and an extra blank cell at the bottom. The values must be in ascending order.

After providing a bin range, type in the /DD (Data Distribution) command. 1-2-3 will request that you:

Enter Values range:

In this worksheet, the values are in the range A4..A99. Type that in, and 1-2-3 will ask that you:

Enter Bin range:

The bin range in this example extends from cell D5 to D10. Type in D5..D10 <RET>, and 1-2-3 will fill in the frequency distribution, as in Fig. 15-11.

```
A1:                                                    READY

         A       B        C       D      E       F     G    H
   1  Data from Income Questionnaire
   2
   3  Age       Annual Income       Frequency Distribution
   4   47       $31,032             (Bin Range)
   5   32       $26,990             20      0
   6   29       $21,630             30     16
   7   27       $19,129             40     38
   8   30       $33,000             50     24
   9   36       $41,932             60     13
  10   57       $61,084             70      8
  11   22       $17,320                     0
  12   61       $87,200
  13   43       $29,992
  14   32       $23,543
  15   34       $22,080
  16   49       $43,005
  17   50       $47,500
  18   21       $16,040
  19   22       $18,000
  20   37       $34,000
```

Fig.   15-11

The frequency distribution shows that nobody in the group is 20 years old or less. Sixteen individuals are in the 21 to 30 age group. Thirty-eight individuals fall in the 31 to 40 age range, 24 in the 41 to 50 range, 13 in the 51 to 60 age group, 8 were in the 61 to 70 age group. Zero individuals were over 70.

A quick and easy way to fill in the values in a bin range is to use the Data Fill command. Position the cell pointer to the top of the bin range. Type in the /DF (Data Fill) command. 1-2-3 requests:

Enter Fill Range:

Type in the range. In the example above, D5 to D10. 1-2-3 asks:

Start: Ø

put in the lowest value, 20 in the example above. 1-2-3 requests:

Step: 1

The step value is 10 in the example, so type in 10 <RET>. 1-2-3 then asks:

Stop: 2Ø47

Type in the highest value, 70 in this example. Press RETURN, and 1-2-3 will fill the cells in the specified range with the appropriate values. This is also useful your other applications, such as filling in a range of years (i.e., 1984 to 1994), or for numbering records in a database.

In this chapter, we've seen a number of extended features of 1-2-3's database management capabilities. The Data Table options provide automated "what-if?" analyses. The database statistical functions provide analyses of an entire database, or only on records that meet a certain criteria. Data Distribution provides frequency distributions, and Data Fill can fill in a series of cells with values that increase in even intervals. In the next chapter we will begin discussing 1-2-3's typing alternative, macros.

MACROS

Chapter 16

MACROS

1-2-3 provides the capability to create macros, collections of keystrokes stored in a cell which can be executed by typing two keys. For example, suppose you have a spreadsheet with five bar graphs. Furthermore, you often try out various "what-if" scenarios with the worksheet, view the various graphs by typing in the many necessary commands to call up each graph, and view it. An alternative to this procedure would be to store all the keystrokes necessary to view all five graphs in a macro. Then, each time you want to view the graphs, you can just press a couple of keys and 1-2-3 will automatically display all five graphs, one at a time, on the screen, and return to the ready mode so you can try out some new assumptions in the worksheet. To view the effects of changes on all five graphs, simply type in the two keystrokes to view the graphs.

MACRO KEYSTROKES

Most commands that you put into a macro appear exactly in the macro as they do typed on the screen. For example, to reformat the worksheet to a global column width of three spaces, you would type in the command /WGC3 (Worksheet Global Column-width 3), and press the return key. This same series of commands, made into a macro, would look like this:

'/WGC3 ˜

The leading apostrophe is a label prefix. All macros must be labels, and therefore the apostrophe is required. The command to set the column widths appears exactly as it would be typed, /WGC3. The tilde at the end of the macro is the macro symbol for "Press the RETURN key."

Several keystrokes are represented by symbols in macros. Keystrokes for moving the cell pointer about the worksheet are listed below:

Macro Symbol	Keystroke Meaning
~	Enter, or return, key
{UP}	Up-arrow
{DOWN}	Down-arrow
{LEFT}	Left-arrow
{RIGHT}	Right-arrow
{HOME}	Position cell pointer to home position
{GoTo}	GoTo a cell (F5)
{PgUp}	Page up
{PgDn}	Page down
{Window}	Change window on split screen (F6)
{End}	End key

There are several other macro symbols that provide for other worksheet tasks. These are:

Macro Symbol	Keystroke Meaning
{Del}	Delete key
{Edit}	Edit key (F2)
{Abs}	Absolute Reference key (F4)
{Table}	Recalculate a data table (F8)
{Graph}	Redisplay a graph
{Esc}	Escape key
{Bs}	Backspace key
{Name}	Display named ranges (F3)
{Query}	Perform database query (F7)
{Calc}	Recalculate (F9)

In addition, macros can use a special symbol to interrupt the execution of a macro, and wait for the user (whoever happens to be sitting at the keyboard while the macro is running) to respond to a prompt. This symbol is the question mark:

Macro Symbol	Keystroke Meaning
{?}	Pause for input from the user, wait for a press on the RETURN key.

We'll soon see how this macro symbol can come in handy.

CREATING MACROS

There are three steps to creating and using a macro: (1) Type the macro into an out-of-the-way cell, (2) Name the macro, and (3) Execute the macro. Here is an example using the macro to automatically set all column widths to 3:

1. The series of keystrokes necessary to set the global column width to three are /WGC3 <RET>. Type these into any cell in the worksheet. In Fig. 16-1, we used cell A5. Be sure to use a label prefix. The label prefix will not appear in the cell, but it will appear in the control panel, as in Fig. 16-1.

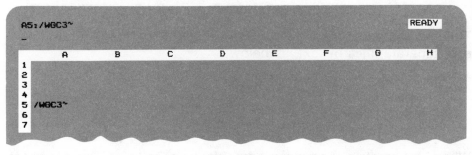

Fig. 16-1

2. Name the macro using the /RNC (Range Name Create) command. Macro names must begin with the backslash character, and have only one letter as their name. In this example, type in /RNC. 1-2-3 will ask that you:

Enter name:_____

Type in \M. You can use any other letter of the alphabet for the name, we selected M at random. 1-2-3 next asks:

Enter range: A5..A5

A5 is the macro cell, so just press RETURN.

3. To invoke the macro, hold down the Alt key (lower left on the keyboard) and press M. All of the keystrokes in the macro are executed, and the worksheet is immediately formatted to column widths of three spaces, as in Fig. 16-2.

Fig. 16-2

This macro is quite simple. Macros can be as large as you like, and can be spread down several rows. For example, here is a long macro to present a graphics slide show:

'/GNU ˜˜˜ {RIGHT}˜˜˜ {RIGHT}{RIGHT} ˜˜˜ {RIGHT}{RIGHT}{RIGHT} ˜

This macro can be made a little more readable by breaking into several separate lines of text, as below:

'/GNU˜
˜˜{RIGHT}˜
˜˜{RIGHT}{RIGHT}˜
˜˜{RIGHT}{RIGHT}{RIGHT}˜

When you create a long macro like this, be sure to use the top-most line as the range when using the /RNC command to name the macro. When you execute any macro, 1-2-3 checks to see if more of the macro is stored in the line immediately below. If so, it continues processing the macro. It stops as soon as it encounters a blank row.

For the remainder of this chapter, we'll describe some useful macros that can be used in a variety of spreadsheets and databases.

QUICK SAVE OF A WORKSHEET

As we have mentioned several times throughout this book, it is a good idea to save your worksheet from time to time. Here is a macro that will quickly save a worksheet just by typing in the Alt-F key combination:

/FS˜R

Place the macro anywhere in your spreadsheet, as long as it is out of the way of existing cells, and use the /NRC (Name Range Create) command to name it \F. Then, anytime you want to do a quick save of a worksheet, just type Alt-F. Make sure that you do want to save the current worksheet before you type Alt-F, because this macro immediately overwrites the existing worksheet with the same name as the current worksheet. The macro does not ask for confirmation. Also, the first time you save a worksheet, use the standard /FS command, then use the macro for saving the worksheet in the future.

SPLIT AND UNSPLIT THE WORKSHEET

For this macro example, we will use the ten year projection worksheet. This worksheet was originally described in Chapter 9. In its normal state, it looks like Fig. 16-3.

	A	B	C	D	E	F
1	Ten Year Projection for Commercial Real Estate					
2	With Internal Rate of Return					
3	===					
4		Increase				
5	Description	Rate %	1984	1985	1986	1987
6	---					
7	Tenant 1	0.12	$15,000	$16,800	$18,816	$21,074
8	Tenant 2	0.15	$10,000	$11,500	$13,225	$15,209
9	Tenant 3	0.16	$5,000	$5,800	$6,782	$7,804
10	Tenant 4	0.18	$5,000	$5,900	$6,962	$8,125
11	---					
12	Maintenance	0.13	$11,000	$12,430	$14,046	$15,872
13	Insurance	0.13	$7,500	$8,475	$9,577	$10,822
14	Debt	0.10	$10,000	$10,000	$12,100	$13,310
15	Mngmt Fee	0.14	$9,000	$10,260	$11,696	$13,334
16	---					
17	Cash Flow		($2,500)	($2,165)	($1,688)	($1,035)
18						
19	IRR Guess:	0.16				
20	IRR Actual: 0.24255					

Fig.   16-3

The first macro described below will automatically split the screen, display the years 1991-1994 in the righthand window, and reposition the cell pointer to cell B7 so that other assumptions can be tried out and viewed at year 10 immediately. Once the macro is keyed in, typing Alt-S will produce the worksheet shown in Fig. 16-4.

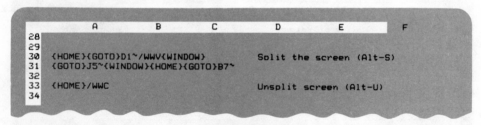

```
        A         B       C    J      K        L        M
1  Ten Year Projection for Comm 1
2  With Internal Rate of Return 2
3  ============================  3  ===============
4            Increase           4
5  Description  Rate %    1984   5  1991     1992     1993     1994
6  --------------------------    6  -----------------------------------
7  Tenant 1     0.12   $15,000   7  $33,160 $37,139 $41,596 $46,588
8  Tenant 2     0.15   $10,000   8  $26,600 $30,590 $35,179 $40,456
9  Tenant 3     0.16    $5,000   9  $14,131 $16,392 $19,015 $22,057
10 Tenant 4     0.18    $5,000  10  $15,927 $18,794 $22,177 $26,169
11 --------------------------   11  -----------------------------------
12 Maintenance  0.13   $11,000  12  $25,879 $29,243 $33,044 $37,340
13 Insurance    0.13    $7,500  13  $17,645 $19,938 $22,530 $25,459
14 Debt         0.10   $10,000  14  $19,487 $21,436 $23,579 $25,937
15 Mngmt Fee    0.14    $9,000  15  $22,520 $25,673 $29,268 $33,365
16 --------------------------   16  -----------------------------------
17 Cash Flow           ($2,500) 17  $ 4,288  $6,628  $9,545 $13,168
18                              18
19 IRR Guess:     0.16          19
20 IRR Actual: 0.24255          20
```

Fig. 16-4

The "unsplit" macro will instantly return the worksheet to its natural format.

We will store the macros in rows 30 to 33. Fig. 16-5 shows the macros as typed into the screen:

```
        A          B          C          D          E          F
28
29
30  {HOME}{GOTO}D1~/WWV{WINDOW}           Split the screen (Alt-S)
31  {GOTO}J5~{WINDOW}{HOME}{GOTO}B7~
32
33  {HOME}/WWC                            Unsplit screen (Alt-U)
34
```

Fig. 16-5

The macro to split the screen is in rows 30 and 31. Breaking this macro into its component parts will help clarify its steps:

{HOME}{GOTO}D1˜ This step positions the cell pointer to the home position (cell A1), then positions the cell pointer to cell D1, where the window separator is to appear.

/WWV This step executes the /WWV (Worksheet Window Vertical) command, causing the screen to split at the cell pointer's current position (column D).

	To split the screen at some other column, change D1 to the appropriate column letter.
{WINDOW}	This step places the cell pointer into the right side of the window.
{GOTO}J5˜	This causes the cell pointer to jump to the 1991 column, which is the column that is to appear at the left edge of the right window. This assures that the columns for the years 1991 to 1994 will appear in the right edge window.
{WINDOW}{HOME}	This section puts the cell pointer back into the left portion of the split screen, then positions the cell pointer to cell A1 (Home).
{GOTO}B7˜	This element places the cell pointer to the range of assumptions. Cell B7 is the first percentage increase rate cell.

Once the macro is keyed in, name it using the /RNC (Range Name Create) command. Give it the name \S, and the range A30. To split the screen after creating the macro, just type Alt-S after naming the macro.

The "unsplit" macro is in row 33. It is a small macro which provides this function:

{HOME}/WWC	Positions the cell pointer to the home position (cell A1), then issues the /WWC command (Worksheet Window Clear).

Place the macro into cell A33, and use /RNC to give it the name \U. Its range is A33.

A TRUE GRAPHICS SLIDE SHOW

One of the most amazing and powerful uses of macros is to create a true graphics slide show. In this example, the macro is included with a ten year financial projection system. You can use the worksheet to try out various assumptions. To view the assumptions on a variety of series of graphs, simply press Alt-G. A bar graph will appear on the screen. Press any key when finished viewing the graph, and another graph will appear immediately. When done viewing that graph, press any key, and a third graph will appear immediately. Press any key, and the worksheet will appear on the screen in the Ready mode. You can then change any assumption, or many assumptions, then press Alt-G again, and the graphs will again appear in slide-show form, but they will plot the new data based upon the changes in the assumptions.

For this example, we've again used the ten-year financial projection system. Furthermore, we created three graphs, a bar graph of the cash flows, a line graph of the cash flows, and a stacked bar graph of the tenant incomes. Each bar graph was given a name using the /GNC (Graph Name Create) command. The macro works like this:

First, it invokes the /GNU (Graph Name Use) command, then issues a return key to draw the first graph (since the graph name pointer will be highlighting the first graph name in the list). When you press any key to stop viewing the graph, the macro then issues two return key commands, to select the Name and Use options, then elicits a right-arrow key to move the pointer to the second graph in the menu of named graphs, and issues a RETURN to view the second named graph. When you press any key to erase the second graph displayed, the macro again issues two RETURN key commands to select the Name and Use commands, and then moves the graph name pointer to spaces to the right to select the third-name graph. Another RETURN key issued by the macro displays the third named graph on the screen. After viewing that graph, the macro then selects the Quit option from the Graph menu, and returns the worksheet to the Ready mode.

The macro will work in any worksheet, as long as there are three named graphs associated with the worksheet. It does not matter what the names of the graphs are. The macro looks like this:

```
'/GNU˜˜˜{RIGHT}˜˜˜{RIGHT}{RIGHT}˜{RIGHT}˜
```

Of course, you are not limited to displaying three named graphs. Here is a macro that can display five named graphs in a row, then return to the worksheet in the Ready mode:

```
/GNU˜˜˜{RIGHT}
˜˜˜{RIGHT}{RIGHT}
˜˜˜{RIGHT}{RIGHT}{RIGHT}
˜˜˜{RIGHT}{RIGHT}{RIGHT}{RIGHT}
˜{RIGHT}˜
```

Fig. 16-6 shows the ten year projection program with the macro for a five-graph slide show in it.

```
          A          B         C         D         E          F
1   Ten Year Projection for Commercial Real Estate
2   With Internal Rate of Return
3   ===============================================
4              Increase
5   Description  Rate %     1984      1985      1986       1987
6   ---------------------------------------------------------------
7   Tenant 1      0.12    $15,000   $16,800   $18,816    $21,074
8   Tenant 2      0.15    $10,000   $11,500   $13,225    $15,209
9   Tenant 3      0.16     $5,000    $5,800    $6,782`    $7,804
10  Tenant 4      0.18     $5,000    $5,900    $6,962     $8,125
11  ---------------------------------------------------------------
12  Maintenance   0.13    $11,000   $12,430   $14,046    $15,872
13  Insurance     0.13     $7,500    $8,475    $9,577    $10,822
14  Debt          0.10    $10,000   $10,000   $12,100    $13,310
15  Mngmt Fee     0.14     $9,000   $10,260   $11,696    $13,334
16  ---------------------------------------------------------------
17  Cash Flow             ($2,500)  ($2,165)  ($1,688)  ($1,035)
18
19  IRR Guess:    0.16
20  IRR Actual: 0.24255
21
22  /GNU~~~{RIGHT}
23  ~~~{RIGHT}{RIGHT}
24  ~~~{RIGHT}{RIGHT}{RIGHT}
25  ~~~{RIGHT}{RIGHT}{RIGHT}{RIGHT}
26  ~{RIGHT}~
28
```

Fig. 16-6

Each line of the macro has an apostrophe as the label prefix. Once the macro is keyed in, you can name it by typing in the /RNC (Range Name Create) command, and when it asks for the name of the range, type in a backslash and the letter G (\G). Press RETURN. 1-2-3 will ask for the range, type in A22 <RET>. Now to see your graphics slide show, press Alt-G. Be sure though that you have first created and named at least five graphs.

The slide show macro has to be seen to be appreciated. Its real value can't be appreciated until you try it. The ability to try a "What if" assumption, and then use it immediately graphed in a series of graphs brings a whole new meanig to the concept of electronic spreadsheets. You'll wonder how you ever got along without it.

CUSTOM HELP SCREENS

If you develop worksheets that are to be used by people other than yourself, you might want to provide the other users with custom "help" screens that provide instructions on using your worksheet. In the following example, the help system provides instructions for using the financial projection worksheet as well as the split-screen, "unsplit" screen, and slide show macros.

When the user first calls up the worksheet, it looks like Fig. 16-7.

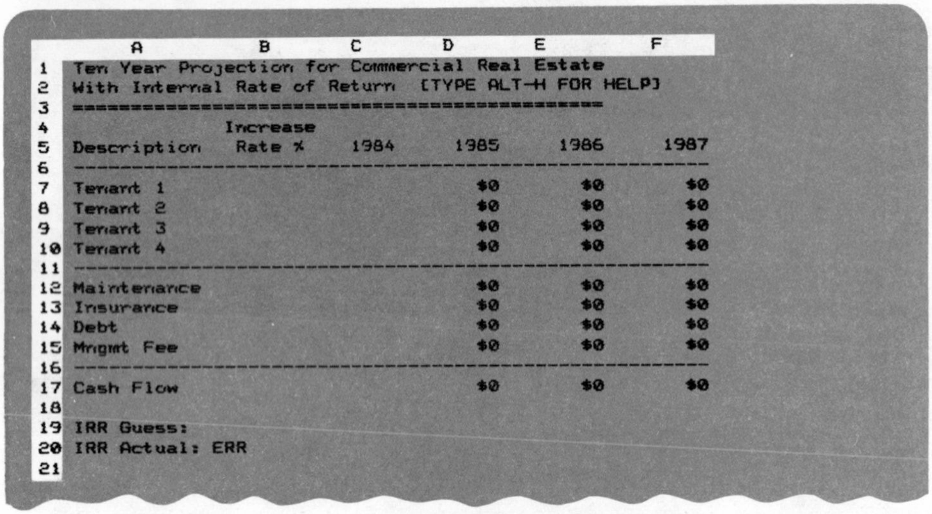

Fig. 16-7

Notice the instruction in row 2 which reads:

[TYPE ALT-H FOR HELP]

Add this instruction to the worksheet by simply positioning the cell pointer to cell D2 and then type in the instruction as you would any 1-2-3 label. When the user types and holds down the Alt key and presses H, a series of instructions appear on the screen, as shown in Fig. 16-8.

As soon as the user is done reading the instructions, he can press the Enter key, and the worksheet will reappear on the screen with the cell pointer in cell B7, which is the cell for filling in the first year assumed percentage increase rate.

To create the help screen, simply position the cell pointer to cell A48 and type in the sentences shown above. For the sentences that begin with numbers (i.e., 1., 2., and 3.), be sure to use the apostrophe (') label prefix before typing in the sentence.

We placed the help macro between the macros we've already discussed for this worksheet. The macro could actually be placed

```
        A         B         C         D         E         F         G
46
47
48  To use the financial worksheet, follow these instructions:
49
50  1. For each tenant and expense category in column B,
51     type in an assumed increase rate, follwed by a percent
52     sign and a press on the Enter ((--') key (e.g. 16%).
53
54  2. For the first year, 1984 (column C) fill in the assumed
55     first year amounts for rental income and expenses.
56
57  3. In cell B19, type in an estimated value for the internal
58     rate of return.  If the symbol ERR appears, try other
59     estimated values.
60
61     Other options are:
62     Alt-G    (Graph) See graphics slide show.
63     Alt-S    (Split) Split worksheet to see more years.
64     Alt-U    (Unsplit)  Return to normal worksheet.
65              PRESS ENTER TO RETURN TO THE WORKSHEET
```

Fig. 16-8

anywhere on the worksheet, its position does not affect its performance. Fig. 16-9 shows the macro in row 28 between the existing macros.

We have already discussed the slide show and split screen macros. The "help screen" macro is stored in cell A28, and looks like
this:

$$\{GOTO\}A46 \tilde{}\, \{?\}\{HOME\}\{GOTO\}B7 \tilde{}$$

This macro performs the following steps:

{GOTO}A46 ˜	This step tells 1-2-3 to go to cell A46, which is the start of the help screen. This causes the help screen to appear on the screen.
{?}	This step causes the macro to halt execution and wait for the user to press the ENTER key. Therefore, the help instructions stay on the screen until the user presses the ENTER key.
{HOME}{GOTO}B7 ˜	This step sends the cell pointer to the home position (cell A1), then places the cell pointer in cell B7, which is the first input cell.

After typing in the macro, use the /RNC (Range Name Create) command to give the macro the name \H. The range is A28..A28.

```
        A        B        C        D        E        F        G
22  /GNU~~~{RIGHT}                            Slide show macro (Alt-G)
23  ~~~{RIGHT}{RIGHT}
24  ~~~{RIGHT}{RIGHT}{RIGHT}
25  ~~~{RIGHT}{RIGHT}{RIGHT}{RIGHT}
26  ~{RIGHT}~
27
28  {GOTO}A46~{?}{HOME}{GOTO}B7~            Help macro (Alt-H)
29
30  {HOME}{GOTO}D1~/WWV{WINDOW}             Split screen (Alt-S)
31  {GOTO}J5~{WINDOW}{HOME}{GOTO}B7~
32
33  {HOME}/WWC                              "Unsplit" screen (Alt-U)
34
35
```

Fig. 16-9

YEAR-TO-DATE ACCUMULATOR

Year-to-date accumulations in electronic worksheets often present a problem. This is because of the *circular reference* issue. A year-to-date accumulation, for example, would have to be the sum of the present year-to-date value (itself), plus the current month-to-date value. Whenever a formula refers to itself, as the year-to-date value does in this example, we say that that it performs a circular reference. The problem is that the circular reference grows enormously, because every time a new value is added to the worksheet, all the circular references reaccumulate, even before they should, which usually makes the year-to-date value grow at an inaccurate and rapid rate.

The problem can be solved by making sure that the accumulation procedure only occurs once a month. A macro can take care of this quite well. Observe the worksheet in Fig. 16-10. It presents a simple income statement for a single month.
With data filled in, the worksheet might look more like Fig. 16-11.

For the first month, January, the year-to-date values are identical to the month-to-date values. We could just copy them over with the Copy command, but in this example we want to create a macro that can provide a year-to-date update at the end of each month. So, we will use a temporary data file to store the values in the month-to-date column, and then add them to the year-to-date values. For the first month, this must be performed manually. Here are the instructions to do so:

1. After the first month's data are in the worksheet, type in the command /FXV (File Extract Values), and when 1-2-3 asks for a file name, give it the name TEMP (for temporary). 1-2-3 will ask for the range, and in this example it is all the month-to-date values, D4..D20. This will create a small worksheet file called TEMP.WKS.

2. Position the cell pointer to cell D4, and type in the command /FCAE (File Combine Add Entire file). When 1-2-3 asks for the name of the file to combine, type in TEMP <RET>. At that point, the worksheet looks like Fig. 16-12.

Once the first month is done, a macro can handle future year-to-date accumulations. The macro can be stored anywhere on the worksheet, and should look like this:

{GOTO}D4˜
/FXVTEMP˜D4..D2Ø˜R
{RIGHT}
/FCAETEMP ˜

Once the macro is typed in, use /RNC to give it a name (such as \ Y). At the end of each month, typing Alt-Y will automatically update the year-to-date values based upon the current month's data. Let's examine the macro more carefully.

{GOTO}D4˜   This step positions the cell pointer to the top of the MTD column.

	A	B	C	D	E	F	G
1	Income Statement			January, 1984			
2							
3	Revenues from Sales			MTD	YTD		
4	Gross Sales.....						
5	Returns & Allow.						
6	Discounts.......						
7	Total...............			+D4-(D5+D6)			
8							
9	Cost of Goods Sold						
10	Materials.......						
11	Freight-in......						
12	Total...............			@SUM(D10..D11)			
13							
14	Operating Expenses						
15	Selling Expense.						
16	Salaries........						
17	Depreciation....						
18	Supplies........						
19	Total...............			@SUM(D15..D18)			
20	NET INCOME..........			+D7-D12-D19			

Fig. 16-10

Fig. 16-11

Fig. 16-12

/FXVTEMP ˜ D4..D2Ø ˜ R

This step selects the File eXtract Values command, names the extraction file TEMP, specifies the range of the month-to-date values (D4..D20), and replaces the existing TEMP file (last month's current values) with the current month's values.

{RIGHT}	This step moves the cell pointer over to the top of the year-to-date column.
/FCAETEMP ˜	This step selects the File Combine Add Entire file command, and names TEMP as the file to combine. The current month's values will be added to the existing year-to-date values.

In February, you will add some new month-to-date figures. These will not directly affect the present year-to-date values. Fig. 16-13 shows February's income statement prior to performing the accumulation procedure:

```
         A         B        C       D           E         F      G     H
 1  Income Statement                    February, 1984
 2
 3  Revenues from Sales              MTD         YTD
 4      Gross Sales.....           $15,000     $12,000
 5      Returns & Allow.             $700        $500
 6      Discounts.......             $650        $750
 7  Total...............          $13,650     $10,750
 8
 9  Cost of Goods Sold
10      Materials.......             $900      $1,000
11      Freight-in......             $175        $250
12  Total...............          $1,075      $1,250
13
14  Operating Expenses
15      Selling Expense.           $1,600      $1,400
16      Salaries........           $3,000      $2,500
17      Depreciation....             $230        $250
18      Supplies........             $400        $300
19  Total...............          $5,230      $4,450
20  NET INCOME..........          $7,345      $5,050
```

Fig. 16-13

Now, to accumulate the year-to-date values, just type Alt-Y (the alt key followed by the name of the macro). The macro will send the month-to-date values to the file named TEMP, then add these to the year-to-date column on the worksheet. The result is displayed in Fig. 16-14.

You must make sure that you only request the updating procedure once a month, or the year-to-date values will increase inappropriately during a single month. For each new month, just type in the current amounts, double check for accuracy, then perform the update using the Alt-Y macro.

```
     A        B        C        D         E          F        G
 1  Income Statement              February, 1984
 2
 3  Revenues from Sales           MTD       YTD
 4       Gross Sales.....      $15,000   $27,000
 5       Returns & Allow.       $700     $1,200
 6       Discounts.......       $650     $1,400
 7  Total...............      $13,650   $24,400
 8
 9  Cost of Goods Sold
10       Materials.......       $900     $1,900
11       Freight-in......       $175      $425
12  Total...............      $1,075    $2,325
13
14  Operating Expenses
15       Selling Expense.     $1,600    $3,000
16       Salaries........     $3,000    $5,500
17       Depreciation....      $230      $480
18       Supplies........      $400      $700
19  Total...............     $5,230    $9,680
20  NET INCOME..........     $7,345   $12,395
```

Fig. 16-14

PASSING MACROS AMONG WORKSHEETS

As you build up a store of useful macros, you may want to use them in new worksheets that you create. There is no need to retype the macro in the new worksheet, since you can just pass them from worksheet to worksheet. For example, you could place all the macros in the worksheet above into a separate file, and give that file a name like "Macro." Then when you begin to create a new worksheet, you can pull all the macros into the new worksheet using the /F command.

The worksheet we've been working with so far has the macros stored in rows 22 to 33, as shown in Fig. 16-15.

To send the macros to their own file, type in the command /FXF (File eXtract Formulas) and provide a file name, such as MACROS <RET>. 1-2-3 will ask that you:

Enter xtract range: A22..A22

The macros are in the range A22..E33 (if you include the comments off to the side). Type in this range. 1-2-3 will create a file called MAC- ROS.WKS on disk.

To transfer the macros to another worksheet, be sure to first save the current worksheet using the /FS (File Save) command. Call up another worksheet, or create one. In this example, we'll call the macros into a blank worksheet. First, position the cell pointer to the

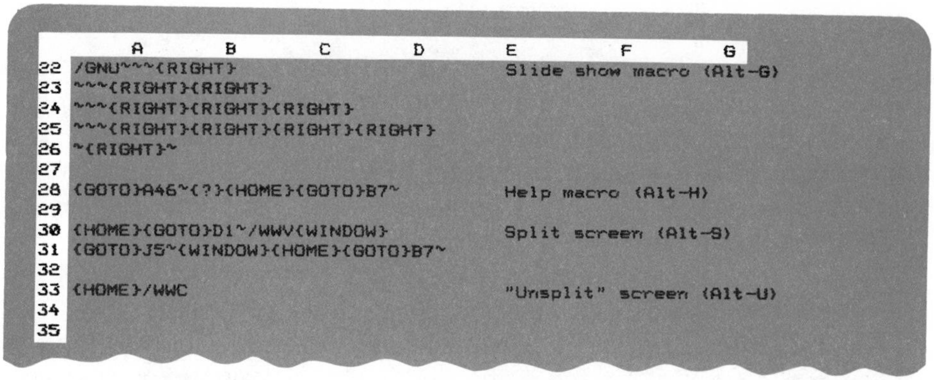

Fig. 16-15

place where you want the macros to appear in the new worksheet. Type in the command /FCCE (File Combine Copy Entire file). 1-2-3 requests:

Enter name of file to combine:

Type in MACROS <RET>. The macros will come into the new worksheet starting at the current cell position. In Fig. 16-16, the cell pointer was placed in cell A30 prior to typing in the command /FCCE, so the macros appear in rows 30 to 42 in the new worksheet.

The macros do not have names in the new worksheet. The extraction process did not carry range names. To give the macros names in the new worksheet, just use the /RNC command as usual.

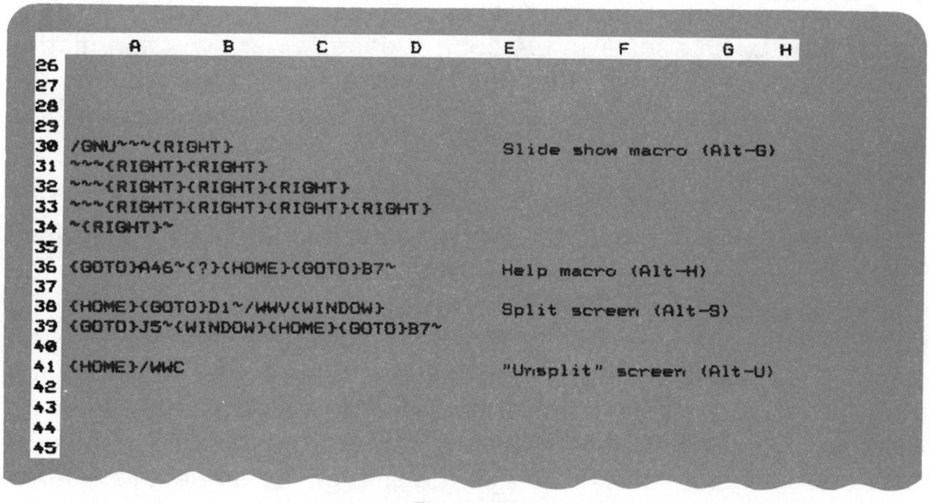

Fig. 16-16

DEBUGGING

Macros do not always perform as you may have expected. 1-2-3 always does exactly as the macro says, which is not always exactly what you meant. When a macro does not perform as expected, you are going to have to change it to get it to work properly. Fixing things that don't work properly in the computer world is called *debugging* (getting the bugs out).

When you create a macro, you should first manually do all the steps that the macro is to perform. Every time you press a key, jot down on a piece of paper the key you just pressed. Then to type in the macro, simply place the same sequence of keystrokes that you wrote on paper into a worksheet cell. The macro *should* perform perfectly, but if it does not, follow these steps:

1. Work through the intended macro procedure manually again. Except this time, follow your own keystroke sequences that you wrote on the paper. At some point, you may notice that you left out a keystroke on the paper.
2. If you had to change the keystrokes you wrote on paper, then you will need to make the same change to the macro. If your handwritten sequence of keystrokes worked fine on the second test, then there is a discrepancy between the actual macro and the sequence you wrote on paper. Study the macro carefully to locate the discrepancy.
3. When you find the discrepancy, position the cell pointer to the cell with the macro in it, and press the F2 (Edit) key. The macro will appear in the control panel, where you can modify it. Press RETURN after making corrections. Try executing the macro again, and repeat these steps until the macro works correctly.

If that procedure does not help, you can slow down the execution of the macro so that you can watch it happen a step at a time. First, press Alt-F1 to put 1-2-3 into single-step mode. The mode indicator displays the message STEP. Next, type the Alt-(letter) sequence used to execute your macro. 1-2-3 will process one step of the macro, then wait for you to press any key. After you press a key, the next step in the macro is performed, and so on. This allows you to watch each step of the macro in slow motion, and at some point your error should become clear. To exit the single-step mode and resume normal processing, press the Alt-F1 key again.

In general, when you create a large macro, try to make a habit of creating only a small portion of the macro at a time. For a large macro you can enter a small piece of the macro, name it, and execute it. When the little piece works, create another piece by either adding it to the end of the existing macro using the Edit key, or by putting the next step on the line below the existing piece. Create a small macro, test it, correct it, then add a little more, test it, correct it, and so forth. Building your macro in this way allows you to work in small steps which are easy to correct should you make an error.

Chapter 17

PROGRAMMING 1-2-3

Macros can contain more than keystrokes and worksheet commands. They may include macro commands which are similar to commands used in most programming languages. These allow you to develop very sophisticated macros which allow you to custom program a worksheet to automate many tasks.

MACRO COMMANDS

All the macro commands use the symbol /X. They are summarized in Table 17-1. If you happen to be a programmer, these will be pretty obvious based on their descriptions. If you are not a programmer, the examples in this chapter will explain these commands more clearly.

The best way to learn about macro commands is to try them. We'll present some powerful macros below.

A LOOPING MACRO

The Lotus manual provides an example of a looping macro that changes all the formulas in a column to their calculated values. The formulas themselves are eliminated from the worksheet. We'll use a similar example here, but a different approach.

Fig. 17-1 shows a worksheet in /WGFT (Worksheet Global Format Text) format. Cell A1 contains the number 10, and the remaining cells display formulas. Cell B2 contains the number of formulas in column

Table 17-1. Macro Commands

Macro Command	Function
/XI	Performs an If..Then procedure. If the condition being tested is true, then the macro processes the rest of the cell. Otherwise, it continues processing the macro at the next cell below.
/XG	Makes the macro skip to another cell to continue processing. Provides a branching (GOTO) capability.
/XC, /XR	/XC calls a procedure from within the macro, and /XR returns execution to the position just beyond the /XC call. (Operates as a subroutine capability, like the BASIC GOSUB and RETURN commands.)
/XQ	Quits execution of the macro and returns to ready mode.
/XL	Pauses macro execution, displays a message in the control panel, and waits for a response. The response is treated as a label and placed into a specified location on the worksheet.
/XN	Same as above, but treats the user input as a number.
/XM	Creates a menu of choices in the control panel, waits for user to select a menu item, then executes a macro based on user's choice.

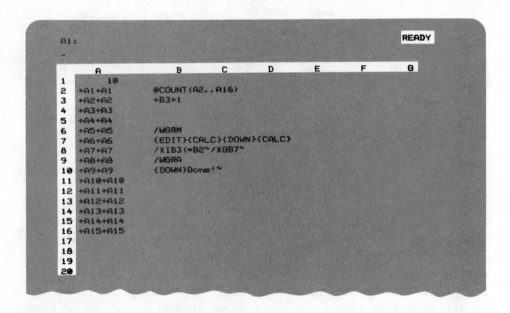

Fig. 17-1

A, calculated with the @COUNT command. Cell B3 contains the formula B3+1, which will grow by 1 each time the worksheet recalculates. Since it refers to itself, it adds one to itself each time the worksheet recalculates, therefore it can serve as a counter.

Cells B6..B10 contain the macro. Each step in the macro is explained below:

/WGRM	Worksheet Global Recalculation Manual. This is necessary so that the macro can control when a recalculation takes place. The {CALC} symbol in the macro causes the worksheet to recalculate.
{EDIT}{CALC} **{DOWN}{CALC}**	The {EDIT} symbol brings the cell's contents to the control panel for editing. Pressing {CALC} while a formula is in edit mode causes the formula to disappear, and its value to replace the cell's contents. The {DOWN} symbol moves the cell pointer down to the next cell in the column, and the second {CALC} symbol causes the worksheet to recalculate. The recalculation causes the circular reference in cell B2 to add one to itself.
/XIB3<=B2˜/XGB7˜	This command uses the /XI macro symbol to determine whether or not the counter in cell B2 is less or equal to the number of formulas to be converted. If so, the /XG command causes the macro to loop back to cell B7, which performs the conversion for a single cell and moves down to the next cell. If the value of cell B3 is not less than or equal to cell B2, the /XI command will automatically cause the macro to start executing in the cell below.
/WGRA	This command sets the worksheet back to automatic recalculation.

{DOWN}Done! ˜   Moves the cell pointer down one cell and puts the word "Done!" in it.

To see the macro in action, use /RNC to name cell B6 to \C. Position the cell pointer to cell A2, the first cell to be formatted. Then, type Alt-C. The macro will convert each of the formulas in the column to numeric values. The formulas are permanently erased.

CUSTOM MENUS

The 1-2-3 menus all work on the same principle: The menu choices are displayed on the screen, and a brief description of the highlighted choice is always displayed under the menu. When you move the menu pointer to another option on the menu, its description appears on the screen. You select menu options by either positioning the cell pointer to the option and pressing RETURN, or by typing the first letter of the option.

You can create your own menus in 1-2-3 that work in exactly the same fashion. Fig. 17-2 shows two macros that provide for automatic sorting of the database. They are set up to be menu options, so that when the user types Alt-S, the control panel reads:

Names   Zips
Sort alphabetically by name

Moving the menu pointer to the Zips option changes the brief description below it, like this:

Names   Zips
Sort by zip code

Selecting the names option instantly sorts the database by name, selecting Zips automatically sorts the database by zip code. The macro to perform this task appears in Fig. 17-2.

In this example, the macro is stored in the range of cells near the lower right corner of the screen, columns IA and IB, and rows greater than 2000. Cell IA2000 contains the label /XMSub1. The /XM macro command specifies a menu located in cell IA2001. Cell IA2001 is the top-left portion of the menu. Its row contains the two menu choices, Names and Zips. The line immediately below the menu options must contain the brief messages associated with the menu option above it. Therefore, row 2002 contains two descriptive statements. 1-2-3 will

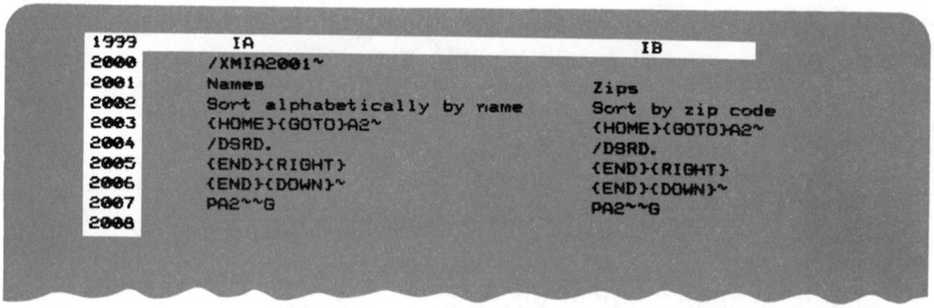

```
1999        IA                                      IB
2000        /XMIA2001~
2001        Names                                   Zips
2002        Sort alphabetically by name             Sort by zip code
2003        {HOME}{GOTO}A2~                          {HOME}{GOTO}A2~
2004        /DSRD.                                   /DSRD.
2005        {END}{RIGHT}                             {END}{RIGHT}
2006        {END}{DOWN}~                             {END}{DOWN}~
2007        PA2~~G                                  PA2~~G
2008
```

Fig.   17-2

display the menu choices in the control panel, and display the descriptive message for whichever is highlighted.

If the user selects Names from the menu, the macro in column IA, Rows 2003-2007 is executed. If the user opts to sort by zip, the macro in rows 2003-2007 in Column IB is executed.

The structure of the macro command is always the same. The /XM command contains cell address for the upper-left corner of the menu. The first line contains the menu choices, the second line contains the descriptive messages, and the remaining lines the actual commands to be performed for each menu option. The structure for the macro menu is illustrated n Fig. 17-3.

You can have up to 8 choices in a custom menu, and as many steps as you want for each menu option.

Once the custom menu macros are typed into the worksheet, use the /RNC (Range Name Create) command to give the cell with the /XM command in it (cell IA2000 in the preceding example) a macro name, such as \M. Then, to execute the macro and see the menu in

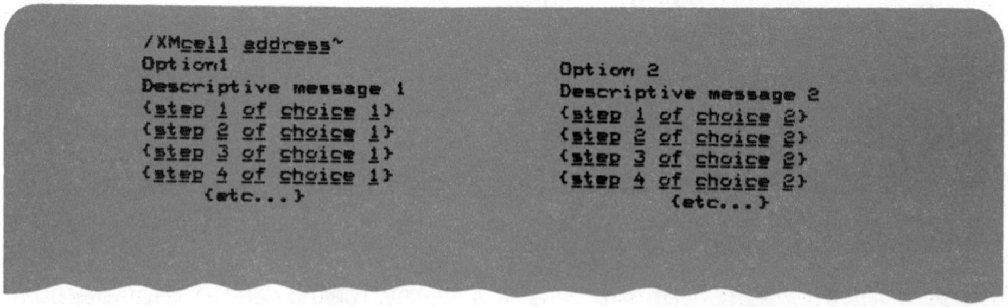

```
/XMcell address~
Option1                          Option 2
Descriptive message 1            Descriptive message 2
{step 1 of choice 1}             {step 1 of choice 2}
{step 2 of choice 1}             {step 2 of choice 2}
{step 3 of choice 1}             {step 3 of choice 2}
{step 4 of choice 1}             {step 4 of choice 2}
        {etc...}                         {etc...}
```

Fig.   17-3

the control panel, type Alt-M. Then menu choices will appear, and behave just like any of 1-2-3's built-in menus.

We will deal with the specifics of the macros that do the actual sorting later in the chapter.

A MENU-DRIVEN DATABASE SYSTEM

In this section we will develop a database system with fully automated sorting, searching, and other capabilities. When you first use /FR to retrieve the file, it appears on the screen with a menu of choices, as shown in Fig. 17-4.

```
Add   Delete   Sort   Print   Lookup   Worksheet
Add new names to the directory
        A           B           C           D           E         F           G
  1  Lname      Fname      Address      City        State    Zip
  2  Smith      Sandy      234 B St.    San Diego    CA      91234
  3  Adams      Andy       123 A St.    SD           CA      90011
  4  Koss       Caron      111 Elm      New York     NY      01234
  5  Johnson    Jackie     213 Bragg    San Diego    CA      90012
  6  Richards   Ricky      911 S St.    Berkeley     CA      91234
  7  Smith      John       450 SL St.   Los AngelesCA        91234
  8  Jones      Janet      333 C St.    New York     NY      12345
  9
 10
 11
 12
 20
```

Fig.   17-4

If you select Add from the menu of choices, the cell pointer drops the first available record on the database, and moves across each field as you type in data. It will also automatically put in label prefixes for the address and zip codes. If you select option 2, the control panel will ask:

Enter person's last name:

After you fill in the last name, it will then ask:

Enter person's first name:

and you fill in the first name; it will automatically delete that person from the database. If you select the Sort option, a new menu will appear which reads:

Names   Zips
Sort alphabetically by name

If you select Names, the macro will immediately resort the records by name. If you select Zips, the names will immediately be sorted by zip code. If you select Print, the directory will be displayed on the printer. The Lookup option will ask:

Look up whom?   :

You type in a name, and it will be highlighted on the screen immediately. The Worksheet option returns to normal 1-2-3 Ready mode.

The beauty of a system like this is that it is easy to use fast. Also, it creates all its own Input and Criterion ranges automatically, so you don't need to bother with those steps. We will use the /XM command to display the menus, and the /XL command to provide prompts, such as "Look up whom?."

The macros are stored in the lower right portion of the worksheet. Fig. 17-5 shows the macros as they appear in the worksheet.

The main macro is stored as a series of six menu choices across row 2001. The options are Add, Delete, Sort, Print, Lookup, Worksheet. Line 20001 contains descriptive statements for each of the menu choices. Cell IA2000 contains the macro command /WMMenu˜ . "Menu" is the cell name for cell IA2001. The cell name was created with the /RNC (Range Name Create) command. It is a good idea to use cell names rather than actual addresses in macros, because if you insert or delete a row or column in the worksheet, and the macros move to another location, then the cell reference in a macro will be incorrect. If the reference to a cell in a macro is a range name, then any time the macro moves, the range name will adjust accordingly and everything will still work properly.

Each menu choice has a macro that performs a specific task associated with it. We'll discuss each below.

MACRO TO ADD A RECORD

When the user selects the Add option from the menu, the cell pointer automatically moves to the next available record in the database. The user types in the first field, presses RETURN, and the cell pointer automatically moves to the next field. The macro also

```
        IA                      IB
2000   /XMmenu~
2001   Add                     Delete
2002   Add a new name          Delete a name
2003   {HOME}                  /XLEnter person's last name: ~H2~
2004   {END}{DOWN}             /XLEnter person's first name: ~J2~
2005   {DOWN}                  {HOME}
2006   {?}{RIGHT}              /DQRI.{END}{RIGHT}{END}{DOWN}~
2007   {?}{RIGHT}              CH1..J2~
2008   '{?}{RIGHT}             DDQ
2009   {?}{RIGHT}              /XMMenu~
2010   {?}{RIGHT}
2011   '{?}{DOWN}
2012   {END}{LEFT}
2013   /XMMenu~
2014
2015
2016
2017   /XMsub1~
2018   Names                   Zips
2019   Sort alphabetically by name    Sort by zip code
2020   {HOME}{GOTO}A2~         {HOME}{GOTO}A2~
2021   /DSRD.                  /DSRD.
2022   {END}{RIGHT}            {END}{RIGHT}
2023   {END}{DOWN}~            {END}{DOWN}~
2024   PA2~~G                  PF2~~G
2025   /XMMenu~                /XMMenu~
```

```
        IC          ID                  IE                  IF
2000
2001   Sort        Print               Lookup              Worksheet
2002   Reorganize  Print the Directory Find an individual
2003   /XMsub1~    {HOME}              /XLLook up whom? ~H2~
2004               /PPCRR              {HOME}/DQRCH1..H2~
2005               .{END}{RIGHT}       I.{END}{RIGHT}
2006               {END}{DOWN}~G       {END}{DOWN}~
2007               /XMMenu~            F{?}{ESC}Q
2008                                   /XMMenu~
```

Fig. 17-5

ensures that street address and zip code automatically start with a label prefix. Also, since the cell pointer automatically moves to the right, you can enter data with the numeric keypad, because you don't need the arrow keys to position the cell pointer.

After filling in the new record, the menu reappears on the screen. To add another record, simply select the Add option again, or select any other option from the keyboard. Here are the steps of the macro:

Add   This is the menu choice for the /XM command.

Add a new name **{HOME}**	This is the menu descriptive statement.
{END}{DOWN}	This places the cell pointer in cell A1. Moves the cell pointer to the last record in the database.
{DOWN}	Moves the cell pointer to the first record below the last record in the database (next available record).
{?}{RIGHT}	Pauses to let the user fill in the LNAME, then moves the cell pointer to the right after the user presses RETURN.
{?}{RIGHT}	Pauses to allow the user to type in FNAME, then moves the cell pointer to the right.
'{?}{RIGHT}	Places the apostrophe label prefix into the address cell, then waits for the user to type in the address. (You must enter this macro with two leading apostrophes, ''{?}{RIGHT}).
{?}{RIGHT}	Pauses to allow the user to enter the city, then moves the cell pointer to the right.
{?}{RIGHT}	Pauses to allow the user to enter the state, then moves the cell pointer to the right.
'{?}{DOWN}	Adds the apostrophe label prefix to the zip field, and waits for the user to type in the zip code, then moves the cell pointer down.
{END}{LEFT}	Moves the cell pointer to the beginning of the next available record.
/XMMenu~	Redisplays the custom menu.

MACRO TO DELETE A RECORD

When the user opts to delete a name, the control panel asks:

Enter person's last name:

and waits for the user to type in the last name of the person to delete. Then the control panel asks:

Enter person's first name:

and waits for the first name of the person to delete. Then, the macro deletes this individual from the database, and moves all records below the deleted person up a notch. Here are the steps in the macro:

Delete	Menu option name.
Delete a name	Menu descriptive message.
/XLEnter person's last name:˜H2˜	Asks the user to type in the last name of the individual to delete, and stores that last name in cell H2.
/XLEnter person's first name:˜J2˜	Asks for first name of person to delete, and stores the name in cell J2.
{HOME}	Puts the cell pointer in cell A1.
/DQRI.{END}{RIGHT} **{END}{DOWN}˜**	Selects /DQR (Data Query Reset) to eliminate previous data ranges. Then I selects Input Range. The period (.) anchors the cell pointer. The end, right, end, down sequence draws the range of the entire database as the Input Range.
CH1. .J2˜	C selects the criterion range, and H1. .J2˜ defines cells H1 to J2 as the Criterion Range. Cells H1 and J1 always have the labels LNAME and FNAME, respectively. The names typed-in in response to the preceding /XL commands are stored in cells H2 and J2, so the Criterion Range is set up properly for this specification.
DDQ	Selects Delete, Delete (on double check from 1-2-3), and Quit from the Data Menu. This step performs the actual delete.
/XMMenu˜	Brings the custom menu back to the control panel.

Cells J1 and H1 must contain the labels LNAME and FNAME in this example, as these are the top line of the Criterion Range.

SORTING MACRO

The sorting macro asks the user if they want to sort by Names or Zips, and instantly sorts the database accordingly. In the main macro, the sort option is very small:

Sort	Menu option.
Reorganize	Menu descriptive statement.
/XMsub1˜	Calls up a submenu at a cell location named sub1.

The location sub1 is actually a cell address for the beginning of the sort options menu. The sort options menu looks like this:

/XMsub1˜

Names		**Zips**
Sort alphabetically by name		**Sort by zip code**
{HOME}{GOTO}A2˜		**{HOME}{GOTO} A2˜**
/DSRD.		**/DSRD.**
{END}{RIGHT}		**{END}{RIGHT}**
{END}{DOWN}˜		**{END}{DOWN}˜**
PA2˜ ˜G		**PF2 ˜ ˜G**
/XMMenu˜		**/XMMenu˜**

/XMsub1˜	
Names	Menu option from submenu.
Sort alphabetically by name	Descriptive statement for menu choice.
{HOME}{GOTO}A2˜	Positions the cell pointer to cell A2.
/DSRD.	Selects the /DSR (Data Sort Reset) command to eliminate previous range specifications. Then selects Data Range from the Data menu, and anchors the cell pointer with the period key.
{END}{RIGHT} **{END}{DOWN}**	These two steps "draw" the entire database as the Data Range.
PA2˜ ˜G	P selects the primary sort range, and names cell A2 (the first name in the LNAME column) as the range to sort on. The two ˜ commands enter the new range, and select Ascending order from the next prompt. G selects the Go option, which sorts the data.
/XMMenu˜	Returns the main custom menu to the control panel

The macro for sorting by zip code works in exactly the same fashion, but selects cell F2 as the Primary key, in the macro step which reads: PF2 ˜ ˜G.

MACRO TO PRINT A REPORT

This macro sends a list of all names and addresses in the database to the printer. Its steps are:

Print	Menu option name.
Print the directory	Menu option descriptive statement.
{HOME}	Moves cell pointer to cell A1.
/PPCRR	Selects command Print Printer Clear-Range Range:
{END}{DOWN}˜G	as the range to print, then select Go.
/XMMenu˜	Returns the custom menu to the control panel.

LOOKUP MACRO

The Lookup macro asks the user:

Look up whom?

and allows the user to type in a last name. Then it immediately high-lights that individual on the screen. It automatically creates its own Criterion Range, but requires that the top half of the Criterion Range already exist. This can be accomplished by simply typing the word LNAME into cell H1.

Here are the steps it follows:

Lookup	Menu option name.
Find an Individual	Menu option descriptive statement.
/XLook up whom? ˜H2˜	Asks the user who to look up, then places that person's name in cell H2.
{HOME}/DQRCH1..H2˜	Selects the Data Query Reset command to reset previous range specifications. Then it selects the Criterion option from the menu, and specifies H1..H2 as the Criterion Range.
I.{END}{RIGHT}	Selects the Input range option from
{END}{DOWN}˜	menu, and draws the entire database as the Input range.
F{?}{ESC}Q	Selects the Find command which immediately highlights the name being searched for. Then, it pauses until the user presses the RETURN key. It then

Escapes from the Find mode, and
Quits the Data Query menu.

/XMMenu˜   Redisplays the custom menu in the
control panel.

The Worksheet option from the custom menu has no macro
associated with it. When the user selects this option, the custom
menu disappears from the control panel and the worksheet returns
to the basic Ready mode.

Once all of the macros are typed in, use the /RNC (Range Name
Create) command to give cell IA2000 the macro name \M. Then anytime you want to use the automated database management system,
just type Alt-M.

AUTOMATIC MACRO EXECUTION

If you want a macro to start up as soon as the worksheet is
loaded onto the screen with the /FR (File Retrieve) command, give it
the macro name \0 (backslash zero). This special macro name makes
any macro execute immediately as soon as the worksheet is loaded.
In the above example, you could give cell A12000 two range names.
The \M name will execute the custom menu any time you type ALT-M.
If you also give it the name \0, the custom menu will appear on the
screen as soon as the worksheet is retrieved from disk.

Installing
1-2-3

When you first buy 1-2-3, you need to go through some installation procedures so that the program can function properly on your computer. You only need to perform this procedure once, and if 1-2-3 is already functioning properly on your computer, then you can skip this Appendix altogether.

Since various computers may require different installation procedures, we can only provide general instructions here. Version 1A of Lotus 1-2-3 comes with a pamphlet called "Getting Started," and there is also a section in the Lotus Manual called Getting Started. Refer to these for additional instructions.

MAKING 1-2-3 "BOOTABLE"

The first step for installing 1-2-3 is to make it "bootable." That is, you want to be able to insert the Lotus disk into your computer, turn on the computer, and have 1-2-3 ready to go on the screen. This is often called "booting up," because inside the computer, it is "picking itself up by the bootstraps." Technically, the computer is testing and preparing itself.

INSTALLING FOR A FLOPPY DISK SYSTEM

For a computer with two floppy disk drives (such as the IBM PC or Compaq), follow steps 1 through 4 below. If you have a hard disk system (such as the IBM XT), follow the instructions under "Hard Disk System" below.

1. Remove all five Lotus disks from their packet at the back of the Lotus manual. (Be sure you read the License Agreement first.) If any of the disks have write-protect tabs on them (a small adhesive strip on the right edge of the diskette), remove them.

2. Insert your DOS diskette into drive A of your computer, and turn on the computer. If your computer asks for the date and time, you can fill these in or skip them by pressing the RETURN key (labeled ↵ on the IBM keyboard). You should see the A> prompt.

3. (NOTE: Perform this step only if your computer has 320K or more of RAM and you are using DOS version 1.10.) Remove the write-protect tab from the DOS disk (if any), and reinsert it into drive A. Place the Lotus disk labeled "Utility Disk" into drive B. Type the command B:FIXDOS and press the RETURN key.

4. Place the Lotus disk labeled "System Disk" in drive B, and type in the command B:INSTALL, then press the RETURN key. You will see a message asking you to make sure the proper disks are in their drives. When you have double-checked, press any key to continue. The installation procedure will then take a few seconds, and let you know it is finished.

5. Repeat step 4 for each of the disks listed below. Check them off here as you install them:

☐ System Disk (Backup Copy)

☐ PrintGraph Disk

☐ Utility Disk

When done with this step, move to the section in this Appendix on Installing the Drivers.

INSTALLING FOR A HARD DISK SYSTEM

1. Remove all five Lotus disks from their packet at the back of the Lotus manual. (Be sure you read the License Agreement first.) If any of the disks have write-protect tabs on them (a small adhesive strip on the right edge of the diskette), remove them.

2. Turn on your computer, and log onto the hard disk. For example, if your hard disk is drive C, type C: and press the RETURN key (labeled ↵ on the IBM keyboard).

3. Place the Lotus disk labeled System Disk in drive A.

4. Type in this command:
COPY A:*.*
and press the RETURN key.

5. Repeat steps 3 and 4 for these other Lotus diskettes:

☐ PrintGraph Disk

☐ Utility Disk

☐ Tutorial Disk (optional)

6. Your hard disk should also contain the various DOS utility programs. If it does not, you can transfer these by placing the DOS diskette in drive A, and typing this command:

COPY A:*.*

and pressing the RETURN key.

7. (NOTE: Perform this step only if your computer has 320K of RAM or more, and you are using version 1.10 of DOS.) Place the Lotus Utility Disk in drive A, and type in the command:

A:FIXDOS

then press the RETURN key.

INSTALLING THE DRIVERS

The Lotus drivers custom configure 1-2-3 to your computer. Installing the drivers is an easy process. Follow these steps:

1. Make sure the A> prompt is showing on the screen. If not, type A: and press the RETURN key.
2. Place the Lotus Utility disk in drive A. We will refer to drive A as the *source drive.* The other disk drive will be the *target* drive. If you are using a system with two floppy disk drives, the target drive will be B. On a hard disk system, the target drive will be the hard disk, probably C.

Type in one of the following commands depending on which type of monitor your computer uses. In each example below, the X: refers to the target drive (B for floppy, C for hard disk).

If you have a regular monochrome screen, with no graphics capability, type in the command:

MONO X:

and press the RETURN key.

If you have the regular monochrome screen and the Hercules card, type in:

HERCULES X:

and press the RETURN key. If you have a black-and-white graphics screen, type in the command:

B&W X:

and press RETURN. If you have a color graphics screen, type in the command:

COLOR X:

and press RETURN. If you have both a monochrome and a graphics screen, type in the command:

BOTH X:

and press RETURN. If you are using the COMPAQ computer, type in the command

COMPAQ X:

Once you have successfully identified the type screen your computer uses, and the target drive, the Lotus installation program will provide instructions for installing each diskette. The screen will tell you when it is finished installing all of the Lotus diskettes. After you have installed each diskette, place a write-protect tab over the small slot on the right edge of the diskette.

INSTALLING THE PRINTER

Complete instructions for installing a particular printer to 1-2-3 are provided in the Appendices section of the Lotus manual, under the heading "Configuring 1-2-3." To install a particular printer, insert the Lotus System disk into drive A of your computer. If the computer is not on yet, switch the power to "on." If the computer is already on and the A> prompt is showing, type LOTUS and press the RETURN key.

A menu of choices will appear, with the 1-2-3 option highlighted. Press the RETURN key. A copyright notice will appear next, along with instructions to press any key to continue. Press any key, and the 1-2-3 worksheet will appear on the screen.

Type in the command /WGD (Worksheet Global Default) to configure your printer. Follow the instructions in your copy of the 1-2-3 manual to install your printer. If you need technical information about your printer's interface cable, contact your dealer.

Index

☐ **BEST BOOK OF: SYMPHONY™**

Symphony is a complete set of integrated applications programs and therefore can be overwhelming to the first-time user. This book takes a feature-by-feature approach to explaining and demonstrating the full capabilities of the package. Alan Simpson.
ISBN 0-672-22420-8 . . . . **$14.95**

☐ **THE BEST BOOK OF: dBASE II/III**

dBase II® and dBase III® have long been recognized as comprehensive data base management packages, but they also gained a reputation for being difficult to use. This book simplifies a very complicated product and allows you to get greater utility from this software. Ken Knecht.
ISBN 0-672-22349-X **$19.95**

☐ **DISCOVERING MS DOS™**

The Microsoft generic version of DOS for the IBM PC is given the unique Waite touch. From complete description of the basic command set through analysis of architectural implications, you will gain a complete understanding of this operating environment. Kate O'Day.
ISBN 0-672-22407-0 . . . . **$15.95**

☐ **MS DOS BIBLE**

In the *CP/M® Bible* tradition, *MS-DOS Bible* brings you instant access to MS-DOS keywords, commands, utilities and conventions. If you find yourself using MS-DOS by choice or by chance, you'll need this clear and comprehensive guide. Steven Simrin.
ISBN 0-672-22408-9 . . . . **$18.95**

☐ **PC DOS™ COMPANION**

DOS need no longer be a mystery. This clearly written, abundantly illustrated introduction to PC DOS 1.0, 1.1, and 2.0 for PC and PC/XT™ users covers PC DOS commands and the relationship of DOS to applications software. Tips on the best use for each command and a handy command reference card complete this vital reference book. Murtha and Petrie.
ISBN 0-672-22039-3 . . . . **$15.95**

☐ **UNIX™ PRIMER PLUS**

Another excellent Waite book. For those who want to learn about the amazing UNIX operating system, this primer presents UNIX in a clear, simple, and easy-to-understand style. This classic is fully illustrated and includes two handy removable summary cards to keep near your computer for fast reference. Waite, Martin, and Prata.
ISBN 0-672-22028-8 . . . . **$19.95**

☐ **HANDBOOK FOR YOUR IBM® PC**

To use a telephone you need a phone book. To use your IBM PC you need this book. Beginner to intermediate PC users will learn about IBM and non-IBM hardware and software, programming, graphics and peripherals. All commonly used commands, procedures, and controls are clearly presented. Frenzel and Frenzel.
ISBN 0-672-22004-0 . . . . **$15.95**

☐ **THE LOCAL AREA NETWORK BOOK** 📗

Defines and discusses localized computer networks as a versatile means of communication. You'll learn how networks developed and what local networks can do; what's necessary in components, techniques, standards, and protocols; how some LAN products work and how real LANs operate; and how to plan a network from scratch. E. G. Brooner.
ISBN 0-672-22254-X **$7.95**

☐ **DISCOVERING KNOWLEDGEMAN™**

Dynamic, powerful learning tool that quickly shows you how to use the KnowledgeMan information management system. Introduces KnowledgeMan's data management and spreadsheet capabilities, and goes on to teach you how to use each feature by actually working with the program in a step-by-step approach. Excellent tutorial. Micro Data Base Systems, Inc.
ISBN 0-672-22415-1 . . . . **$19.95**

☐ **COMPUTER DICTIONARY (4th Edition)**

There are 33% more definitions in this new edition, which instantly translates state-of-the-art computer terminology into language you can understand. An indispensable computing tool, unmatched for clarity, depth and scope. Charles J. Sippl.
ISBN 0-672-22205-1 . . . . **$17.95**

☐ **COMPUTER LANGUAGE REFERENCE**
REFERENCE GUIDE (2nd Edition)

Build on your existing knowledge. If you know at least one programming language, this newly updated reference now helps you understand eight more! New chapters focus on C and FORTH, while others feature revised and expanded coverage of ALGOL, BASIC, COBOL, FORTRAN, LISP, Pascal, and PL/1. There's a keyword dictionary too. Harry L. Helms, Jr.
ISBN 0-672-21823-2 . . . . **$9.95**